China's citizenship challenge

MANCHESTER
1824
Manchester University Press

China's citizenship challenge

Labour NGOs and the struggle for migrant workers' rights

Małgorzata Jakimów

Manchester University Press

Published by Manchester University Press
Altrincham Street, Manchester M1 7JA

www.manchesteruniversitypress.co.uk

British Library Cataloguing-in-Publication Data
A catalogue record for this book is available from the British Library

ISBN 978 1 5261 5399 9 hardback

First published 2021

Typeset
by New Best-set Typesetters Ltd

Contents

Appendices

List of figures

Acknowledgements

'A journey of a thousand miles begins with a single step', says an old Chinese adage. This journey certainly proved to be much longer and more unexpected than anything I had imagined when embarking on this research nearly ten years ago. And remembering to take it one step at a time was the only way to make arriving at the destination possible. But the journey's lessons are not drawn from admiring landscapes or reaching faraway destinations – rather from meeting people who make the furthest corners of the world, and knowledge, just a bit more familiar. For helping me along on that journey I have the deepest gratitude for so many mentors and peers. For taking the time to read the whole or parts of the manuscript in its various renditions I wish to thank Michael Dutton, Guo Zhonghua, Elena Barabantseva, William A. Callahan, Japhy Wilson, Katherine Morton, Heather Zhang and William Schroeder. For their supportive comments on my work and confidence in my abilities, I wish to thank Guo Taihui, Rachel Murphy, Renata Enjuto Martinez, Deborah Davies, Rosita Armytage, Walter Lee, Julia M. Famularo, Chris Chan, Chun-Yi Lee, David Tobin, Eva Pils, Chenchen Zhang, Paola Pasquali and Jane Hayward. I would also like to thank my previous department at Sheffield University's School of East Asian Studies, and particularly Zhang Zhong, Chen Yu, Hugo Dobson and Peter Matanle for their helpful comments and suggestions on drafts of the book. I also bear a debt of gratitude to my current department, the School of Government and International Affairs at Durham University, and particularly John Williams, Gordon Cheung, Christopher Finley and Emma Murphy for their advice and understanding about the project. For help with parts of the fieldwork, my deepest gratitude goes to Zhang Yihong, Tzu-Chi Ou, Zhang Zhong, Yuan

Fasen, and others who enabled my access to the field but cannot be listed here for ethical reasons: you know who you are. And, last but not least, I wish to thank the labour NGO staff, international activists and migrant workers I was privileged to encounter, and who, regretfully, I also cannot name in the book: your courage and optimism made me reconsider the meaning of perseverance and the limits of the possible.

I am also grateful for the sponsorship of several institutions, without whose generous support I would never have been able to conduct this research: the University of Manchester Centre for Chinese Studies, the University of Manchester Norman Chester Fund, the University of Manchester Sir John Zochonis Grant, the University of Manchester Research Institute for Cosmopolitan Cultures, the Universities' China Committee in London and the British Inter-University China Centre.

This journey also led me to the most precious of relationships. Words could not express the depths of gratitude I hold for my husband, José, whose intimate understanding of every high and low of the writing process made it possible for me to continue, for my son Felix for sweetening the toughest of days with just one smile, and for my dear parents: my mother who taught me never to recoil from hard work, and my father who bestowed on me the passion for all things political.

List of abbreviations

AC	Action for the Children
ACFTU	All-China Federation of Trade Unions
ACLA	All-China Lawyers' Association
ACWF	All-China Women's Federation
BWH	Beijing Workers' Hotline
CCP	Chinese Communist Party
CPPCC	Chinese People's Political Consultative Conference
CSR	corporate social responsibility
EC	European Commission
ET	Empowered Together
FA	foreign actor
FJ	Fighting for Justice
GONGO	government-organised non-governmental organisation
ICFTU	International Confederation of Free Trade Unions
ILO	International Labour Organisation
IMH	Injured Migrants' Home
INGO	international non-governmental organisation
IO	intergovernmental organisation
JM	Justice for the Miners
LHC	Legal Help Centre
MOCA	Ministry of Civil Affairs
MVD	Migrant Village Defenders
MWU	Migrant Women United
NBW	New Beijing Workers
NHC	New Hangzhou Citizens
NGO	non-governmental organisation
NPC	National People's Congress
NPO	non-profit organisation

PRD	Pearl River Delta
SA	Students in Action
SAIC	State Administration of Industry and Commerce
SC	Safer Construction
SFI	Saving From Injury
SOE	state-owned enterprise
SWS	Solidarity with the Sick
TNC	transnational corporation
UA	United in Action
ZFTU	Zhejiang Federation of Trade Unions

They want us to come quietly and leave quietly, our sleeves just brushing, without asking for wages. But how about if we sell our land back home? What would happen to us if we just stayed here in the city? They are afraid that we will say that this world is full of bubbles and what we see is only an illusion! Let us burst the bubbles, let us breathe fresh air! We are determined to speak out the truth!

(from the play *Our World, Our Dreams*, 2009,
New Beijing Workers)[1]

Notes

1 All the translations in this book are my own, unless stated otherwise.

Introduction
Labour non-governmental organisations (NGOs) and the citizenship challenge

It was a cold autumn day in 2011, when I boarded a bus from central Beijing to take me to a migrant village on the outskirts of the city. Leaving the prosperous skyscrapers of Chaoyang district behind, the expensive cars soon gave way to noisy tuk-tuks and crowds gathered around low-storey shops offering street food, disco music blasting from the speakers. As the bus emptied of suited white-collar workers rushing to work in central Chaoyang, it was filled by clearly less prosperous migrants: men carrying sacks and women chatting loudly in incomprehensible dialects. The exceptionally blue October sky was soon marred by dust rising from the road. Two hours later, as I finally exited the bus, I witnessed an alternative urban landscape. A collection of low-rise houses, many of them derelict, the stray dogs staring at me, and dust swirling in the air from noisy scooters passing by. Walking through the village's labyrinth of alleyways, I managed to find my way to the place I was looking for: a local migrant worker-founded NGO – New Beijing Workers (NBW).[1] Greeted by a young man with unruly hair and a suspicious attitude, I quickly introduced myself, taught by experience: 'I am not a journalist'. 'No, don't worry, I came by myself. Nobody knows about my visit here.' It took me a while to soften his unwelcoming facade, but eventually he took me to the building I came to see – a museum built by NBW from the gifts and input from both local and faraway migrant workers. As I passed through the makeshift rooms, I saw pictures representing bleeding hands and feet, children's drawings of their teary faces when confronted with the demolition of their schools, and a tricycle cart positioned proudly in the centre of the final exhibition room. This would be the first of several visits I paid to the village.

Two years before my visit, the NGO put on a countrywide festival celebrating migrant workers' culture, the first such event in China. A crowd of wannabe migrant stars strutted their talents. A female migrant worker called Yan Jun positioned herself on stage, casting her eyes down on the paper while reading her poem:

> Hands are no longer hands
> They are now the resources of economic growth
> The fast food of factory machines
> And legs are no longer legs
> They are the wheels which help roll out the old era
> Now buried under grinding tools and reinforced concrete
> It seems that
> Countless people have lost their smiles and health in
> order to survive
> Countless people have had their dreams evaporated in
> the bright sun
> A shuttered heart
>
> Yan Jun, 'Hands and Legs'

Among the performances some common themes could soon be discerned: the factory regimes were inhuman, they turned people into machines, they took their hands and legs through industrial accidents, they offered pay that was always too low or too late, and the bosses were too cruel. The experience of coming to Beijing was one of hope, which soon turned bitter, with feelings of marginalisation, police surveillance and hardship in the daily life of the city. Increasingly pushed away from the city centre to the outskirts, migrants have constantly found themselves on the move, from one demolished urban village to another already scheduled for demolition. Through the festival and the museum, NBW created an independent, grassroots platform which would enable migrants to relate these stories, as expressed in the opening address of the festival:

> We often hear that it is the government's role to create a stage for people to perform and express themselves. But don't we have the ability to create such a stage ourselves? All of us here have this one very deep experience: that is, if we do not have our own stage on which we can perform, we don't have a place to express our own voice; we can then only ask to be allowed on other people's stages. But do we really have no culture? We do have our own culture! But

> our culture is not yet visible, it does not have its own stage, it does not have a recognisable style and has not yet found a space in which it can be displayed. (Migrant Worker Song Festival, NBW founder, 2009)

Yet, 'setting the scene' and 'acting' can also take on a different meaning for some other migrant worker-founded NGOs. In April 2014, in the city of Dongguan in China's southernmost Guangdong province, an unprecedented event was taking place: thousands of migrant workers from the Yu Yuan shoe factory took to the streets. They were vocal about their dissatisfaction with the local government-backed lax implementation of the social insurance law and (more informally) the lack of worker-appointed trade union representation (Tang, 2014; *The Economist*, 2014).[2] The protest was treated with suppressive measures by the local government and armed police (*wujing*),[3] in conjunction with the factory management: many strikers were detained, including some activists from United in Action (UA), a Shenzhen-based migrant worker NGO, who had provided them with independent legal advice. Mr Zhao,[4] UA's founder, who provided legal aid to the strikers, said to me in an interview later: 'Once the Public Security dragged us into their cars, I overheard the guard saying that the strike rounded up 60,000 people, making it the biggest strike in China's history.'[5]

Mr Zhao, himself originally a migrant worker from the Hunan countryside, has long fought for justice for migrant workers. Injured in a work-delivery traffic accident in the 1990s, he went through many courtrooms to claim accident compensation, and came across many migrant workers who, like himself, would never have received justice. He then learned the law through self-education and started to run an NGO which helped migrant workers to understand their rights and find affordable or free representation for court hearings. In time, his fight would become increasingly radical, including assisting striking workers, which landed him under arrest, led to divorce with his wife and saw his co-workers abandon him one by one. His car was scratched, his work vilified as 'socially harmful', he was called a swindler and forced to move his office fifteen times in the space of just one and a half years. Finally, he was arrested in 2019 and only released in April 2020 after fifteen months in custody without access to a lawyer. When asked why he persisted despite such obstacles, he told me:

> I have experienced a lot of hardship in my life, when I did *dagong* and after, and because of that I can deeply identify and sympathise with the injustice that other migrant workers are subjected to every day, as I experienced them myself. Our group needs people who are committed to our struggle. Luckily, I feel I can help. Of course, I cannot say I can help many people, as I can do so only within a limited scope, but I know that what I do has value and meaning. The government's crackdowns happen because they know they are not fulfilling their legal responsibilities and obligations towards society. But it is their problem, not mine. Even if I switched to another kind of work, these issues would haunt me and I would not be able to ignore them after a while. As I live in this country and I am part of this society, I cannot help but notice the labour problems around me. If I stopped doing this, I would feel constantly conflicted.[6]

The stories above illustrate how, in the absence of established institutions of political representation, migrant workers set up their own organisations, which become channels allowing, supporting and sometimes driving migrants' activism against their subjugated status in urban China. Emerging from the stories are claims which concentrate on three broad areas of concern: those related to civic organising, labour and space. Civic organising-related claims stem from the absence of migrant workers' own channels of political representation and the silencing of their grievances in the public debate. Labour-related claims stem from the experience of hardship and a feeling of inferiority linked to their working conditions and working-class status. What can be broadly conceived of as spatial claims arise from the experience of marginalisation within the cities, resulting in an existence suspended between rural and urban, producing a profound experience of non-belonging. This book presents how labour NGOs come across, and consequently are forced to address, the question of citizenship as a key unifying factor behind such treatment of migrant workers in China.

Migrant workers' citizenship in China has traditionally been discussed in relation to the infamous *hukou* system, which constitutes a legal foundation denying migrant workers access to rights in urban China. Yet the migrants' citizenship discrimination in China also stems from wider social, political and economic factors, which are closely tied to the three areas of claims outlined above. The wider limitations in exercising political, civil and social rights of citizenship, while not targeted against the migrant population in particular, constrain their ability to undertake civic activism aimed at changing their subjugated status and workplace exploitation. The popular *suzhi* (quality) discourse denigrates migrant workers as second-class citizens due to their level of education, appearance, speech, wealth or origin. These factors, paired with their limited access to jobs, services and space in urban China, result in their marginalisation within the cities. This book shows how, in order to effectively address the migrants' plight, NGOs which seek to represent them must address, and often contest, such variegated aspects of citizenship formulation in contemporary China. To do so, they must challenge the established idea of who a citizen is, what a citizen can do and who defines citizenship.

It has been recognised that other types of NGOs, and wider groups of so-called social entrepreneurs, can co-shape certain aspects of citizenship, usually by contributing to state-prescribed forms of citizenship, such as those defined through the *suzhi* discourse (Hsu C., 2017). This book looks at an opposing phenomenon: it documents cases when civic actors seek to question and challenge state-defined aspects of citizenship. While labour NGOs largely employ a conciliatory activism towards the state, in order to truly engage with migrant workers' issues, they must challenge the systemic features of structural citizenship which result in inequality and mistreatment of migrant workers. Moreover, the very fact that these NGOs are mostly set up by what is considered an underclass of migrant workers already challenges the prescribed citizenship practice in China. Civic engagement of such a 'low *suzhi*' group disrupts the traditional notions of politics as the prerogative of the educated classes (or 'high *suzhi*' individuals), who traditionally set up NGOs in China (He, 2012; Hsu C., 2017), challenging the idea of who can be an activist citizen.

This is one way in which labour NGOs can undertake the citizenship challenge in China. But in recent years, Xi's party-state has come to treat labour NGOs' activism as quite another type of 'citizenship challenge'. With growing worker unrest, it has begun to equate such forms of citizenship challenge with a political threat to its power. After all, the authoritarian state is an actor who maintains power by monopolising the citizenship-making process: from defining who is fit to be a citizen to designating the limits of what a citizen can do. Yet, in this book I argue that NGO-initiated citizenship challenge is rarely threatening to the state: if resistance is taking place, it tends to engage with the state language and prescribed channels (such as the law) and is centred on the wider change in the citizenship condition of migrants in China, and not the subversion of the political system. Indeed, as the following pages will reveal, by challenging the poverty, inequality and exclusion experienced by migrant workers in China, migrant NGOs are addressing the ripening social conflict in the country, so their activism largely aligns with the state's long-promoted goal of 'maintaining stability'.

Approaching migrant workers' citizenship in China

Why is the issue of citizenship so central to migrant workers? And why has challenging citizenship become such a controversial form of activism in Xi's China? One of the reasons for the state's attention to labour NGOs' activism is the sheer size of the population which can be labelled as migrant workers in China. In 2018, more than 288.4 million so-called 'migrants' (or more precisely, non-local-*hukou* holders) lived in urban China (National Bureau of Statistics of China, 2019).[7] Out of this group, around 70 per cent were rural migrant workers (Woodman, 2017: 755). Indeed, in the last thirty years this social group has been driving the largest ever peacetime migration in human history. In the process, migrant workers became the engine of China's so-called 'economic miracle' and an essential link in the global economy of production, as they constitute a large percentage of the workforce in China's export-orientated manufacturing zones, such as those in the Pearl River and Yangzi River Deltas – 'the factory of the world'. The social condition of migrant workers is defined by two issues: the exploitative working conditions and their citizenship status in urban China. The precarious type of work they tend to engage in is commonly depicted in Chinese by the word *dagong* (working for a boss). Behind that word often lurks a reality of fourteen-hour shifts, near-slavery living conditions, exploitative employment conditions and the social costs of migration. All this has long fuelled the influx of cheap goods to Western countries through transnational corporations. The *hukou* system limits migrant workers' access to basic citizenship rights, such as education, free healthcare or housing in urban China, particularly in the largest cities. This treatment of migrant workers in China has been a key foundation of the country's economic model and it has far-reaching political implications. This is the main reason why the state is particularly sensitive about political contestation of this state of affairs.

It is mainly, but not solely, in response to the conditions of labour exploitation that most migrant workers' social activism has been taking place – mainly through strikes in their industrial workplaces and construction sites, but also through the formation of grassroots organisations (NGOs). Yet the representation of migrant workers solely as labour activists prevents us from understanding the absolute centrality of migrant workers in the formulation and transformation of citizenship in China.

This centrality has been targeted by the *hukou*-focused literature. The predominant focus of this literature has been on the inequalities in rights distribution brought about by the *hukou* system. Dorothy Solinger's (1999) study of migrant workers' citizenship was the first to deal with the subject from the perspective of a critique of the *hukou* system. Many scholars have followed in Solinger's footsteps, and, like the China-based scholar Chen Yingfang, for example, equated migrants with 'non-citizens' because of their restricted citizenship rights in the cities (Chen, 2005: 121). Others have emphasised the social prejudice stemming from the *hukou*-instigated divisions, such as the prejudice entailed in the language used to refer to migrant workers or negative attitudes from the urban-*hukou* holders (Mao, 2008: 52; Chen, 2005: 131–132; Wang, 2009: 135). However, this *hukou*-centred approach to citizenship reflects the predominance of the liberal tradition of citizenship studies, which focuses on the legal connections between the state and citizens, and ignores other aspects of citizenship. Indeed, there is more to citizenship than the citizenship rights angle can provide us with. What about the informal ways in which we build our place in society as political subjects? What is the meaning and substance of citizenship for those who already possess legally defined citizenship? What about those who are treated as second-class citizens because of their ethnicity, class or gender, rather than *hukou*? And what about the civic consciousness and the activism that runs counter to the established sets of laws and practices?

Some of these questions are partially addressed by the rich scholarship on *renkou suzhi* (population quality) in China. *Suzhi*, associated with both rural–urban and class hierarchy, underlies the public discourse towards migrant workers, and together with the class and rural–urban divides forms a kind of 'cultural citizenship' (Fong and Murphy, 2006). In the *suzhi* discourse, a citizen is defined not by rights, but by the desired and approved ways of acting, looking and thinking, most of which comes with the 'civilising' effects of education (Murphy, 2004: 2; Jacka *et al.*, 2013: 165). The *suzhi* discourse serves to define who the 'proper citizen' is in this cultural sense and prescribes what needs to be done to become one (Murphy, 2004; Lin, 2017; Sun, 2009; Yan, 2008). In that sense, the state encourages citizenship transformation, but a transformation which is within the state-prescribed project of who is a desirable citizen in China (Lin, 2017: 10). Indeed, those social entrepreneurs who frame their NGOs' work within this rationale of raising poor populations' quality are accepted and even aided by the state (Hsu C., 2017). These social entrepreneurs usually sit high in the *suzhi* hierarchy themselves: they have college degrees and work in white-collar jobs (Hsu C., 2017: 13). In line with the *suzhi* discourse logic, due to coming from such privileged backgrounds they see themselves as having authority over those they regard as 'low *suzhi*' (Lin, 2017: 67). Yet, if professionals who are supposed to address migrant workers' discrimination hold such preconceived ideas, wouldn't they tend to reimpose the same hierarchies they are supposedly struggling against, and in effect further disempower migrant workers? If the majority of citizenship transformation is driven by the state and/or middle classes and intellectuals, is there any space for those low in the *suzhi* hierarchy, such as migrant workers, to influence their own citizenship?

To understand how existing citizenship formulation can be challenged, not by the state and middle-class 'social entrepreneurs', but by those actors who themselves are the objects of civilising and educational missions – that is, migrant workers – this book focuses on civic organisations which are predominantly set up and run by migrant workers themselves. If citizenship hierarchies are reinforced by state agents and social actors cooperating with the state, can organisations set up by the subaltern actors provide a viable challenge to such entrenched citizenship formulation? Can they challenge the underlying *suzhi* discourse? Can they transform civic participation? Are they shaping new civic practices? Are they contributing to the production of more inclusive laws? Or are they entrenching existing hierarchies and mechanisms instead? To accurately account for the ability of these actors to transform citizenship, an expanded approach to citizenship – beyond the *hukou* and *suzhi* debates – is required.

The definition of this expanded citizenship must account for its legalistic aspects (*citizenship status*), for its behavioural aspects (*citizenship practices*) and for its ideological foundations (*citizenship discourse*) (see Figure I.1 below). *Citizenship status* consists of rights defined by the *hukou* system, but also sets of laws defining wider citizenship rights. These rights are best conceptualised with the use of the Marshallian triad (Marshall, 1992 [1950]) of civil rights (to voice, to assembly, to fair trial, etc.); political rights (to vote, to stand in elections, to organise politically, etc.); and social and economic rights (to the minimum wage, to a minimum welfare guarantee, to free primary education, etc.).[8] But apart from the codified and institutionalised citizenship status, it is equally important to account for the *citizenship practices*. These can be understood as a set of conventions and behaviours which are unwritten, yet define everyday actions towards other members of a polity. Citizenship status and practice form the *citizenship regime*. They are underscored by an overarching *citizenship discourse* that, in the case of China, draws on the Confucian ideology and discourses of modernity, postcolonialism and development through the 'othering' mechanism of 'internal Orientalism', which rejects the non-modern, not-educated, non-urban and non-Han from being regarded as 'proper' citizens. Indeed, if we read history through 'rupture', 'discontinuity' and marginalised voices against which the dominant discourses have been formed (Foucault, 1972: 4, 75), we can find that the excluded groups have played an important, if not crucial, role in the discursive formation of citizenship (Isin, 2002: 4). In the case of China, the peasant population – and, consequently, migrant workers – served the important role of the Other to the urban Self, which helped forge the dominant formulation of who is a 'proper' and 'desirable' Chinese citizen (Jakimów, 2012; Jakimów and Barabantseva, 2016). Such a citizenship discourse is co-produced by and co-productive of the citizenship regime, and together they constitute the contemporary

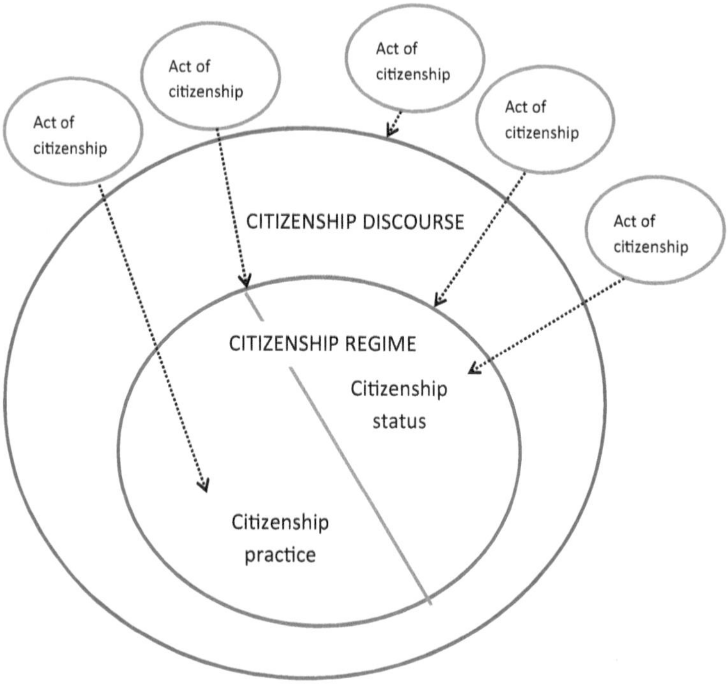

Figure I.1 The analytical framework illustrating the structural aspects of citizenship (*citizenship formulation*) and the acts of citizenship.

formulation of citizenship in China, defining the structural aspects of citizenship.[9]

Citizenship approach to labour NGOs in China

Much of the above discussion centres on the role of the state and structural factors in the formation of citizenship. But the story of citizenship in China cannot be told without accounting for the non-state actors' role in that process, despite political obstacles to the involvement of citizens in negotiating citizenship in China. The structural aspects of citizenship are so fundamental to migrant workers' conditions that, if NGOs seriously seek to challenge the inferior position of migrant workers in China, they must engage in reshaping a variety of aspects that form structural citizenship. In order to convey how citizens' action can impact structural citizenship, this book engages with critical theories of citizenship, and most prominently the 'acts of citizenship' framework (Isin and Nielsen, 2008).

An 'acts of citizenship' approach is useful because it allows for the agent-centred view of citizenship as a process in the making, rather than a purely state-defined construct. Similarly to Yuval-Davis' definition, the framework conceives of citizenship as 'the participatory dimension of belonging to a political community' (Yuval-Davis, 2011: 46). In this framework, a citizen is not only someone who has been endowed with rights by the state; people can become citizens by 'acting as citizens' – that is, claiming their political subjectivity through activism. This type of citizen can be labelled an 'activist citizen' – a citizen who is able to affect some aspects of structural citizenship by 'writing the script and creating the scene' (Isin, 2008: 38; 2009: 381). An activist citizen is different from an active citizen: while an active citizen consciously uses the rights they are given and adopts the prescribed ways of acting, an activist citizen aims to contest this legal and behavioural status quo. The instances of such interventions into citizenship status, practice and/or discourse are called 'acts of citizenship' (Isin, 2008). Acts of citizenship can transform structural citizenship, because they 'rupture socio-historical patterns' of status (embedded in law) and practice (informed by discourses) (Isin and Nielsen, 2008: 2). For activism to be recognised as an act of citizenship it should go beyond existing laws, borders and conventions. It should question the law, and even break it, but, most importantly, it should eventually affect it (Isin, 2008: 39). In the original framework of acts of citizenship, 'citizenship transformation' or 'citizenship challenge' refer specifically to instances where structural citizenship (laws, practices and discourse) are put into question, challenged or changed.

This conceptual framework is a useful starting point in the study of migrant NGOs' activism in China. While such a strongly formulated republican approach may appear at odds with the authoritarian (or increasingly totalitarian) context of Chinese state–society relations, it is actually highly relevant, because it does not distinguish between the democratic and non-democratic regime, as it is not the state or the structure, but the agent who establishes themselves as a citizen through an act of citizenship (Isin, 2008: 36–37). Moreover, while the approach was primarily designed in a Western context, it was formulated to respond to the condition of actors who had no rights and no say in the political context of Western democracies: the downtrodden, the foreign, the non-citizens, *sans papiers* and migrants without rights. When approached in this way, an 'acts of citizenship' framework can be surprisingly effectively transferred to help account for the role of the similarly underprivileged population in the authoritarian context of China. Nevertheless, this book aims to extend and contribute further to this framework so that it can account effectively for a non-democratic context. By tracing the distinction between activist and active citizens in such a context, the book aims to bring new insights into how citizens can affect their condition in an authoritarian context, and also how this process differs from a democratic context.

To do so effectively, it is important to first understand how this approach can contribute to existing studies of state–society relations, labour activism and the struggle for the right to the city in China. The existing studies on NGOs in China ask largely about the content of the relationship between the state and civil society, and the ways in which NGOs carve up space for their activism (Teets, 2014; Fu, 2017; Hsu J., 2017; Hildebrandt, 2013). The question of the NGOs' autonomy from the state has been particularly central to this literature. The widely shared view that NGOs in China lack independence from the state has led many to either tweak the concept of 'civil society' to suit China or reject its suitability altogether.[10] The state corporatist tradition, in particular, emphasises the primacy of the state in defining the scope of action and the character of NGOs in China (Unger and Chan, 1995; Shieh, 2009; Teets, 2014; Hsu J., 2017; Hsu, Hsu and Hasmath, 2016). Alternatively, neo-Gramscian, resource mobilisation social movement theory and social capital-focused studies are more interested in the economic motivations of organisations and the effectiveness of their activism (Hildebrandt, 2013; Franceschini, 2014; Howell, 2015). Some of these scholars deromanticise social movements by revealing the instances of self-interest and short-term profit-seeking of civil society actors (e.g. Hildebrandt, 2013; Franceschini, 2014; Lee and Shen, 2011). In sum, the NGO literature emphasises the importance of the state and donors in the shaping of NGOs in China, and focuses on

NGOs' strategies of survival under the authoritarian state. Partially overlapping with this literature is labour studies' focus on the wider activism of migrant worker groups in China. The studies falling into this category mainly employ a Marxist framework of relations of production, class struggle and class self-identification to explain the motivations behind wider migrant workers' activism, which they unequivocally label 'labour activism' (Froissart, 2014; Howell, 2009; Friedman, 2014; Sun, 2014; Chan, 2012a, 2012b; Pringle, 2011; Franceschini and Nesossi, 2018). Urban studies scholars, on the other hand, consider how uneven citizenship is reproduced by spatial organisation of cities (Lin, 2016; Fan, Allen and Sun, 2014; Song *et al.*, 2008; Zhang, 2001, 2002; Wang, 2010). Rather than focusing on labour-related claims, they approach migrants' agency by examining their ability to put forward claims to the 'right to the city' – that is, a right to have full access to the city's resources and ultimately participate in the decision-making of the city (Qian and He, 2012; Shin, 2013; Wong and Liu, 2017). These scholars argue that, while migrant workers might access some form of belonging to the city by creating alternative citizenship and alternative ways of interacting with urban space (Solinger, 1999; Zhang, 2002; Kochan, 2019), effective access to the right to the city would need to involve a deeper social and political change (Ren, 2012; Qian and He, 2012; Swider, 2015). All the above-mentioned approaches have brought important insights into the structural aspects of migrant workers' exploitation and provide informative analyses of citizen activism in China.

This study builds on these works by providing an account of how migrant worker NGOs initiate an incremental process of transformation aimed at all three aspects usually treated separately in the existing studies: state–society relations, labour exploitation and access to urban space. I argue that the unifying factor underlying the struggles around these three areas of claims is the migrant workers' citizenship positionality in China. Only activism targeted at transformation of structural citizenship, which takes place through acts of citizenship, can address these three major sources of migrant workers' disempowerment. By focusing on citizenship, this book's theoretical approach differs from the existing studies of NGOs in terms of the questions it asks and the methods it employs.

The citizenship approach helps us to appreciate how labour NGOs contest the structural factors, even when they must abide by the limits on civic activism imposed by the state. As much of the literature has noted, NGOs rarely direct their activism against the state: instead, they seek to boost their relationship with state actors as this provides protection and assistance in their work (Ho, 2008a; Hildebrandt, 2013; Teets, 2014; Hsu J., 2017). The strategies NGOs employ to do so have been called variously: 'embedded activism' (Ho, 2008a), 'policy entrepreneurship' (Mertha, 2008) or 'contingent symbiosis' (Spires, 2011), to name but a few. Studies on labour NGOs also note some discursive strategies of depoliticisation which serve a similar purpose (Gleiss, 2014; Franceschini, 2014: 483, 487; Hsu, 2009; Hsu J., 2017). Some scholars show how such strategies might bring about social or political change: Kevin O'Brien and Lianjiang Li (2006) observe how atomised civic actors launch forms of 'rightful resistance' – that is, resistance to power elites (usually at a local level) who have failed to implement the existing law or did not meet a promise. However, the transformative impact on the formulation of citizenship of migrant NGOs I discuss in this book (which might as well be shared by other NGOs) is not well captured by these concepts. 'Resistance through accommodation' is intended to fill this gap. It relates to the strategy of organisations that use state-approved channels (e.g. law) or vocabulary (e.g. communist slogans) to push for change in the position of migrant workers. This form of resistance does not necessarily take the state, either local or central, as its target; the target of resistance is dispersed and not clearly articulated. It is usually labelled as 'the social system' (*shehui zhidu*) by migrant worker NGOs, and, depending on the context, might refer to the policies, capital–labour relations or derogatory discourses on migrant workers. In conceptualising this strategy I draw on Michel de Certeau's idea of 'hidden tactics' – that is, the 'practices of the weak', their 'calculated' yet 'isolated actions' – which subvert the dominant order of things by 'seizing the opportunities' to 'constantly manipulate events', the pre-given language, rules and space into which the weak are forced (de Certeau, 1984: xix, 37). Akin to such tactics, the strategy of 'resistance through accommodation' uses the dominant resources and language to 'create new transcripts', which can have transformative power. By decentring the long-standing question of civic actors' autonomy from the state, this approach allows us to engage with the proximity of state and society in China, without losing sight of the instances of civic action which challenge established structural citizenship. Therefore, the main interest of this study is not to assess NGOs' autonomy from the state, but to reveal the ways in which NGOs claim citizenship, define it and, eventually, transform it.

This study is also intended to contribute to the labour studies literature. While most labour scholars see material grievances as the main motivation of migrant workers' activism, the critical citizenship theory points to the importance of identity, civic consciousness and claims beyond labour as equally stimulating aspects of this struggle. Indeed, as the book shows, the requests for both rights of status (legal and material) and rights to identity are clearly present in the narratives of migrant worker NGOs, which confirms other citizenship studies scholars' findings that 'social action is shaped as much by narratives, myths, ideational regimes, and cultural codes as it is by … economy, the state, the class structure, and so on' (Somers, 2008: 23). Fieldwork material in this book also illuminates how some labour activism can be regarded as conducive to 'the establishment of a common political identity among diverse democratic struggles' (Mouffe, 1993: 6). This approach can help us to see the struggle of migrant workers not just as a struggle for subsistence and the implementation of legal labour rights, but also as the struggle for the rights beyond labour and beyond legalism: rights to voice, participation, space and identity. It is particularly the inclusion of identity (claims for recognition, not just redistribution) (Isin and Wood, 1999; Somers, 2008: 23) which makes it different from the Marxist focus on class dominating the literature on migrant worker activism in China.

This book also theorises the importance of space as a crucial element in both the formulation and transformation of citizenship. I do this by investigating how the process of challenging citizenship utilises existing spaces (both material and discursive) and creates new spaces, a work already initiated by urban studies scholars (e.g. Zhang, 2002; Kochan, 2019). Building on the work of Li Zhang (2002), Chapter 1 highlights how, in the process of the historical development of citizenship in modern China, rural citizens, and consequently migrant workers, were defined as 'below' and 'behind' urban citizens. In the final part of the book I discuss how NGOs engage with this hierarchical spatial imaginary. There, I discuss the ways in which NGOs promote the alternative role of migrant workers in the citizenship discourse, defying the established spatial imaginaries of citizenship. I also point to alternative ways of practising citizenship through cultural and virtual spaces and through mobilisation of spaces available in the city.

Finally, this research contributes some important findings that can be applied beyond China. First, it contributes to the studies on the role of migrants in shaping structural aspects of citizenship (Bottomore, 1992; Isin and Wood, 1999; Hardt and Negri, 2000: 399–400; Walters, 2008). In comparison to studies which take transnational migration as their point of departure, this book investigates an unusual type of migrant – intranational migrants – who, nationality-wise, are citizens of the country they live in, but are second-class citizens legally, substantially and socially. The treatment of these migrants is often akin to the treatment of non-nationals in host countries, or even worse (see Kovacheva *et al.*, 2012). Yet studying the struggle for citizenship performed by China's domestic migrants is worthwhile, as it shows the different types of tools, discourses and solidarities that these domestic migrants engage compared to transnational migrants. By outlining these differences, the study contributes to a deeper understanding of the depth and breadth of migrants' struggles for citizenship, further divorcing understanding of citizenship from nationality.

Second, this study highlights how citizenship transformation, as performed through acts of citizenship, can take place in authoritarian, as opposed to democratic, regimes, for which the framework was initially designed. While this book uses the framework as an analytical toolkit to consider how NGOs' activism can be understood as transforming citizenship, the findings of the study contribute new insights into the framework of acts of citizenship, extending the understanding of how and when acts of citizenship take place in an authoritarian context. One of these insights is the difference that civic actors' engagement with the law bears upon structural citizenship. The assumption inherent in most studies on the sociology of law in China treats the law predominantly as an instrument of state control (Teets, 2014; Gallagher, 2006, 2017; Froissart, 2014). The theory of acts of citizenship also adopts the view that for the act to be regarded as an act of citizenship it has to go beyond the established practices and laws. However, in an authoritarian state like China, the laws are often deliberately vaguely formulated and arbitrarily implemented; the rights enshrined in legal documents are not exerted in practice, and practices are themselves exclusive of civic actors like NGOs. In such a citizen-hostile environment, actions such as attempts to uphold the law and train fellow excluded migrants in how to utilise the law for self-empowerment can transgress prescribed citizenship practices. Moreover, the effectiveness of the acts of citizenship performed by NGOs often comes precisely from their engagement with the law and state-approved channels, because the pressure for change applied through these channels is more difficult to suppress, as it does not attempt to break the law, but simply to uphold it. This approach to law differs from the original approach of the acts of citizenship framework, yet is an important aspect of how underprivileged actors can affect citizenship in an authoritarian context.

The third important theoretical extension to an acts of citizenship framework is the study of how one-off 'acts' become practices and how such practices remain transformative of citizenship. Acts of citizenship are understood as one-off actions, which rupture the established structural citizenship because of their uniqueness (such acts could be, for instance, protests and demonstrations, petitions, performances, etc.). However, it is also through everyday practices, which do not have to be orientated at changing citizenship itself, but which end up shaping and redefining citizenship, that the actual change may even more effectively take place (de Certeau, 1984; Hann and Dunn, 1996). In order to enact a lasting influence on citizenship, some of the acts must be repeated over and over again, until they become 'practices'. While each act of citizenship is unique in time, the number of acts which can be subsumed under the same type (e.g. 'organising') will eventually form a practice, even if it is enacted differently each time. Therefore, in tracing different forms of NGO activism in this book, I seek to ascertain two characteristics of this activism. First, I seek to judge whether these actions have a transformative impact on citizenship, and therefore whether they can qualify as acts of citizenship. Second, I seek to enquire whether such 'acts' are one-off instances which have only temporarily ruptured structural citizenship, or whether they have already formed a practice which has a more long-lasting effect on citizenship. Such a focus on citizenship practices and its transformative impact follows in the footsteps of the recent turn in Chinese citizenship studies literature, initiated by several studies of migrant workers' ability to negotiate citizenship inclusion in China (see Woodman, 2017; Guo and Liang, 2017; Xiong and Li, 2017; Xia and Guan, 2017; Yang, 2017).

The above-presented analytical approach to NGOs in China was developed to respond to the conditions found during fieldwork in China in the years 2011–2016. However, since the introduction of the 2017 Overseas NGOs Management Law, which cut many organisations off from foreign sources of funding, paired with the post-2015 crackdown on labour NGOs across China, few NGOs are still able or willing to engage in activism which has a tangible impact on migrants' citizenship (see Amnesty International, 2019; Franceschini and Nesossi, 2018; as well as Chapters 2 and 3). Indeed, some organisations discussed in this book have been forcibly closed and their staff detained and eventually sentenced. Those which survived the crackdown are now facing lack of funding due to the 2017 law. This situation pivoted many organisations into less contentious forms of activism, often resulting in less engagement with labour or citizenship issues (as discussed in Chapter 2). In addition, at the time of submitting this manuscript for publication, the COVID-19 pandemic had brought drastic restrictions on citizen movement within China, further limiting NGO activism, especially when involving assistance to migrant workers in person. COVID-19 has also further reinforced invasive state-control technologies, including face-recognition cameras, movement-tracking technologies and 'neighbourly vigilance' practices (Palmer, 2020). The discrimination against migrant workers whose *hukou* happened to be Hubei-based during the pandemic illustrates that citizenship-related discrimination is taking new forms, in addition to more established ones. The longevity of the COVID-19 extra security measures and discrimination against migrant workers is currently not easy to judge, but they are likely to further contribute to a period of inactivity or demise of some NGOs discussed in this book.

In the light of this dramatic change in the past three years, the activism which falls under the label of 'resistance through accommodation' is the only remaining way to enact some impact on wider citizenship. However, at the time of submitting this monograph, even this kind of conciliatory activism is largely lying dormant, as labour NGOs have been either shut down, are under threat of disappearing due to lack of funding, or have shifted their activism to an area which does not influence structural citizenship. But the question of citizenship, as discussed in this book, continues – arguably more than ever – to affect the life chances of migrant workers. As the grievances which gave rise to the emergence of labour NGOs are unlikely to disappear any time soon, it is highly possible that the types of activism discussed in this book will resurface, and if not these, then new activists are likely to continue the struggle for migrant workers' rights.

Introducing labour NGOs

The first migrant/labour NGOs[11] emerged in the 1990s in Guangdong province. From their inception, they were set up by both middle-class 'social entrepreneurs', such as journalists, academics or social workers, and migrant workers themselves. Two of the earliest organisations set up in the Pearl River Delta (PRD) in the late 1990s, the Migrant Women Network and Panyu Migrant Workers Centre,[12] reflect this variety. Migrant Women Network was set up by a renowned Hong Kong-based academic, Pun Ngai, and a cohort of Hong Kongese social workers, incrementally including mainland female migrant workers to help with running the organisation. Panyu Migrant Workers Centre, though initially set up by a rural migrant worker self-educated in law, was quickly taken over by a lawyer called Zeng Feiyang. Both these NGOs are influential, because they coached the next generation of migrant NGOs in the 2000s (Huang, 2012), which, in turn, were mostly set up by migrant workers themselves. Meanwhile, a range of NGOs started to form outside of Guangdong, particularly in Beijing. Of the nineteen organisations included in this study, fourteen were set up by migrant workers and five were set up by non-migrant workers (lawyers, academics and a journalist). All but one are *minjian zuzhi*, a term used to describe grassroots civic organisations set up by non-state actors.[13]

In comparison with other types of NGOs, such as those concerned with poverty alleviation, LGBT or environmental issues, migrant/labour NGOs are treated more suspiciously by the state as presumably more capable of 'subversive action' due to their focus on rights defence and the empowerment of an underprivileged – and therefore potentially explosive – group (Fu, 2017; Ho, 2001; Fulda, 2013). The 'political sensitivity' of these NGOs has resulted in their relatively low number. According to my interviewees and other sources (e.g. Fu, 2017: 36), there are currently about 50 to 100 migrant worker NGOs in China, but the numbers vary widely due to the insecure and volatile environment for labour NGOs, particularly under Xi's administration. Consequently, the capacity of these organisations is severely limited and they are very small in size (employing on average between two and five people), with little impact on wider policy-making. They rely heavily on pro bono lawyers, migrant workers and university student volunteers. Many of them also cooperate with academics based in Chinese universities, and they use these connections to receive professional advice on legal matters and to conduct research underlying their advocacy attempts.

While these NGOs are most commonly referred to as 'labour NGOs', the label 'migrant' or 'migrant worker' NGOs better reflects these organisations' predominant focus on aiding migrant workers (rather than all workers), so I use all these names interchangeably in the book. The label 'migrant NGO' also better describes a rather variegated group of organisations, which focus on a wide range of activities, many going beyond labour issues, and focusing instead on community building and migration. A renowned supporter of migrant NGOs, labour rights lawyer Duan Yi, once divided labour organisations into three types: 'service type' (*fuwuxing*), 'rights protection type' (*weiquanxing*), and 'labour movement type' (*gongyunxing*). He also argued that there was a progression from the first type to the last, indicating the labour movement in the making (Duan, 2015). While there definitely was momentum among some NGOs in the PRD towards labour movement-type activism from the early 2010s, this was only limited to a small group of organisations in Guangdong province, with the rest of the NGOs, particularly those outside of Guangdong, focusing on less controversial activism. For that reason, I have divided these organisations' activities slightly differently, as falling within four areas: service delivery and education; advocacy; rights defence (legal action); with only a small portion committed to supporting striking workers ('collective bargaining', *jiti tanpan*) (see Figure I.2 below). The service delivery type of activism includes personal development and community-building services, providing entertainment, psychological support, training, art, education and discussion centres. Advocacy-orientated activism includes NGOs' own research on migrant workers, often in cooperation with universities, and attempts to advocate with policy-makers. Legal action-orientated activism includes representation of migrants in court, negotiation with employers and sometimes local governments, as well as provision of legal training for migrants to enable their self-sufficiency in court. The NGOs which undertake the riskiest form of activism – that is, supporting striking migrant workers and extending legal action activism to include collective bargaining cases – are in the minority of the organisations I reached. While some NGOs work in only one clear-cut area, most conduct activities in several broad areas depending on the political environment related to their activism, sources of funding and local needs.

The fieldwork for this study was conducted between 2011 and 2016 with nineteen migrant worker NGOs based in four broad locations: Beijing, Zhejiang province (Hangzhou, Yongkang), Hunan province (Shiyan) and Guangdong province (Shenzhen, Guangzhou and Foshan). In order to conduct a study which was geographically broad and qualitatively in-depth, the fieldwork was based primarily on ethnographic participant observation as well as interviews – semi-structured, individual and group.[14] The participant observation was conducted in four NGOs in particular. I worked as a part-time translator (three to four days a week) in Beijing Workers' Hotline (BWH) for nearly three months between February and May 2012. I also participated in various activities conducted by NBW and two Hangzhou-based organisations – New Hangzhou Citizens (NHC) and Students in Action (SA) – in 2011 and 2012. Participant observation has been sparsely used in research on Chinese NGOs in the past, making this book one of very few studies which rely on this method in researching NGOs in China.[15] Such fieldwork enabled me to compare information gathered via interviews, and provided better access to the field through extended socialisation. Additionally, I conducted nearly fifty in-depth formal interviews (both individual and group) with the founders and employees of the NGOs, as well as seventeen foreign actors (FAs) (comprising funding organisations, such as international non-governmental organisations (INGOs), foreign embassies, businesses and representatives of intergovernmental organisations (IOs)) and four Chinese academics. Apart from the

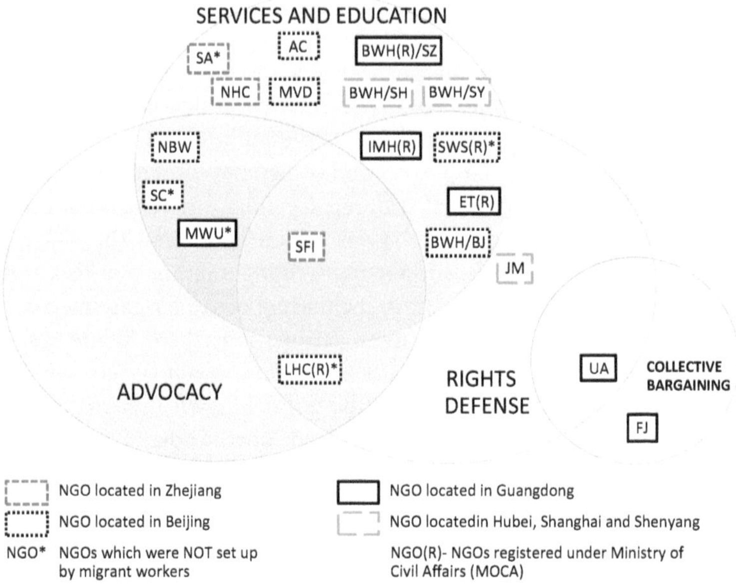

Figure I.2 Map of NGOs included in the study. This figure presents the NGOs by their area of activism, location and registration status.

formal, semi-structured, and mostly recorded interviews, I also conducted many informal face-to-face conversations, interviews over social media, and maintained correspondence with NGO leaders, migrant workers coming to these NGOs, FAs and academics in China – in some cases long after I had finished my participant observation part of the fieldwork – which brings the total number of interviews to around a hundred.

The cities of Beijing, Shenzhen and Hangzhou were selected as key research locations because they receive high numbers of inflow migrant workers. Moreover, Beijing and Shenzhen are two locations with the greatest number of labour NGOs, and are therefore key locations to study and compare. Beijing and Shenzhen are classified as 'first-tier' cities, while Hangzhou is classed as 'second-tier' by the central Chinese government, or 'new first-tier' by some business analysts. All three host a population of over 10 million, making their municipal policies particularly restrictive to extending citizenship rights and local *hukou* to the rural migrant population under the 2014 National New-type Urbanisation Plan, the newest iteration of '*hukou* reform' (as discussed in detail in Chapter 1). Beijing and Shenzhen are comparable in terms of national importance, size and their GDP income. Hangzhou, while smaller, is a desirable migration destination. Moreover, Zhejiang in general and Hangzhou specifically are important locations to study in terms of migrant activism, because despite Zhejiang being the second largest inflow migration destination in China, the activism of labour NGOs in this province is virtually unknown in the academic literature. Only one NGO based in inner provinces is included in this study – the Hubei-based NGO Justice for the Miners (JM). I discuss its activism and the specific challenges it faces in detail throughout the book.

While a detailed discussion of the variegated treatment of migrant NGOs by local authorities in these three core locations will be presented throughout this book, it is important to highlight here the main differences between the municipal policies and their impact on NGOs. The discussion needs to be complemented with Chapter 1's introduction of these three municipalities' policies towards migrant workers more generally, which paints a fuller picture of the reasons behind the location-specific activism of migrant NGOs. It is important to note that while the local governments' attitudes to civic organisations used to differ considerably between these various locations under the leadership of the Hu-Wen administration, they have somehow converged under Xi due to centrally driven repression of labour NGOs, removal of foreign funding opportunities and their replacement with government funding.

As to Beijing's environment for migrant NGOs, the capital authorities are generally extremely vigilant towards any form of activism which could be seen as contentious (NGOs providing court representation or strike support would fall under this category). This has resulted in NGOs specialising in less contentious areas of activism, such as catering for local migrant communities – NBW, Migrant Village Defenders (MVD), Action for the Children (AC); providing health and safety training – Safer Construction (SC); helping victims of occupational diseases – Solidarity with the Sick (SWS); or providing state-approved assistance to migrant workers in claiming forfeited wages – BWH. Only a semi-GONGO (government-organised non-governmental organisation) with close links to the government, the Legal Help Centre (LHC), is able to undertake more 'contentious' activism, such as providing legal representation for migrants in court.

Some of the above-mentioned NGOs would also stretch their activism to doing research on migrant workers' conditions, liaising with universities or even providing policy advocacy (see Figure I.2 for details of how these activities overlap). However, despite the rather stringent attitude of the municipal authorities, the particularity of Beijing as a global hub and the location of many foreign embassies and INGOs has meant that until recently, these organisations have had better access to foreign funding than labour NGOs located inland (see Chapter 3 for a detailed discussion). Under Xi's administration, the Beijing government has also widened provision of government funding (through the so-called 'procurement of social services' – *goumai fuwu*), which migrant NGOs can access through local All-China Federation of Trade Unions (ACFTU) branches in Beijing. Since the introduction of the 2017 Overseas NGOs Management Law, public procurement projects have become the main source of funding for migrant NGOs across China. In Beijing, like elsewhere, NGOs have been further compelled to redirect their activism from borderline contentious 'workers' representation' or 'legal support' to areas of community service or health and safety training, as the discussion in Chapter 2 will highlight.

Guangdong province, by comparison, has witnessed the fastest and largest development of civic organisations in China in the last three decades. There are two reasons for this. First, the province, particularly under the leadership of the liberal-minded Wang Yang (up to 2012), had introduced a particularly relaxed environment for NGOs, allowing many of them to operate in what, elsewhere, would be considered unacceptably contentious areas of activism: education in labour rights, court proceedings and class-building consciousness – Migrant Women United (MWU), Injured Migrants' Home (IMH); court representation – UA, Empowered Together (ET); and even collective bargaining and strike support – UA, Fighting for Justice (FJ). Second, the province, and Shenzhen city in particular, borders Hong Kong, which is the main location of many INGOs working in the area of labour rights. These INGOs have been an important source of funding for the Guangdong-based grassroots NGOs. However, the situation has drastically changed since 2012, as discussed in detail in Chapter 2. Despite the 2012 introduction of a simplified registration procedure for civic organisations, the Shenzhen government initiated a crackdown on labour NGOs, which intensified over the following years, resulting in arrests and the sentencing of some prominent NGO leaders. Ever since, the process of redirecting activism towards less contentious areas has been taking place. However, in comparison to Beijing and Hangzhou, Shenzhen municipality does not deliver funding through ACFTU, but rather through the Bureau of Civil Affairs,[16] which further marginalises the ability of labour NGOs to access funds, as they have to compete with non-labour organisations in areas such as 'urban communities' or 'child education'.

The municipal authorities of the final location, Hangzhou – and more generally Zhejiang province – have taken a quite conservative approach to migrant NGOs. The authorities would limit and obstruct NGOs' activism if they refused to form official partnerships with government agencies or ACFTU. For instance, ZFTU, the Zhejiang branch of ACFTU, has delegitimised labour organisations in the past, even when they received support from the local Bureau of Civil Affairs (Howell, 2009: 186–189). Saving from Injury (SFI), an organisation operating in the Yongkang area of Zhejiang province, is also an example of that trend. SFI works in the area of health and safety and labour rights education. It has also been helping migrants to negotiate compensation from employers. Its activities were deemed too contentious for the provincial and municipal authorities, and it has been targeted several times since 2012 in personal attacks on the NGO's founder, and then by cutting the organisation off from foreign funding. Similarly, the municipal authorities in Hangzhou have strived to co opt any emerging migrant NGO, and channel their activism towards non-contentious issues. Such was the fate of NHC – an NGO which mostly delivers community service and entertainment for migrant workers, and which was accommodated as early as 2010 to state-funded procurement schemes under the local trade union, ZFTU.

The organisation of the book

China's Citizenship Challenge untangles the complex way in which NGOs engage with the impact of structural citizenship on migrant workers' lives by discussing their activism through the prism of acts of citizenship. Not every act is an act of citizenship, but tracing those which can be seen in this way is helpful in mapping the impact of NGOs on structural citizenship in China. Throughout the book, I present these various acts, and investigate when and why they can be conceived of as acts of citizenship. In order to account for the main motivating factors behind these acts, I introduce an analytical framework of 'sites' around which the acts are performed: civic organising, labour and space. 'Sites' are understood here as 'fields of contestation around which certain issues, interests, stakes as well as themes, concepts and objects assemble' (for example, urbanism, the law, but also material spaces like courts or streets) (Isin, 2009: 370). Civic organisation, labour and space can be understood as sites of activist citizenship because it is through them that migrant NGOs respond to the forms of discrimination suffered by migrant workers, by putting forward claims to new forms of citizenship discourse, practice and status. The acts performed around these sites cut through the urban/rural geographical scales which have come to define the citizenship of migrant workers in China.

Within these three sites, activism related to civic organising is aimed at producing an institutionalised form of representation of migrant workers' interests under the pressures of the authoritarian state and limited funding. Acts which target labour as their main area of concern relate to labour rights protection, pressure for better working conditions and the shaping of workers' identity against the backdrop of the labour–capital conflict. Acts revolving around the site of space are related to urban redevelopment, discursive spatial marginalisation and forms of spatial activism aimed at addressing the rural–urban dichotomy. While these three sites are separated for analytical reasons, they are often imbricative and mutually reinforcing in the migrant workers' claims discussed in this book.

In Part I of this book (Chapter 1) I focus on the structural aspects of citizenship in China. In a largely chronological manner, the chapter presents a history of the mutual co-constitution of the citizenship regime and discourse. I argue that the current formulation of citizenship in China is founded not only on the formal legislative aspect of the *hukou* system, but also on the underlying citizenship discourse, which stems from the processes of modernisation, urbanisation and nationalism, underlined by the new economic divisions created by market reforms. In this chapter, I trace genealogies of citizenship in China in order to reveal how it has been constructed through the mechanism of the spatio-temporal 'othering' of the rural/migrant worker population. I then set out the attempts by central and local governments to reform the *hukou* system, arguing that despite much debate about reforming the system since 2003 and particularly since 2014, not enough has been done to truly transform the citizenship status of migrant workers in China. I also discuss state-prescribed citizenship practices, which are enforced both through the law and through public campaigns and school education, and reflect on what type of citizen they promote. The final section of the chapter presents how these various historical and contemporary discourses have been entangled locally in China in the form of the municipal authorities' policies and narratives towards migrant workers in Shenzhen, Beijing and Hangzhou, the main fieldwork sites.

Having sketched out how structural citizenship defines migrant workers' positionality in China, the next three parts of the book evidence if and how NGOs go about challenging this. In Part II (Chapters 2 and 3) I discuss how NGOs work in relation to the first 'site' of citizenship contestation: civic organising. I focus, in particular, on instances when the acts of organising and networking can be recognised as acts of citizenship – that is, when they transform the wider citizenship structure. Organising and networking are tied to citizenship, because they are shaped by the limitations to civil and political rights of citizenship in China. I discuss how these acts can push for new practices of activist citizenship, such as volunteerism and inter-NGO networking. Through the act of 'organising', which is often undertaken under many financial, political and legal constraints, migrant workers who set up NGOs manifest their resolve to take action over the circumstances in which they live. By doing so, they assert the right to voice, which they are not normally granted in the public space, and the right to organise, negotiating the role and function of citizen-formed organisations in China, thereby reshaping citizenship practices. Through the act of networking, NGOs challenge the limitations of the hostile environment for inter-organisational networking and assembly in China, redrafting what is regarded as 'acceptable' civic interactions. However, both acts come across tremendous obstacles from the constrictions of political space and the transformation in the state's approach to foreign funding under Xi Jinping. This has impacted the degree to which NGOs are willing to undertake citizenship challenge in recent years:

from the fear of state repression to their accommodation to donors' agendas in search of funding, NGOs are rarely still able to translate their activism around the site of civic organising into genuine change in citizenship.

The focus of Part III (Chapters 4 and 5) is on the ways in which NGOs perform labour-focused activism, and how this activism impacts migrant workers' citizenship. This part demonstrates that NGOs' demands revolving around labour cannot be divorced from wider citizenship rights, such as the right to voice, assembly, striking, recognition, representation and political participation. However, labour rights play a special role in the negotiation of citizenship in China, because claims to those rights are usually positioned as 'legal', which makes them different from claims to civil or political rights of citizenship, such as those voiced through the site of civic organising, or the claims related to inequality in the *hukou* system and the right to the city voiced through the site of space. Unlike these aspirational kinds of rights, labour rights are usually framed as already existing 'legal rights' (*hefa quanyi*), which simply need to be 'respected', and until recently, this made activism around them somehow less contentious. Finally, labour is also an important site of citizenship transformation because it endows migrant workers with vocabulary in their struggle for identity and recognition. Chapter 4 analyses two acts, 'defending rights' and 'educating in legal rights', which utilise state-designated channels (in this case, labour laws), and therefore do not challenge the state directly. I reflect critically on when these acts can have transformative effects on citizenship and when they help to maintain the status quo, by comparing cases when they help to produce active and informed citizens, and when they do not. Chapter 5 presents three further acts: 'educating beyond rights' (that is education on the forms of exploitation and control), 'advocating and petitioning' (for changes in laws) and 'claiming the rights' (to independent labour representation, collective bargaining and strikes). These acts are not performed through state-defined legal channels, and instead seek to transform the law itself. I ultimately argue that, while the activism of NGOs performed around labour affects the citizenship structure in a variegated way, some of the NGOs recognised citizenship transformation as a precondition to successfully tackling labour issues in China.

In Part IV (Chapters 6 and 7) I look at space as yet another site around which migrant worker NGOs perform acts of citizenship. Chapter 6 looks at the production of the figure of worker-citizen as a response to the discrimination against migrants in the public discourse and an attempt to rectify them as rightful citizens. I trace the process of how this identity of worker-citizen is constructed through acts of 'voicing' (of migrants' grievances), 'challenging marginalisation' (embedded in the citizenship discourse) and 'constructing a new identity' for migrant workers. The NGOs which engage in this form of activism aim, though not always successfully, to liberate migrant workers from the hierarchical spatio-temporal rural/urban, backward/modern and economically useless/useful binaries entrenched in structural citizenship. Consciously cast in the language of class and the value of labour, their figure of worker-citizen rejects both *suzhi* discourse and the *hukou* system's denigration of migrant workers as second-class citizens, and is aimed at reshaping migrants' relationship to both the rural and the urban. Chapter 7 focuses on the migrant NGOs' claims to the city through acts of 'integrating into the city' and 'claiming the right to the city'. Urban citizenship here is understood not only as a legal right to belong to the city, but also as a process of building community within the city and participating in the building of the city, both materially and culturally. This chapter also analyses whether various forms of engagement and intervention within the urban spaces, which take place through those acts, can challenge the powerful discourses around urbanisation, prescribed practices of passivity and the legal constructs at the heart of urban citizenship. This is observed through examples of creating spaces of belonging, defending the last house standing in a demolished urban village, or establishing schools for migrant worker children in defiance of urban development policies and the *hukou* system constraints. As with the previous chapters, this chapter takes into account the obstacles to such citizenship transformation by reflecting critically on the structural limitations put up by the state and the capital to bar migrant workers from successfully claiming the right to the city.

In the conclusion, I further reflect on the internal and external limitations to migrant worker NGO-driven citizenship transformation, particularly in light of the crackdown in recent years on activists and NGOs under Xi Jinping. I ask what this crackdown signifies given that the main organisations targeted are labour NGOs, and what role the 'citizenship challenge' has played in instigating the state's harsh response. The book highlights the fact that migrant worker NGOs do not intend to work against the state, but actually, to a great degree, help its quest for 'maintaining social stability' by targeting and addressing the abuse experienced by migrant workers. However, the ability to effectively target such injustice ultimately calls for a wide-ranging citizenship transformation. As migrant worker NGOs' activism highlights, any such transformation would need to create space for a greater political participation by migrant workers. As migrant worker NGOs tap into that need, they are perceived as a political threat to the state, despite their non-confrontational behaviour. However, the state's attempts to limit migrant-led citizenship transformation in China are counterproductive as long as its attempts at reforming citizenship fail to address the inherent inequality in the formulation of Chinese citizenship. By preventing migrant worker NGOs from helping to resolve this inequality, the state's crackdown will only heighten social discontent and increase social instability in China.

Notes

1 All names of NGOs in this book are pseudonyms, unless otherwise stated.
2 Further discussion on the motivations behind these claims can be found in Chapter 4.
3 All Chinese words used throughout this book are listed in Appendix 5 (Glossary), both in pinyin and in simplified Chinese characters, and with English translations.
4 A pseudonym: all names in the book are pseudonyms.
5 Interview no. 42.
6 Interview no. 42.
7 I use the terms 'migrant workers', 'rural migrants' and 'migrants' interchangeably throughout this book to define the same social group, most commonly called *nongmingong* (literally, 'peasant workers') in Chinese, that is the rural-to-urban migrant workers. While some migrant workers might be those who migrate between different cities, in this

book, by the term 'migrant workers' I refer exclusively to those migrant workers who possess rural *hukou*.

8 I would also add cultural rights (identity-based, sexual, technological, environmental, etc.) to this triad.

9 The definitions of citizenship status and practice are based largely, though not literally, on Engin Isin's own definitions dispersed across several of his publications (see for example Isin, 2002: 17; Isin, 2009; Isin and Wood, 1999: ix). The notions of citizenship regime, citizenship discourse and citizenship formulation are influenced by the writings of Engin Isin and Michel Foucault, but the definitions applied in this book are largely my own. See Jakimów (2015) for further discussion of the role of citizenship status, regime and discourse in the citizenship formulation in China.

10 An example of this adjustment of the concept of civil society can be found in the notions of 'partial civil society', where civil society's autonomy is not institutionalised and protected (Kerr, 2015) 'state-led civil society' (Frolic, 1997), 'nascent civil society' (He, 2003), 'many civil societies' (Howell, 2004: 167), or 'new civil society', where the boundary between the state and society is blurred (Callahan, 2012). Examples of rejection and replacement of 'civil society' altogether are concepts of 'embedded activism' (Ho, 2008a), 'spaces of exchange (between state and society)' (Hsu J., 2017), or 'negotiating the state' (Saich, 2000).

11 For the full names of NGOs and detailed descriptions of their origin, sources of funding and activities, see Appendix 4, Table A4.1. For detailed reflection on the methodology and ethical consideration of data collection see Appendix 1. See Appendix 2 for the list of interviews, Appendix 3 for the list of fieldwork sites, and Appendix 4, Table A4.2, for details of FAs who sponsor these NGOs.

12 These are the real names of these NGOs. They still may figure in this book under pseudonyms.

13 When analysing the grassroots organisations set up by migrant workers I use the term non-governmental organisations, or NGOs, instead of non-profit organisations (NPOs), a term used to depict civic organisations registered under the Ministry of Civil Affairs (MOCA). The legal names given to NGOs when they register with MOCA are: social associations (*shehui tuanti*), social service organisations (*shehui fuwu jigou*) and foundations (*jijinhui*). The reason I prefer to use the label NGO is because of the majority of these organisations' unregistered status. Also, these organisations prefer to call themselves 'NGO *zuzhi*' (which means 'NGO organisation' in English). They do so because it signifies the civil, grassroots and self-made character which these NGOs very much identify with, and which is quite different from the more

ideologically neutral label of NPOs. However, the English acronym does not necessarily sound politically sensitive or anti-governmental to them.

14 For details of the methodological design and ethical challenges of the fieldwork, see Appendix 1 (Methodology).

15 For another study using similar research methods see Fu (2017).

16 Interview no. 46.

Part I

Structural citizenship

1

Migrant workers' citizenship, the *hukou* system and local state policies: a genealogical enquiry

The story of citizenship is closely linked to the story of urbanisation: the story of how urban life imposed a different perspective of time and space which forged national consciousness, of how communities transformed from tight, familial networks to self-governing bodies of individuals, of how technology, the mainstream urban cultures and city images shaped urbanites' identity. From Greek polis, to the emergence of medieval cities to the multicultural, global cities of nowadays, city has been central to the shaping of citizenship. Yet, in this story of how urbanisation formed citizens, there is rarely a chapter authored by those who live in the shadows of the city. They are the ones who are given their voice only once they rise, change and move, and once they become fully urban, as if their own experience of what came before is irrelevant. In the Chinese context, these marginal experiences are the experiences of rural migrant workers. Suspended in the world of in-between – not yet fully urban, but already delinked from their rural home – migrant workers are at the forefront of shaping new forms of urban belonging and citizenship in China.

This chapter presents a genealogical enquiry into how rural migrant workers have played such an important role in the shaping of citizenship in China. As discussed in the introduction, in China, the story of migrant workers' citizenship has been predominantly told in relation to the *hukou* system and the *suzhi* discourse. Yet in order to fully grasp the role of migrant workers in citizenship formulation and contestation, it is necessary to go beyond these two aspects, and look at how both discursive and legal aspects of structural citizenship have been shaped in China. The first section presents the role of the rural–urban divide in the formation of the concept of citizenship in China and in the relationship between citizenship discourse and regime. I propose here that the mechanism which unifies both, citizenship discourse and regime, is the spatio-temporal 'othering' imaginary introduced with the onset of Western-influenced modernisation. This mechanism hierarchically identifies urban, modern and Han residents as 'proper' citizens, while excluding migrant workers and peasants as those who are of a 'worse sort' and need to be 'turned into citizens' (*shiminhua*). The citizenship regime, with its cornerstone in the Maoist version of the *hukou* system, was both a consequence of this modernist vision of citizenship, and a driving force behind its contemporary entrenchment. The second section looks at how citizenship has been shaped in relation not only to the rural–urban divide, but also state–society relations. I reflect here on how the concept of citizenship has been shaped at the crossroads of Western and Confucian traditions, and how this tension, in turn, was translated into citizenship education in post-Maoist China, which promoted the paternalistic, state-obedient ideal of citizenship. The final section discusses how the combined forces of the hierarchical rural–urban imaginary, the *hukou* system and the prescribed citizenship practices of obedience and passivity have interplayed with local state policies in urban China. I analyse three cities in particular – Shenzhen, Beijing and Hangzhou – as these are the locations of the majority of NGOs in this study, and three key endpoints of migration. I discuss the variegated municipal policies of these three locations towards both migrant workers and NGOs. This discussion allows exploration of local particularities of state approach to the political, social and material position of migrant workers in urban China.

Migrant workers' role in the historical formation of citizenship in China

In order to grasp adequately the extent to which structural citizenship affects migrant workers' position in China, the hierarchical character of structural citizenship in China should be traced beyond *hukou* and *suzhi* debates, and positioned within the wider context of how citizenship has been forged in modernity. The rural–urban divide has played a crucial role in the process of the modern shaping of citizenship in China, since long before the Maoist-type *hukou* system was introduced. Indeed, it owes much to the way Western experience of modernity filtered into China through semi-colonial encounters with the West. Mayfair Yang (2011) argues that with the appropriation of Western theories in China at the turn of the twentieth century, the Chinese modern elites started seeing anything non-modern as 'backward' and 'shameful'. Such 'Orientalist' self-perception in both the state's and intellectuals' self-image as Chinese in relationship to the West, as well as their approach to the many groups within China, became intertwined with the modern development of citizenship in China.[1]

One important theory which underlay this conceptualisation of citizenship is Max Weber's assertion that citizenship is necessarily an urban (and Occidental) phenomenon (Weber, 1963: 1228; Weber, 1930). This theory, in its original European context, was both a response to urbanisation as the engine of modernisation, and an attempt to disentangle a complex relationship between citizenship and the city. While it was the nineteenth-century condition of industrialisation that especially forcefully created the perception of peasants (and impoverished migrants to the city) as 'savages' and non-citizens (Weber, 1976: 3), a close link between cities and citizenship is recurrent in the history of Europe. Engin Isin (2002) shows how the city, as the space around which citizenship was initially formed in ancient Greece, has been continuously reappropriated throughout history. Even when citizenship became equated with nationality and belonging to the state rather than the city, the characteristics of urban citizenship were retained in the characteristics of state citizenship (Isin, 2009: 374–375). This 'Weberian' understanding of citizenship as necessarily urban has also become a cornerstone of the contemporary understanding of citizenship in China after its contact with the West.[2] This was the decisive impact which influenced the treatment of peasants, and later migrant workers, in China, long before the introduction of the *hukou* system.

In China, before contact with the colonial powers in the nineteenth century, the relationship between city and countryside was strikingly different. Under the early Qing empire, it was based on balanced economic and cultural exchanges between rural and urban, whereby rural life and identities were seen not as inferior, but rather as ideal: the microcosms of the empire (Oakes and Schein, 2006: 4; Duara, 2000: 15). This equilibrium started to shift after the first Opium

War in 1840, and the change was further embedded in the Republican era (1912–1949), when the rapid growth of coastal cities gave rise to new urban elites located in the colonial enclaves, which envisioned the character of Chinese cities as 'global', and 'urban' as modern, in contrast to rural China and to the rural migrants to the city (Yeh, 1997).

Ironically, this modernist tendency continued during Communism. Officially, the Communists strived to renounce anything that they associated with the 'bourgeois' capitalist class of the Republican era, including urban merchants and semi-colonised urban culture (Whyte and Parish, 1984: 10–16; Yeh, 1997: 378). The rejection of the Republican Chinese urban values opened a way to 'ruralise' city culture and organisation. For instance, with the gradual introduction of 'work units' (*danwei*) in the cities after 1949, the entire life-work of an individual or a collective was organised around a particular walled-off, urban, village-like community (Dutton, 1992: 231–232). However, even though the 'rural' was the new ideal to be re-enacted in the 'revolutionary' cities, the Maoist understanding of the 'rural' had little to do with Imperial China's conception of the 'rural' as the microcosm of the empire. Instead of family- or clan-centred identities, the Communists sought to remake both the city and the countryside into a new society (see Mao, 1940), where the old 'feudal' organisation of rural life was to be replaced by classless social relations, a process which peaked in the years of the Cultural Revolution (Cohen, 1993: 152–154). The *hukou* system, established in the late 1950s, was to aid this project by enabling strict monitoring of the ideological education of the peasantry, at the same time limiting movement of the population. By limiting people's movement, the system ensured a steady flow of produce from the countryside to the growing urban areas, ensuring that urban Chinese lived in the comfort of welfare provisions guaranteed by their *danwei*. In the meantime, despite the Maoist rhetoric, peasants continued to be seen as a 'feudal' and 'backward' part of society, which needed to be remade into a new class in order to lead the revolution (Cohen, 1993: 156).

Subsequently, after the 'opening to the world reforms' (*kaifang gaige*), the narratives of development and progress became even more pronounced, while peasant identities experienced a further downgrading as anti-modern. As economic development became the ultimate goal for society and individuals, spatial mobility came to be associated with social mobility (Oakes and Schein, 2006: 7), and the inequality that rural migrants experienced after having moved to the cities could be justified by the state and migrants themselves as a 'necessary sacrifice' for modernity. And so, with migration, not only did the process of marginalisation of the peasantry continue, but the capitalist and market-orientated mindset of urbanites actually led to increased discrimination against rural migrants in the cities. Lacking access to citizenship rights in the cities, until 2003 treated as 'illegal migrants' under the threat of deportation, and experiencing social and vocational discrimination, migrant workers have been excluded from both substantive and figurative 'urban citizenship'.

The tension between the urban and the rural is encapsulated in one of the most common names for 'citizen' in the Chinese language, *shimin* (urban citizen). In contemporary China, the word has lost the Republican meaning of urban citizens' autonomy from the central government, obscuring the Western origin of the word. The notion of *shimin* is somewhat ambiguous: while it means 'citizen' in a figurative sense, it has been predominantly used as an administrative term meaning 'an urban-*hukou*-holder' (Chen, 2005: 120), reflecting the substantive citizenship that urban-*hukou* holders have access to as opposed to rural migrants. The combination of these two connotations underpins the hierarchical formulation of citizenship in China. This exclusionary character of *shimin* is reflected in the notion of *shiminhua* ('becoming a citizen' or 'turning/being turned into a citizen'). In China, the notion of *shiminhua* has been used in the post-Maoist era to describe both the process of transformation from rural to urban (as in the culture, the identity, the sense of belonging) and the attainment of urban citizenship rights (e.g. Cai, 2008: 69–70). In public debates in China, the process of 'becoming citizens' (*shiminhua*) is understood as the migrants' ultimate need and aim. The majority of academics use this kind of migrant–victim narrative to make requests for migrants' 'rightful access to social benefits', 'education rights for their children' and 'respect for physical labour' etc. (Fan and Mao, 2008; Cai, 2008: 69; Chen, 2005: 121). However, this process also means the rejection, rather than acceptance, of the pre-existing (rural) identities of migrants. In this dominant narrative, the process of 'becoming an (urban) citizen' is the process of the replacement of rural identities with one of 'a better kind' – modern and urban.

However, despite such downgrading of the rural, migrant workers have been crucial actors in shaping citizenship in China. After all, it is migrant workers who, by exacerbating the government's fears of mass social unrest and by utilising the limited space created by the more relaxed attitude to migration, have been the primary actors pushing for reform of the *hukou* system (Wang, 2010: 80; Xiang, 2005). Under internal and international pressure, the government has introduced some changes in law, such as the relaxation of the *hukou* system, initially in 2001–2003, and then more decisively since 2014 when the so-called New-type Urbanisation Plan was put in place (Li *et al.*, 2016). However, the reforms so far have been superficial in that they have mainly involved the extension of urban-*hukou* registration to rural-*hukou* holders, rather than the complete overhaul of the system. They have also been geographically uneven, because different cities and provinces have employed varying policies towards migrant workers, often not conforming to central government's national policy (see Wang, 2010; Chan, 2014; Branigan, 2014).

The reform initiated in the years 2001–2003 introduced two broad changes: one was the extension of urban *hukou* to selected members of the migrant population; the other was the change in the cruel repatriation policies towards migrant workers. The first part of the reform was officially labelled '*hukou* in exchange for talent and investments' and it introduced new ways of acquiring an urban *hukou*. Before the reform, rural migrants could attain an urban *hukou* by serving in the army, climbing the Party career ladder, entering university or having their land repossessed, so that it had been reclassified as 'urban' (Solinger, 1999: 16). Following the 2001–2003 reform, the most common way to acquire an urban *hukou* has become the purchase of a property (*goufang ruhu*),[3] employers' sponsorship (granted to those deemed 'beneficial to the city') or simply payment of a substantial bribe (Zhang, 2007: 92–93).[4] Therefore, this reform clearly didn't abolish the urban/rural disparity, as was initially promised, but rather ended up just extending urban *hukou* to a few rich incomers who could afford a property or who fulfilled 'entry conditions' – that is, they possessed skills deemed 'valuable' to the city (Wang, 2010: 83–84). Other important legislation introduced by the reform was the overhaul of the repatriation policy and the *hukou* enforcement system. Prior to 2003, migrant workers were subjected to frequent police checks and, if proven not to have a 'temporary resident permit' to stay in the city, they would be detained (and sometimes beaten and tortured) and then deported to their place of origin. Through reform of the Measures on Aid and Management for Urban Vagrants and Beggars regulation in 2003, the government restricted checks on personal identification cards, and limited the automatic detention and deportation of migrant workers (Wang, 2010: 91). The central government introduced the reform in reaction to the public outrage at the beating to death of Sun Zhigang, a university-educated migrant detained by police in Guangzhou in 2003 for not carrying ID with him. This development should also be regarded as an example of the potential of society to transform laws governing some aspects of citizenship status (Hand, 2006). However, the reforms were short-lived as the rise in the homeless and begging population in the city centres of Shanghai and Beijing prompted the authorities to revise the policy, and resulted in renewed repatriations and checks (Wang, 2010: 92), particularly noticeable around 'mass events' such as the Beijing Olympics, as well as the sixtieth anniversary of the PRC in 2009 and the transfer of power to Xi Jinping in 2012 (as observed by myself during these events in Beijing).

The 2014 National New-type Urbanisation Plan is regarded as yet another important step in the *hukou* system reform. The plan promises 'people-orientated urbanisation' and the overhaul of the *hukou* system through removal of the rural–urban distinction (PRC Government, 2014). In 2014, the plan aimed to grant urban *hukou* to 100 million rural migrants by 2020, to decrease the proportion of the population without an urban *hukou* in cities from 18 per cent in 2012 to 15 per cent in 2020, while giving access to free education to 99 per cent of migrant children and workers (Chan, 2014: 4–5; PRC Government, 2014). However, this bold plan did not specify whether migrants would have access to council housing, which is the crucial challenge for migrant workers' integration in cities such as Beijing, where rental prices are prohibitively high. Indeed, some preliminary studies of the implementation of the reform so far point to the rising housing costs as one of the most visible impacts of the reform (Chen *et al.*, 2019), questioning the 'people-centredness' of the reform (Chen *et al.*, 2018). While, indeed, the reform encourages full access to substantial citizenship rights for migrant workers in cities of up to 500,000 inhabitants, it leaves freedom for interpreting the reform to urban authorities for cities with over a million inhabitants (Branigan, 2014). In the case of cities with more than 5 million residents, the plan calls for tightening of migration control, which makes access to equal citizenship in those cities more difficult than ever (Chan, 2019). This mismatch between the reform's professed aim of abolishing the *hukou* system and the reality of growing exclusion of migrant workers from the largest cities is economically unsustainable in the long run (Hayward and Jakimów, forthcoming 2021). Additionally, despite the proclaimed people-orientated character of the reform, the plan does not clarify the role of grassroots organisations in the implementation of the plan. For instance, the high-level meetings across Beijing with representatives from the National Development and Reform Commission did not encourage input from NGOs in the discussion of the plan; nor did they explain whether the plan would be consulted on with communities at the grassroots level to provide a more holistic and sustainable model of urbanisation (China Development Brief, 2014). This means that the current reforms, in the shape that has been released so far, do not differ greatly from the reforms that have been intermittently implemented since 2001.

Furthermore, while reform of the *hukou* system is crucial for the remaking of citizenship in China, particularly the access to substantial urban citizenship, it is by no means the only reform necessary to change the position of migrant workers in China. Because structural citizenship in China is not just the result of the *hukou* system legislation, but also a product of modernity, market mechanisms and the particular political system, its effects will be very hard to remove even if the *hukou* system is eventually abolished. As the example of inter-urban migrants treated as second-class citizens because of their purported 'low *suzhi*' indicates (Woodman, 2017), the negative social attitudes towards migrants stemming from the *suzhi* discourse will continue to affect migrant workers, even if they attain an urban *hukou*. The limitations in access to other rights of citizenship, such as civil, political, cultural or social rights (not only of rural, but also of urban citizens) will continue to deepen the rural–urban divide because they prevent migrants from co-deciding urban policies concerning their well-being. Apart from restricting legislation, the state continues to promote the overlapping citizenship discourse with hierarchical state–society relations, which further entrenches migrant workers' citizenship positionality in China.

Educating migrants into state-prescribed citizenship

Indeed, the rural–urban divide is only one aspect underlying structural citizenship in contemporary China. Another is the relationship between citizens and the state. It is this concern, rather than rural–urban relations, that dominated the intellectual discussions on citizenship in late Qing and Republican China. For instance, one of the main thinkers who introduced the concept of citizenship to China, Kang Youwei, championed an understanding of citizenship which emphasised China's unity and citizens' responsibilities to the state. For that reason, he used the word *guomin* ('people of the state') to translate the word 'citizen' into Chinese. In contrast to his teacher's (Liang Qichao) preferred notion of *gongmin* ('public people'), which is much closer to the Western tradition of citizen as an autonomous and empowered participant and co-creator of the public realm (Guo, 2015), *guomin* conveyed the idea of a citizen as someone who is state-serving. This preference for such a state-centred concept of citizenship ultimately prevailed under the Republican, and later Communist government, both of which aimed to unify China under a strong state and saw an emancipated citizenry as a potential threat to that project (Goldman, 2005: 11).

Contemporarily, apart from *gongmin* and *guomin*, there are also some other words that can translate as 'citizens', which carry normative meanings and reflect the cultural and political norms for acceptable citizenship practice. The concept of *diaomin* is used to depict the undesirable behaviour of citizens. It translates as 'unruly folk', 'troublemaker' or 'obstinate citizen' and is a pejorative term, which is most commonly used in relation to protestors, strikers or petitioners – the people who might sometimes be regarded as 'activist citizens'. Such labelling reflects the negative official attitudes towards citizenship practices involving active participation of civic actors in negotiation for the rights of groups they represent. This further entrenches the inferior positioning of migrant workers in structural citizenship in China, because it removes the ability to voice grievances by delegitimising activist citizenship. In public discourse, *diaomin* is often posed against *shunmin*, or 'obedient citizen', who trusts in the state's ultimate benevolence and acts 'harmoniously'. Indeed, this Confucian representation of state–society relations, whereby the citizen is depicted as an obedient child protected by a benevolent parent (the state), is actively promoted by the Chinese state, as exemplified by the usage of 'harmony' (*hexie*) and 'family' (*jia*) rhetoric in the Chinese public space and propaganda.

The state's promotion of such prescribed citizenship practices can be traced in school education programmes and public educational campaigns. Prescribing citizenship practices has been central to public campaigns in China since as early as the Republican period (Kennedy, 2013: 5). Also in the post-Maoist period, the above-discussed concepts of citizenship have been continuously integrated into school education. For instance, some of the ideas captured by the concept of *guomin* are closely reflected in the 'patriotic education' introduced especially forcefully in the 1990s as a response to the ideas of liberal democratic citizenship exhibited in the Tiananmen protests, and regarded as politically threatening and 'foreign-instilled' (Zhao, 1998).[5] Similarly to the early twentieth-century Han nationalism cast against the Manchu invaders, this patriotic education sought to instil 'love of the country' by casting the Chinese self against the historical foreign invaders. By renewing the focus on the 'century of humiliation' and the struggle against Japanese invaders, the education programme aimed to nourish a sense of nationalistic pride in being a PRC national (Zhao, 1998). However, in contrast to the early twentieth-century patriotism, this historical education relied heavily on exaltation of the Chinese Communist Party (CCP) achievements in 'saving China', and conflated patriotism with loyalty to the Party. Such patriotic education replaced an earlier focus on Marxism in schools and university entrance exams. The aim of this shift was the search for a new ideological foundation of the CCP's legitimacy: nationalism served this role more convincingly than discredited socialism (Zhao, 1998).

Despite this ideological de-emphasis on Marxism, the idea of 'socialist citizenship' survived in the post-Maoist period in a fragmented and incoherent fashion, and became closely tied to patriotic education. Rather than reflecting socialist ideals of egalitarianism and class struggle, it was refashioned to promote 'collectivism', understood to be integral to a uniquely Chinese conceptualisation of citizenship, and posed against 'liberal individual rights', which were portrayed as an alien and subversive concept. So rather than addressing material and class foundations of inequality which were emphasised under Maoism, 'socialist citizenship' in reform-era China became a justification for the CCP's disregard towards individual rights in the name of building a modern, strong China. A 'socialist citizen' was therefore expected to be both 'patriotic citizen' and 'obedient citizen' (*shunmin*). Indeed, in the reform period, the state started to promote ideas which went quite against the true meaning of socialism (as in egalitarianism): Deng Xiaoping's famous cry 'to get rich is glorious' marked the rise of what Aihwa Ong labelled 'neoliberal citizenship' (Ong, 1999, 2006). The 'neoliberal citizen-subject' was supposed to fend for themselves (*kao ziji*), and show entrepreneurial spirit and a materially orientated mindset (Ong, 2006: 14, 16; Fong and Murphy, 2006). This new understanding of who is a desirable citizen had particular impact on municipal governments' *hukou*-granting policies, targeting the migrant population with 'talent and investments' while excluding those deemed to be 'low-end population', as discussed in the previous section.

Under Xi Jinping, two further changes took place with regard to how state ideology was translated into prescribed citizenship practices and promoted through public and school education. First, the process of 'occidentalising' of Chinese citizenship took a new turn. The 2013 campaign of 'seven speak-nots' (*qi bu jiang*) forbade open promotion of various concepts related to citizenship: 'civil society', 'civil rights', 'universal values', 'freedom of speech', 'crony capitalism', 'judicial independence' and 'the CCP's historical errors' (Bakken, 2018: 3). These concepts, along with 'constitutionalism', 'neoliberalism', 'questioning socialist nature of socialism with Chinese characteristics' and 'free media', were portrayed as part of a 'Western anti-China plot' in the CCP's Central Committee 2013 report on the state of ideology, known as 'Document 9' (CPPCC, 2013). In 'Document 9', and earlier,[6] the CCP targeted the concept of 'civil society' in particular, arguing that its advocates 'set people against the Party' (CPPCC, 2013). Instead, under Hu-Wen's leadership the state sought to replace 'civil society' with the 'public interest' (*gongyi*) concept, stemming from the Lei Feng mythology. However, as discussed further in Chapter 3, the concept of *gongyi* soon became ideologically contested by grassroots actors. While the state promoted a concept of *gongyi cishan* (public-interest philanthropy) in its attempt to involve NGOs in its governance projects, NGOs employed the concept through the phrase *quanmin gongyi* (everyone's public interest), which was more contentious, as it emphasised the importance of grassroots organisations in governance (Wu, 2017: 124; see Chapter 3 for further discussion).

Second, a new spin was put on the idea of 'socialist citizen' by adding a Confucian element in the form of 'Socialist Core Values' and 'moral education', which further displaced Marxism/Maoism from the state-promoted understanding of 'socialism' (Gow, 2017: 97). The 'Socialist Core Values' are closely tied to 'moral education', exerted through Confucian classrooms, Confucian schools, Party schools and public propaganda campaigns such as the 'China Dream'. Confucian morality has formed an important part of citizenship education in China since as early as the 1980s, emphasising values of self-discipline, loyalty to one's country, respect for authority and social responsibility (Yu, 2008). Indeed, Confucianism was part and parcel of the state-promoted 'pastoral state–society relations' approach to citizenship, aimed at perfecting individuals to facilitate the state-building project (Lin, 2017: 59). Xi's re-emphasis on 'moral education' builds on these Confucian values, selectively politicising them in order to preserve the above-described desired ideas of the self-disciplined (economically productive), yet patriotic (CCP-obedient) citizen. This 'moral education' has been promoted through a countrywide public campaign of the 'China Dream/Socialist Core Values', exhibited through slogans and posters throughout China, from construction sites to bus stops. Apart from four 'national' and four 'societal' values, the campaign has a specific set of four values expected of citizens: patriotism, dedication, integrity and friendship (see Figure 1.1). This conceptualisation of citizenship means that a person becomes (rather than is born) a citizen when s/he conforms to the Confucian 'civilised' values (Gow, 2017: 105). Such 'moral education' in Confucian virtues is also currently being extended to the education of the CCP cadres in the form of the 'Three Strict, Three Real' campaign (Gow, 2017: 106). The campaign also promotes the idea of moral, self-disciplined cadres, and is intended to heal the corruption malaise within the Party and improve the perception

Figure 1.1 A Beijing Propaganda Bureau poster presenting 'Core Socialist Values'.

of the moral conduct of its members among the public (Kubat, 2018: 75). The campaigns under the China Dream umbrella in Xi's China emphasise the hierarchy between ruler and subject, as they aim to shape cadres into 'morally superior person[s]' (*junzi*), who are supposed to exert moral and political leadership, albeit in a benevolent manner (Gow, 2017). As Confucianism underlies the tradition of treating politics and participation in public life as a prerogative of elites, not common people, it also helps to further entrench the idea of the 'native' citizenship tradition in China as fundamentally anti-democratic (Yu, 2020: 20). The Confucian 'moral education' exerted through the 'Socialist Core Values' campaign builds on the patriotic and socialist education of the pre-Xi reform period to preserve the state-desired form of citizenship practice. This practice demands compliance with the dominant socio-economic order and unquestioning obedience to state authority, and by conferring matters of politics and public life solely on the state elites, it prescribes citizens' passivity.

These desired citizen behaviours are now being further monitored and enforced through the 'Social Credit System' (*shehui xinyong tixi*). Introduced in 2014, the system uses camera surveillance technology and big data analysis to assess the conformity of individual behaviour to the laws and 'moral values' promoted in Xi's China. Citizens who are deemed 'untrustworthy' (*shixin*) (the punishable behaviours range from serious financial fraud to taking part in strikes and protests, to playing loud music in public spaces or eating on public transport) are barred from access to services and from exercising various rights of citizenship.[7] Defined in state documents as promoting 'a culture of sincerity and traditional values' and 'building a harmonious Socialist society' (State Council, 2014), the system internalises long-standing cultural attitudes to citizenship encapsulated in the 'civilising' objective of the *suzhi* discourse and the Confucian ideas of state-serving and moral conduct (Kostka and Antoine, 2020), captured in the concepts of *shunmin* or *guomin*.

However, this prescribed role of citizens as 'obedient children of a benevolent state' further entrenches the inferior citizenship status of migrant workers. It does so by delegitimising this social group's struggle for change in substantial citizenship by depicting it as 'troublemaking'. In that sense, the authoritarian system contributes to the entrenchment of the socio-economic foundations underlying citizenship in China, as it limits the public debate, solidifies the spatial exclusion within the city and is complicit in maintaining migrant workers' position as docile bodies and neoliberal subjects. This impact of the hierarchical state–society relations embedded in the dominant citizenship discourse is further reinforced in the local strategies of migrant workers' governance in urban China.

Chinese cities as 'spaces of exclusion'

As a consequence of the dual rural–urban and state–society hierarchical citizenship discourse, and the legal aspects which accompany it, migrant workers end up experiencing large Chinese cities as spatial, legal, social and political 'spaces of exclusion'. Spatially, the migrants find themselves delegated to the fringes of the city, because they are unable to afford to own, or even rent, a property within the city proper. This exclusion sometimes takes a legal character, as non-local-*hukou* holders may be specifically excluded from the right to purchase property (as is the case in the largest cities such as Beijing or Shanghai), but even without this, properties in those cities are simply prohibitively expensive. Cities are experienced as 'spaces of exclusion' legally because migrants do not possess rights of urban citizenship, and cannot access services in the city; socially, because migrants' rural origin is a source of discrimination as non-citizens and aliens by the city residents; and politically because migrant workers are excluded from participation in local elections, and any form of political activism is heavily circumscribed and monitored by the municipal governments.

However, it is important to note local differences between the three cities in this study: Beijing, Shenzhen and Hangzhou. These differences illustrate more tangibly how the central citizenship-related policies and discourses affect the actual lives of migrant workers in these localities. The comparison also sketches out the direction of local experimentation and its influence on migrant workers' positionality within structural citizenship. Finally, it provides a fuller assessment of the reasons why labour NGOs' activism differs in each location and what chance these organisations have to influence citizenship regimes in each location in the future.

Beijing

Beijing is perhaps the most striking case of exclusionary policies towards migrant workers. The capital remains one of the most migrant-unfriendly municipalities in China, with severely restricted access to social provisions, and jarring social disparities. While other cities in China also exclude migrants from their housing construction projects, Beijing may be the most extreme case of a city where the production of the image of a 'global' city is exerted directly through practices of exclusion and marginalisation of migrant workers.

Apart from the well-documented lack of long-standing access to basic citizenship rights of education, hospitalisation and communal housing (Xiang, 2005; Solinger, 1999), this discrimination is directly exerted through the policies of urban planning, which often centre on demolition and redevelopment of urban villages. Urban villages, or 'villages within the city' (*chengzhongcun*), are the main areas where migrants live in large cities, because they are often the only places where they can afford to rent. The Beijing municipal government understands urban villages as dirty remnants of past poverty, no longer fit for the city's global ambitions, and seeks to replace them with modern high-rises, which are unattainable for migrant workers. It calls migrant workers the 'low-end' population (*diduan renkou*) (which relies on the citizenship discourse of the migrant population as 'backward', 'unmodern' and 'dirty') in order to justify the destruction and redevelopment of urban villages and the ensuing forced relocation of the migrant population who live there (Hayward and Jakimów, forthcoming 2021). Ironically, while officially presented as a group socially and economically disruptive to the spatial organisation of the city, migrant workers' muscles serve as an instrument of expansion of the physical fabric of the cities.

A prominent example of this hypocritical treatment of the migrant population comes from the 2008 Beijing Olympic Games, intended as a show for a global audience, whereby the Chinese capital was portrayed as a hyper-modern and truly globalised city. However, behind this glossy veneer, the city guards (*chengguan*), operating under the aegis of the Beijing government, were forcefully removing migrant workers from the city centre (Wang, 2010: 92), despite the fact that many of them worked painstakingly on the construction of the Olympic village. Their removal was facilitated by the forced demolition of urban villages: the government scheduled the demolition of 171 urban villages (out of a total of 231) in the run-up to the Olympic games in 2008 alone (Shin and Li, 2012: 2). The demolition of urban villages has continued ever since, and has resulted in continuous relocation of migrant workers to the fringes of the city.

The spatial segregation is also exerted within urban villages themselves. On my visit in 2013 to an urban village in Changping district in north Beijing, beyond the fourth ring road, I met migrant workers from local migrant NGO, AC. This NGO specialises in delivering education to migrant worker children and was founded by graduates of the Beijing Normal University, themselves from rural areas from across China. The NGO staff introduced me to their village, inhabited by about 40,000 migrant workers.[8] As we were walking around, I was shown an open-air exercise ground (*yundong zhongxin*) in the centre of the village, guarded by security guards. As my interviewee explained, the local government ensures that the playground cannot be used by the non-local-*hukou* holders. However, since there are barely any local-*hukou* holders living in the village, the playground stays empty, yet it remains guarded.

While this situation seems curiously arbitrary and unreasonable, the different district levels of Beijing's government are able to take even more drastic measures to limit the movement of migrant workers and their access to public space. In 2008, during the Olympics, the Beijing district government used for the first time the policy of 'sealed management' (*fengbi guanli*) in Laosanyu urban village (Batra, 2012). Sealed management is a practice of fencing off urban villages to control and restrict the migrant population living there. In 2010, the sixteen urban villages in Daxing district and forty-four urban villages in Changping district were walled and an overnight curfew on movement in and out of the village was enforced (Hu, 2010; He, 2010). The official reason for such drastic action was a rise in crime, purportedly linked to the migrant worker population: the widely cited public security report refers to these areas as the 'pain belt' (Yuan, 2011: 244–245, quoted in Hayward, forthcoming). The increased monitoring and control was therefore, as in so many other instances, justified in line with the objective of 'maintaining stability' (*weiwen*).

Since 2017, the plans to 'clean up Beijing' – that is, to expel migrant workers from the capital – have gained even greater traction, as the municipal government has employed the force of law to remove stalls, small shops and the whole markets where migrant workers have traded and worked for decades, deeming them illegal and lacking building permissions (Palmer, 2017; *China Daily*, 2017).[9] The December 2017 mass expulsion of migrants from Daxing district (discussed in more detail at the beginning of Chapter 7) was a culmination of these efforts. The municipal plans capped the population in the capital at 23 million by 2030, which translates into active efforts to remove and limit the migrant population in the capital (Lau, 2017).

Shenzhen

The experience of urban China as 'spaces of exclusion' for migrant workers is not limited to Beijing, but is a common feature of the largest cities across China. Despite being a city famously built entirely through the migrant workforce, Shenzhen has been similarly unwelcoming to the migrant population. Despite the fact that in 2013 nearly 77 per cent of Shenzhen's population were non-local-*hukou* holders (*Shenzhen Evening News*, 2013), the Shenzhen municipal government did not include migrants in the city's welfare schemes. The provincial government's version of the 2011-introduced policies, entitled 'Happy Guangdong', presumably aimed at addressing social inequality among other things (Gore, 2012; Page, 2011), failed to provide a sustainable scheme and the provision of affordable housing has been largely left to 'market mechanisms'. Since slow-return, low-value housing is not financially attractive to investors or the local government, there is a shortage of affordable housing for migrant workers, which also makes it impossible for many migrants to acquire an urban *hukou*.

Since the introduction of the New-type Urbanisation Plan in 2014, the government has made some effort to extend Shenzhen *hukou* to new residents of the city: in 2018 out of 13.6 million inhabitants 65.1 per cent were non-local-*hukou* holders (Shenzhen Bureau of Statistics, 2019), a marked decrease from the 2013 data. However, the current policies of the Shenzhen authorities continue to focus on 'attracting talents' through various generous incentivisation policies (Wu, 2018). The possession of Shenzhen *hukou* allows its holder to apply for housing subsidy (Wu, 2018), which is a particularly attractive incentive for acquiring Shenzhen *hukou*. However, none of these policies are extended to the blue-collar migrant population, in effect excluding them from the city welfare schemes.

Yet, some efforts have been made to transform at least social attitudes towards migrants. An example of this is the recent government-initiated campaigns of appreciation of migrant workers' contribution to China – including the recent trend of setting up migrant workers-themed exhibitions, or even whole museums (Qian and Guo, 2019). There is a permanent exhibition on migrant workers in Shenzhen Museum, which opened in 2008 and is located in the very centre of Shenzhen. In the exhibition I visited in 2013, migrant workers were represented as the constructers of Shenzhen, 'the miracle of China', and an army of producers for the global marketplace. Not surprisingly, in the exhibition the hardship of migrants' lives is quite under-represented: instead, we see migrant women holding hands while running happily to their workshops, and construction site workers cheering in brotherly embrace, proudly displaying their safety helmets (see Figures 1.2 and 1.3). The museum's veneration of the workers' hard work and its positioning within the narrative of nation-state building is actually intended to conceal the discussion of the unequally large price that this group has had to pay for

Figure 1.2 Shenzhen Museum photograph 1.

Figure 1.3 Shenzhen Museum photograph 2.

making reform-era China. Furthermore, the museums across the country uphold the idea of migrant workers as desirable because of their contribution and the idea of their need to rely on themselves (Qian and Guo, 2019), both of which constitute the cornerstone of the 'neoliberal citizen-subject' discourse.

Another visible campaign across the city of Shenzhen consists of slogans and posters, such as the one displayed in the Shenzhen subway in 2016 portraying a happy migrant couple holding a baby, with the inscription 'You are a Shenzhener once you come here' (Figure 1.4). The irony of the poster's message is that very few blue-collar migrants bring their children to the city due to the limited access to free education, the challenges of factory life and limited access to housing. However, the public campaigns seem to envisage Shenzhen as an inclusive and open city – quite an ironic contrast to the haphazard and constraining dormitory regimes in most of Shenzhen's factories and the material exclusion from housing projects. Indeed, the majority of migrant workers are bound by

Figure 1.4 'You are a Shenzhener once you come here'.

their dormitory regimes and overtime work in faraway industrial districts (such as Bao'an and Songgang in the West and Longgang in the East) (see Figure 1.5), rarely having time to venture into the city proper to admire the exhibition in the museum. A former head of ET, a long-serving migrant NGO from Shenzhen, commented on the campaign:

> 'You are a Shenzhener once you come here?' This is just laughable! The real situation of migrant workers in Shenzhen is completely different. There is another saying regarding this: 'You are a volunteer, once you come here' (*Laile, jiushi zhiyuanzhe*), which means that once you come to Shenzhen you just have to pay upfront everywhere, but your salary is nowhere to be seen. If you ask an average migrant worker if they think they can stay in the city, they will say they can't, and they don't want to, because there is really no hope for them here.[10]

Hangzhou

The city of Hangzhou is the capital of Zhejiang province, China's wealthiest province and, after Guangdong, second most popular migration destination (Zai, 2013). According to the 2010 National Census, the city was home to a population of over 8.7 million inhabitants (Zhejiang Provincial Bureau of Statistics, 2014), including

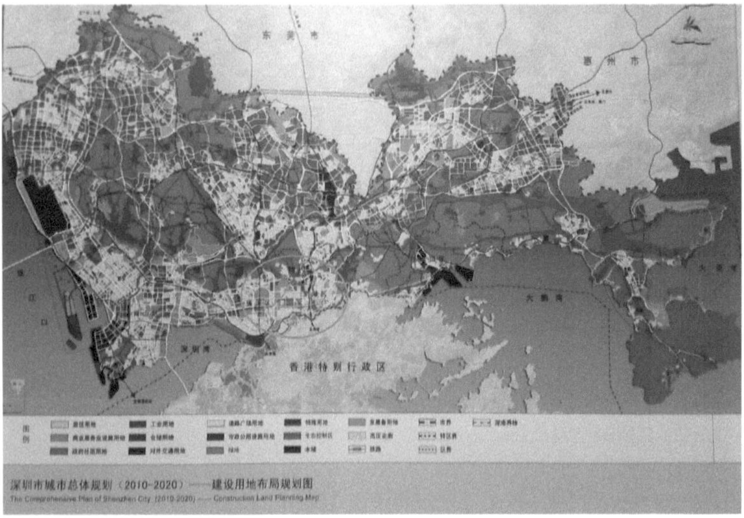

Figure 1.5 The city land use plan for Shenzhen (2010–2020). The area circled in red is the city centre. The areas marked in brown are the factories and industrial zones, where the majority of migrant workers live.

4.2 million migrant workers (Xu Z., 2013: 102). Yet, in 2017 these proportions had changed dramatically, and the number of non-local-*hukou* holders had decreased to only 2.26 million, or 28 per cent of the total population of Hangzhou, which reflects the exclusion of migrant workers from the housing project in the city (Zeng *et al.*, 2019: 73).

In many respects, the city has been implementing similar policies to those of Beijing and Shenzhen. In terms of housing and property development in particular, Hangzhou has also been reluctant to provide affordable housing for migrant workers. The policies behind the slogan 'Hangzhou: the city with quality of life' (*shengmin pinzhi zhi cheng*) have promised access to affordable housing for migrants (Mao, 2008). However, while the local rural-*hukou* population were granted urban *hukou* and given generous compensation after the appropriation of rural land by the municipality (Yang *et al.*, 2008: 75), no constructive measures were taken to provide accessible housing to migrant workers (Mao, 2008). Most migrant workers rent flats in urban villages from local rural-turned-urban-*hukou* holders who, as part of the compensation issued by the local government, received an extra flat, which they then rent to migrant workers (Yang *et al.*, 2008: 75). While urban-to-urban migrants, such as those from Wenzhou, or so-called 'migrant entrepreneurs' (Mao, 2008), have been acquiring urban *hukou* through the purchase of property, further driving Hangzhou's property boom (Zhu, 2012), this route is largely closed off to the blue-collar and rural migrant population. Moreover, recent years have witnessed large-scale redevelopment projects centred on the destruction of urban villages, akin to those in Beijing, which drive migrants away from the city and further prohibit their access to substantial citizenship (Zeng *et al.*, 2019).

Nonetheless, as Mao Dan points out, in comparison to the profit-orientated priorities of other major cities, the Hangzhou government has introduced more welfare-orientated policies towards migrant workers (Mao, 2010: 28). As such, the slogan 'Hangzhou: the city with quality of life' has been underpinned by some concrete legal steps in the form of the Hangzhou Floating Population's Service Management Regulation implemented in June 2012. The 2012 reform opened up access to various welfare measures for migrant workers, such as the right to employment in the same jobs as urban-*hukou* residents, participation in pension schemes, employment insurance schemes, workplace injury insurance, unemployment cover, healthcare schemes and free primary education for their children – therefore, at least in theory, equalising their access to various rights of urban citizenship (*Zhejiang News*, 2012; Xu Z., 2013). The Hangzhou government has also set up insurance schemes for the children of migrant workers and included them in some local healthcare schemes, such as vaccinations (China Labour Bulletin, 2013). Some authors claim that properties became widely available for purchase at 'affordable prices' in sub-centres of Hangzhou (Liu *et al.*, 2011: 720–722).[11] Finally, some studies have found that employer-provided rental subsidies, including a housing provident fund, have been another important factor enabling migrant workers to stay in the city (Zeng *et al.*, 2019).

According to a Chinese official, Xu Zu'e, access to education for migrant workers' children improved greatly after the 2012 reforms (Xu Z., 2013).Yet it was still not easy in early 2012, when I interviewed a representative of NHC, who confirmed that it remained very hard to access public schools, and that many children have to be left in the countryside for their education.[12] Nonetheless, during my participant observation with SA, a Zhejiang University-based association which regularly provides teaching to migrant children and cultural activities for migrant workers on construction sites, I went to both the construction site and the public school for migrant children, where I taught them English.[13] The conditions of schooling were much better (see Figure 1.6) than those I witnessed in Beijing, and access to this particular public school was easier for migrant children. Other studies have found that education in Hangzhou is widely available to migrant children, but it is substandard in comparison to that provided to urban-*hukou* holders (Zeng *et al.*, 2019: 76).

Also, the social discourse around migrant workers is quite different in Hangzhou than in Shenzhen and Beijing. Migrant workers are often called 'new Hangzhouers' (*xin Hangzhouren*) in public discourse,

Figure 1.6 A public school accepting migrant children in Hangzhou. The school is located on the fringes of Xihu District (Hangzhou), in an area inhabited mainly by migrant workers, and accepts migrant workers' children for a small fee.

even by government officials (see *Zhejiang News*, 2012; Xu Z., 2013), or 'new urban citizens' (*xin shimin*) (see Mao, 2008). The attitudes of local residents towards migrant workers were described as more sympathetic than in many other cities.[14]

The municipal government of Hangzhou continues to maintain large barriers to the acquisition of urban *hukou* and even to the granting of permanent residence status. According to the June 2012 regulation, only migrant workers with a high school degree (equivalent to GCSEs in the UK) can be considered for a permanent residence permit (*juzhuzheng*) (*Zhejiang News*, 2012), a form of 'attracting talents' policy forging the ultimate idea of the 'neoliberal citizen-subject' as a desirable type of citizen. Also, because of the lack of a mechanism to allow migrant workers to influence the urban agenda, which makes them 'powerless subjects of government actions' (Zhu, 2012: 451), access to channels linked to claims centred around the 'right to the city' postulate becomes a vital part of the recognition of migrant workers as citizens. However, while the exclusion based on the rural–urban divide still persists in some areas in Hangzhou, in terms of both citizenship discourse and regime, the shift towards the greater inclusion and equality of migrant workers – and therefore the citizenship transformation – has been greater than in the other two case studies discussed earlier.

Conclusion

The genealogical enquiry into the formulation of citizenship and its subsequent impact on the treatment of migrant workers in urban China presented in this chapter exposes the limitations of the mainstream theories of citizenship which conceive of it solely as a legal institution of the *hukou* system. While that system is instrumental in discrimination and segregation practices, the *hukou*-only focus often obscures the presence of wider processes at play which are fundamental to shaping migrant workers' citizenship in China. These wider aspects include the modernity and urbanisation discourses which engendered a hierarchical rural–urban imaginary, as well as the characteristics of the political regime, which resulted in hierarchical state–society relations affecting citizenship regime and discourse. These two fundamental aspects of structural citizenship, paired with a capitalism-orientated logic of development, have driven spatial practices of exclusion and segregation in urban China, which result in migrant workers' experience of cities as 'spaces of (citizenship) exclusion'. While dominant discourses and local policies promise that migrant workers can be included into the urban citizenry, this is only possible once rural migrants attain urban culture and identity, acquire an urban *hukou* and own a property in the city. This excludes the majority of blue-collar workers, who are not able to access an urban *hukou* or afford a city property, nor able or willing to 'transform their culture'. Similarly, the prescribed citizenship practices of passivity and obedience, along with the lack of political rights to participate in urban governance, further entrench the marginal position of migrants in urban China, making them helpless in the face of the combined force of state policies and capital. With local governments reluctant to enable migrant workers' inclusion into the urban citizenry in both figurative and substantive ways, migrant workers are likely to remain second-class citizens, which further entrenches inequality and is likely to contribute to social instability. As central and local governments are unwilling to address the consequences of such differentiated structural citizenship, how can this situation be improved? In particular, to what extent can migrant-orientated NGOs address the underlying aspects of structural citizenship, and how can this improve the position of migrant workers in China?

Notes

1 The concept of Orientalism, a term originally used by Edward Said (1978), is essentially based on the idea of defining 'Self' in contrast to 'the Other', which can be best summarised as the 'othering' mechanism. In China, a similar mechanism has been employed, which takes 'the West' as its 'Other', defined as Occidentalism (see Wang, 2014).
2 Max Weber is one of the most widely cited non-Chinese authors in the Chinese social sciences (Zeng, 2014: 7), therefore his impact on Chinese academia has been crucial.
3 This has not been the case in all cities though; Beijing and Shanghai are still restricting acquisition of *hukou* based on property purchase.
4 The commodification of urban *hukou* has gradually increased from the late 1980s onwards (Zhang, 2007: 92).

5 See Guang (1996) for a comprehensive discussion of the concept of 'democratic citizenship' in the Tiananmen protests.
6 See the 'pitfall of civil society' debate in Zeng (2014): 17, Zhou (2011) and Simon (2013): 8–11.
7 Various forms of punishment have been meted out already to those who are found 'faulty'. Some of the constraints on rights of citizenship include: delaying or refusing access to social services (hospitals and schools), and removing access to financial means (such as loans), to ability to travel (by restricting the sale of rail and plane tickets for instance), to purchase of land, etc. (Creemers, 2018: 14–15). As of June 2019, according to data from the National Development and Research Commission, 26.82 million plane and 5.96 million rail tickets were denied to 'untrustworthy' citizens (Xinhua, 2019). Moreover, in the fashion reminiscent of the Cultural Revolution, the names of citizens found 'guilty' are publicly displayed (online and in public spaces, such as public transport).
8 Interview no. 21.
9 In 2017 alone 120 markets were removed across the city (*China Daily*, 2017).
10 Interview no. 46.
11 Actually, the influx of migrant workers propelled the polycentric development of Hangzhou's property market and job availability, which is very different to Beijing's monocentric urbanisation pattern (Liu *et al.*, 2011: 719).
12 Interview no. 9.
13 Participant observation in December 2011.
14 Interviews no. 1, no. 2 and no. 9.

Part II

Civic organising

2

Organising under the repressive state

As discussed in the previous chapter, migrant workers can expect little support from the government to facilitate their figurative and substantial inclusion as urban citizens. This, combined with the hardship of work in low-paid and often hazardous jobs in the city, means many migrant workers face a difficult choice: either to migrate back to their home towns, or to remain in the cities and agree to degrading conditions of life on the city fringes. Under certain circumstances, migrants seek to change the conditions of life and work in the city: either by going on strike, joining a protest, or through desperate acts such as individual protests and even suicides. While these are specific acts which usually target a certain set of demands, rather than the broader condition of migrant workers' life in the cities, this book focuses on a more sustained and broader type of activism undertaken by migrant workers and other actors sympathetic with their plight: that of creating grassroots organisations in the cities. This chapter will highlight how the very act of creating and running an NGO can be viewed as an act of citizenship.

While the formation of NGOs seems to be a relatively moderate attempt to target injustice suffered by this vast social group in China, it remains rare and fraught with difficulty. But why is organising a migrant NGO so difficult? Is it because of the state's policies, or rather, is it the result of the lack of funding, lack of relationship with appropriate authorities (*guanxi*) or lack of social capital (Franceschini, 2014)? There are certainly all these issues to consider, but they do largely boil down to the underlying problem of uneven state–society relations in China. And these are underpinned by a constant insecurity in the Party about possible challenge to their rule. This insecurity drives the party-state's policies and laws and it results in an array of informal barriers to ensure that NGOs can exist only if their objectives are closely correlated with those of the state. It is ultimately the issue of what citizens can and cannot do, and the fear of challenge from its citizens that defines the repressive relationship between the Party and civic organisations. When trying to organise, the activists face constraints which ultimately derive from the role that is prescribed through this hierarchical state–society relationship. In this chapter I discuss how legal constraints and informal state–society relations have forged a certain understanding of citizenship in China, one which requires its citizens to advise rather than challenge, listen rather than speak and follow rather than initiate. The chapter then highlights the strategies which organisations must follow to organise, and I will reflect how this, in turn, pushes the boundaries of such state-prescribed citizenship.

In doing so, the fieldwork observations contained in this chapter highlight two particular strategies in the way NGOs organise: I call one of these strategies 'resistance through accommodation', and I borrow Jones' notion of 'relational negotiation of citizenship' to describe the other (Jones, 2004: 172). As discussed in the introduction, 'resistance through accommodation' captures how NGOs can perform acts of citizenship (resistance), even if they engage with state actors or state frameworks in their activism (accommodation). 'Relational negotiation of citizenship', on the other hand, refers to the way in which civic actors negotiate citizenship practices and behaviours though a particular relationship with a state agent. These two strategies are interrelated and can be employed interchangeably. Similarly to the strategies described by Ho, Mertha and Spires, 'resistance through accommodation' and 'relational negotiation of citizenship' also take into account the need for civic organisations to enter into a relationship with the state, but unlike them, they focus on attempts by these organisations to stretch and rework the very structure of that relationship, ultimately pushing for a change in the role of citizens in state–society relations.

The legal constraints to organising in China

Since the reforms initiated by Deng Xiaoping, law has become an important instrument in the state's control of society. Unlike the

Maoist-era rule-by-man approach, or the lawlessness and arbitrariness characteristic of the Cultural Revolution, law was reinstated as a necessary stepping stone in the reforms of the Chinese economy. Yet, the law also became an important instrument in the Party's hands to extend its control over society. This designation of law as a control mechanism is visible in the array of new regulations regarding NGOs, passed from the 1990s onwards, introducing increasingly tighter control over civic organisations.[1]

However, while these reforms were intended to weed out the NGOs deemed to be threatening to the state (those involved in advocacy, legal action, labour rights, ethnic issues, religion and human rights) and obstruct the formation of NGOs without strong state connections, they also increased transparency and provided new sources of funding for NGOs deemed socially useful and those which could establish a relationship with a state agency or a GONGO. These regulations aim to limit the emergence and survival of undesirable types of NGOs by blocking access to formal registration, and therefore funding. According to the 1998 Regulations on the Registration and Management of Social Organisations, all NGOs have to register under the Ministry of Civil Affairs (MOCA) through a two-step, so-called 'dual management' procedure. First, the NGO needs to find a sponsoring unit (*guakao danwei*) which acts as an initial organ to review the application, check the 'legality' of the NGO's declared scope of activities and then direct the approved application to MOCA, under which NGOs are formally registered as non-profit organisations (NPOs). The sponsoring units are usually government or Party agencies, and they are overwhelmed with applications (Lau, 2009: 8). In addition, they must bear responsibility for the NGO's actions, so they are unwilling to act as a sponsor. In consequence, throughout the 1990s and 2000s, few organisations ever succeeded in registering legally as NGOs (Saich, 2000: 130). Additionally, the law stipulates that only one organisation of a certain sub-type (out of the six sub-types of NGOs that are specified in this law) can be registered as an NGO in a certain geographical area (such as a city district), and that their activities should not go beyond this administrative area. In consequence, after the introduction of the law, many NGOs started adopting evasive practices, among which registering as a business through the State Administration of Industry and Commerce (SAIC) is the most common.

In 2012, a new, simplified procedure of registering directly with MOCA, without the need of a 'mother institution', was introduced in Guangdong (Doyon, 2012). Moreover, in 2014 new legislation was introduced in Guangzhou removing the 1998 legislative requirement of only one organisation per administrative area (Hsu J., 2017: 53). The revisions to the Regulations on the Registration and Management of Social Organisations (still a draft at the time of writing this book) further entrenched the experiments initiated in Guangzhou in 2012 of a simplified registration procedure allowing 'less sensitive' NPOs to register directly with MOCA (China Development Brief, 2018). This draft introduces a requirement for all NPOs to install Party cells inside those organisations, requires that an NPO must have more than fifty members in order to register, and only permits four 'less sensitive' types of NPOs.[2] Therefore, while registration has been largely simplified for 'less sensitive' types of NGOs and those with links to the government, the migrant NGOs I researched still struggled to access the registration process at the time of writing this book. This confirms that while the registration process was facilitated for some types of NPOs, it is still prohibitive to others, and the new law is likely to make access to registration even more restrictive.

Apart from the above-mentioned 2018 revision of the 1998 regulations, two more legal documents governing the functioning of civil society were introduced under the Xi administration: the 2016 Charity Law and the 2017 Overseas NGOs Management Law. The Charity Law promulgated in 2016 was an important and long-awaited reform to regulate philanthropy in China, a sector that had been frequently tainted with corruption scandals,[3] and one which needed greater legal and fiscal operational clarity. Yet, as with other legislation, the law clearly privileges organisations with strong links to the government, big budgets and a large number of staff members, as only those organisations are allowed to receive charity status. For these organisations, there are substantial tax exemptions, and lowered barriers to receipt of public donations. Small grassroots organisations, such as most migrant NGOs, are highly unlikely to benefit from the law. Moreover, many articles in the law are arbitrary and vague. For instance, art. 5 specifies that 'the government supports organisations representing the core values of socialism and promoting the traditional morals of the Chinese nation', which leaves room for intervention against practically any NGO deemed to be 'promoting non-Chinese morals'.

An accompanying reform which even further restricts NGOs' freedom of association is the Overseas NGOs Management Law promulgated at the start of 2017. This reform was preceded by the 2010 Notice of the State Administration of Foreign Exchange on Issues concerning the Administration of Foreign Exchange Donated to or by Domestic Institutions, which put more bureaucratic requirements on NGOs and tightened the state's control over NGOs, as banks were supposed to report any donations they deem 'suspicious' (State Administration of Foreign Exchange, 2010). The reform hit small, grassroots NGOs in particular, as large organisations with governmental links are exempted from these requirements. The 2017 Overseas NGOs Management Law introduced a new level of restrictions on domestic NGOs' access to foreign funding. According to this law, all INGOs must register with the Public Security Bureau and find partner organisations within China. As in the case of the Charity Law, the organisations which are welcomed to register must operate within the 'less politically sensitive' areas, such as education, economy, science, technology, health, sports, culture, environment, poverty alleviation and disaster relief. The law severely limits the ability of foreign foundations to support small grassroots NGOs in China, particularly those perceived as 'politically sensitive', such as labour, legal action and human rights organisations.

This carrot-and-stick treatment of NGOs is part of the wider approach to civil society under the Xi administration. After a relatively non-interventionist period in the 2000s, with many NGOs remaining unregistered and benefiting from the legal grey zone, the five-year plan of 2011–2015 introduced the 'social management innovation' strategy, which aimed to increase the ability of the party-state to coordinate social organisations in service of the state-led development process. This strategy, also defined as 'consultative authoritarianism', emerged from local experiments in places like Yunnan, and allowed the party-state to strengthen its influence over civil society (Teets, 2014). It was also a prelude to Xi's new model of 'social governance', which was presented as a 'governance partnership' between NGOs and the state in the 2013 Third Plenum Decision of the 18th Central Committee (ICNL, 2017). Yet, given the effects of the laws promulgated in recent years on the NGO sector, it should rather be seen as part of a wider attempt to curtail the growing internal unrest in China. In this new strategy, the 'governing the country in accordance with the law' (*yifa zhiguo*) rhetoric and the new laws serve as a tool of repression on what the party-state perceives as a threat to its power.

The difficulties that the law poses to the mere act of organising a migrant NGO are indeed substantial. Very few labour NGOs manage to register with MOCA, even despite the simplified procedures since 2012. Moreover, the new legislation helps the Public Security forces to more easily intervene and crack down on organisations seen as a 'public security threat', making the law an effective tool of control. Indeed, the state is using these laws to disperse labour NGOs, particularly in Guangdong province, as the cases of sentencing of labour activists in 2016 and 2019 illustrate.[4] Therefore, to organise often requires actions which grab space within the existing laws to circumvent them without breaking them, which sometimes leads to an expansion in the meanings and scope of permissible activism. In this process, NGOs might occasionally go against established practices, but more often they organise by using the strategy of 'resistance through accommodation' and 'relational negotiation of citizenship', which allow them to transform citizenship through negotiation with state agents or by using established state channels and vocabulary. Law is one such area through which NGOs may expand the permissible remits of citizen action in China.

Circumventing the law as an act of citizenship

Under these circumstances, organising an NGO has long been conducted through circumvention of the restrictive laws, without necessarily breaking them. By circumventing these legal constraints migrant NGOs question and reshape the existing prescribed citizenship practices and even challenge aspects of the citizenship regime. They do so through expansion of the space for civic activism *despite* the stringent legal frameworks. One such way of circumventing the law is registering as a business, which makes the NGO a legal, registered entity. This strategy is by far the most popular: among all nineteen NGOs discussed in this book, only five are officially registered under

MOCA, and the majority are registered as businesses under SAIC.[5] While the cost of this strategy is the compulsory taxation, it also affords some benefits. Apart from the 'legalised' status, NGOs can also overcome the geographical restrictions put on officially registered NPOs, and gain greater independence from government agencies than MOCA-registered organisations. This allows these NGOs to utilise some spatial strategies to perform their activities in the cities (and beyond). Some of these spatial strategies help overcome the rigid legal regime that constrains NGOs' activism in China, creatively designing new channels for outreach and citizen engagement.

One such spatial strategy is the intentional location of NGOs within the cities (for example in the city centre), so that migrants from all around the city can easily reach the organisation (BWH, for instance, employed this strategy at the time of the fieldwork). Other NGOs can undertake their activities in a broader number of localities, which they could not have done had they been registered with MOCA. For instance, they can travel around the city or country, allowing them to extend their outreach. NBW is an example of an organisation which, although based in a suburban area of Beijing, has a much wider outreach than just its immediate community. Although mainly catering for the local community, they give concerts and distribute publications to migrants throughout China, and have played concerts across Beijing for a variety of audiences: migrant workers, Beijing's middle class (as I witnessed myself), and even for CCP members. Their national tour in 2012, co-sponsored by the International Labour Organisation (ILO), reached places such as Wuxi (Jiangsu province), Kunming (Yunnan province), Guangdong and many cities in Hunan province.[6] Another channel which circumvents administrative constraints on NGOs' outreach is the internet (social media, microblogging and emails), which is an important tool for contacting migrant workers and potential donors.

Some other spatial tactics noted during the fieldwork concerned the circumvention of restrictions on overseas financial transfers put in place by the 2010 regulation. Activists, the media and academics have argued that this particular regulation had an adverse effect, especially on small grassroots NGOs (Davis, 2010; Ford, 2010), as it mounted bureaucratic requirements and obstructed the only source of funding these NGOs were able to receive. Before 2017, some

NGOs had circumvented the regulation by opening bank accounts in Hong Kong, by setting up internet banking accounts such as Zhifubao, a Chinese equivalent of PayPal,[7] or by setting up business rather than non-profit accounts, which is the most common way of evading the restrictive legislation (though it requires NGOs to pay taxes). However, the 2017 Overseas NGOs Management Law has further entrenched the state's control over overseas fund transfers and made many of the circumventing practices very difficult. Even before it was passed, in 2015, a Zhejiang-based NGO, SFI, for instance, was unable to access funds from a European Union-funded project which it secured through open competition. Of course, there was no clear justification why this was done: the bank simply refused to exchange the sum into renminbi and pay it out to the organisation.[8] The 2017 law created an ever greater obstacle for migrant NGOs to receive funding from abroad, which has indeed negatively impacted many, especially more 'politically sensitive' labour NGOs in the PRD (Franceschini and Nesossi, 2018).

Up until recently, most NGOs still managed to design largely successful methods to help them evade the restrictions imposed by the nationwide laws, or even to turn these restrictions to their advantage. Moreover, these acts of circumventing legal constraints or utilising legal loopholes also challenge the rigid state-defined administrative territorial boundaries or even national territorial boundaries. These channels of horizontal networks or interactions, internet and city spaces become 'spaces of citizenship transformation', as they help NGOs to question the prescriptive citizenship practices and circumvent the national laws which limit migrants' civic organising. As such, organising can be understood as an act of citizenship performed with the use of de Certeau's 'tactics': the manipulating of events, language, rules and spaces into which these organisations are forced (de Certeau, 1984: xix, 37) – the manipulation which at times leads to 'resistance through accommodation'. The spatial tactics described above use and overcome the limitations of territorial spaces, ridicule the ineffectiveness of the law, utilise the gaps between the law and its implementation, and ultimately question the legitimacy of both. While the ever more effective laws under Xi's leadership are likely to put an end to many of these practices, the NGOs' entrepreneurial search for ways to overcome these restrictions makes organising an important act of citizenship.

Organising under the local state: relational citizenship negotiation

While the legal constraints discussed above obstruct the act of organising by labour NGOs, until the 2017 Overseas NGOs Management Law came into force, these could have been largely evaded or diffused by a variety of tactics. This state of affairs had long been caused by the fact that what had a much greater impact on the success or failure of organising a migrant/labour NGO was the quality and management of relationships between NGOs and the local state's many agencies.

Organisations I reached have come into contact with several such local government agencies. In their attempts to register, they came across local bureaus of MOCA and SAIC. In their legal action work as workers' court representatives they came across local Labour Bureaus and courts. They also receive regular visits from State Security agents who are tasked with monitoring the possible threat that the NGOs pose to the state. NGOs' direct contacts with the Public Security Bureau are usually reserved for cases of crackdowns on organisations as well as indirect harassment. Some activists I interviewed have also come in contact with powerful politicians within the city government. These relations proved to be important for some NGOs' development, while saving others in times of trouble, as will be highlighted in the following sections. Finally, many NGOs come into contact with ACFTU, which proved to be an important source of funding and support for some of the NGOs, but which has also acted in an increasingly confrontational manner towards others. ACFTU and GONGOs such as the All-China Women's Federation (ACWF) and All-China Lawyers' Association (ACLA) are important bodies which can act as sponsoring units in the process of official registration under MOCA.[9] While Party directives from as early as 1999, both centrally and locally, have treated labour NGOs as a threat to the party-state (Fu, 2017: 53–54), these various agencies of the local state had long been engaging selectively with the existing legal framework on the functioning of NGOs as well as the Party directives, for a long time turning a blind eye on tactics used by organisations to circumvent the regulations.

The relationships with the above-listed agencies have determined, and to a degree, even under Xi, continue to determine, the experience of operating a labour NGO in China. The importance of these relations' impact on shaping citizenship is well-captured by the concept of 'the relational negotiation of citizenship', first used in the context of South America (Jones, 2004: 172). This concept describes how the scope of civic activism is malleable through negotiations with the local state, rather than fixed through the formal citizenship regime based on the law. It is useful in the Chinese context, where everyday issues and challenges tend to be addressed through established practices of *guanxi* (relationship-building), rather than institutionalised channels.[10] Consequently, the degree to which the act of organising has the potential to change the prescribed citizenship practices depends greatly on the way in which NGOs interact with the local state. Their relations with local government officials and state agencies often determine the way NGOs organise, and then also the ways they can push the boundaries of citizenship. In this context, establishing *guanxi* is an important tactic of exerting change. However, not all NGOs succeed in establishing such relations. In this section I will discuss instances of cooperation, neutrality and confrontation in relations between NGOs and the local state, trade unions and businesses, and whether these relations challenge or maintain the established citizenship practices in China.

NGO–local state relations: from 'resistance through accommodation' to repression

Despite much emphasis on the confrontational interactions between civil society actors and the state in authoritarian regimes, NGOs' relationship with the local state should not be viewed solely as confrontational. Indeed, while the 'times of confrontation' are strongly pronounced in news reports and research, cooperation with the state is important and desirable for all the organisations in this study, while confrontation is avoided and rarely intentionally provoked by the organisations (also see Hsu J., 2017). It takes some years to form a sustainable relationship with the local cadres, and many NGOs, even those which care about maintaining their independent status, crave good contacts with their local government agencies. For some NGOs, however, a relationship with the government is very difficult to form, because small, low-profile organisations do not have much chance of networking with Party officials. Consequently, some NGOs in my study (e.g. MVD or AC) are regretful about not having any such relationship. Having a constructive, or at least a non-obstructive, relationship with local government agencies not only facilitates the NGOs' work; sometimes it also determines their long-term sustainability, public outreach and even survival. It is therefore important for NGOs' long-term ability to negotiate citizenship practices. Moreover, an established relationship with local officials does not necessarily translate into either surveillance of the NGO or subservience towards the state's goals. While NGOs with established relationships feel obliged to obey some more or less institutionalised rules, such as adopting state-promoted language and using the state-approved legal channels, they can use these to facilitate their activism rather than obstruct it.

Several of the NGOs in my study had a good or at least non-obstructive relationship with the local government agencies, which facilitated such relational negotiation of citizenship. Beijing-based BWH,[11] for instance, is an organisation which evolved from an information hotline for migrant workers into a workplace mediation committee under the aegis of the local government, and up until 2014 was an example of an all-round successful NGO, which skilfully balanced its interactions with both the government and FAs. The organisation was set up by a migrant worker from Henan province, who himself had experience of *dagong* as a peddler in Beijing in the 1990s. When it began its mediating activities in the early 2000s, the NGO was approached by district-level government officials who, after learning about its work, allowed it to operate and even officially certified its activities as a mediation committee in 2004. This status enhanced the NGO's position vis-à-vis the employers and secured trust from the migrant workers. While BWH's leader did not disclose this information to me, I was informed by one of the NGO's foreign funders that he formed a relationship with a highly positioned official in the municipal government, which up to 2013 greatly facilitated the NGO's work.[12] The NGO also maintained its relationship with government by attending some government-organised events for social workers, such as the Lei Feng Day (a training day for volunteers) or attending training sessions for lawyers organised by ACLA.[13]

However, this did not mean that the NGO staff were not critical of the government: as the staff became used to my presence in the office, the criticism of cases of corruption and dissatisfaction with the systemic constraints on NGOs' functioning in China would emerge in their conversations. Though some NGO volunteer lawyers became wary of my presence in the office, saying that 'they shouldn't wash dirty laundry in front of a foreigner',[14] some other employees would be more vocal and angry about the issues, insisting that there is a need for an open discussion. Of course, there is a possibility that the NGO had a more direct exchange with local government, that I was not told about or aware of at the time of my stay with the organisation. It is very likely that the organisation regularly reports its doings to the State Security (*guobao*) agents, as the majority of migrant NGOs are by default regularly interrogated (or 'invited for tea' (*qing hecha*)) by State Security agents.[15] However, at the time of my fieldwork with the organisation in 2012 no visits from the local state agents were paid to the office itself and no visits of the NGO staff to the local government that I was aware of. Indeed, the fact that they regularly employed foreign individuals like myself in the organisation testified to its secure status via-à-vis the local government. Perhaps one of the reasons for that state of affairs is the ability of BHW to present their work as aiding the government's efforts, such as 'the creation of harmonious society' and 'helping to resolve social conflicts'.

IMH is another case in point. IMH is a Foshan-based NGO created in 2012 after some activists split from the Guangzhou-based NGO, FJ, in order to focus only on injury-related cases, rather than general labour issues which usually related to wage arrears and collective bargaining. Unlike FJ, at least initially, IMH specialised in dealing with workplace injury-related training, and withdrew from representing migrants in court, directing them to the government's Labour Bureau for arbitration instead. Because of this compliant type of activism, the NGO was allowed to register under MOCA soon after it was established. When interviewed in 2013, the employee from IMH explained to me that this formal registration status was important because it boosted the NGO's legitimacy in the eyes of workers, as they felt more confident if they could see a formal, legal certificate on the wall. My interviewee emphasised on several occasions that apart from this, the status did not help with anything. Indeed, the government did not provide any funding for the NGO and it relied on funds provided by a German INGO instead.[16] The registered status didn't help the organisation during the 2015 crackdown in

Guangzhou either, when its founder was arrested and put on trial with charges of embezzlement, reflecting the abrupt changes in authorities' attitudes under Xi Jinping, and the lack of security even for a 'legalised' organisation.

The above cases illustrate the advantages, but also the limits to benefits that come with forging relations with a local state. The common denominator in the activities of these NGOs who boast good links with party-state agencies is their strong self-censorship, transparency and very clear-cut activities. (Each of these NGOs tends to specialise in one area only, which is clearly approved by the government.) However, such a relationship may force NGOs to concentrate their efforts on maintaining rather than transforming the status quo, including migrants' citizenship status.

Moreover, because such relationships are often formed on a personal, rather than institutional basis, they are usually time-limited, fraught with risk and lacking transparency. The possession of an official NPO registration status or an established relationship with the local state does not guarantee protection from arbitrary actions by state agencies, including bureaucratic obstacles, more or less indirect clampdowns and even closure, as indicated in the examples of crackdowns on the Shenzhen branch of BWH and Foshan-based IMH. BWH's leader had an established relationship with a local Party official, and IMH was officially registered under MOCA, yet both NGOs suffered in the crackdowns in 2014 and 2015 respectively. Indeed, the 'good times' seem to have been limited to the early Hu-Wen period, when even more contentious organisations prospered, as one NGO activist noted:

> When I set up the organisation [in 2004] many officials supported the idea ... Back then the government realised that they needed us, labour NGOs, to help migrant workers, as they knew about the horrible working conditions and workers' hardship ... They might pressure you in your work and add difficulties, but they wouldn't shut you down. If you just went to court to represent workers and did the 'rights defence', they would not make your life too difficult.[17]

However, since the law obstructs the formation of migrant NGOs and is often arbitrarily implemented, NGOs frequently have little choice but to try to create good relations with state actors. This makes the citizenship regime in China 'relational', rather than just institutionalised, as the boundaries of citizenship practice can be negotiated through individual relationships between state and society actors. It also emphasises the state's domination over the process of defining when NGOs can negotiate civic organising-related citizenship rights and practices.

While reliance on personal relationships and the goodwill of the party-state doesn't remove NGO's vulnerability, those NGOs which do not have such relations, or cross the Party-permissible line, especially in times of institutional crackdown, face an even greater struggle to operate and survive. This is the case of many NGOs located in Shenzhen, who have been subjected to changing experiences of harassment throughout their existence. Under the Hu-Wen leadership, such harassment did not impact the effectiveness of the 'resistance through accommodation' approach, as it was infrequent and often just a 'warning sign'. For instance, in this period many crackdowns used to occur around internationally or nationally 'sensitive' events, such as around the time of the 2005 'Colour Revolutions' in Ukraine, Georgia and Kyrgyzstan, when all social organisations registered as businesses or commercial entities were called on to renew their licences (Ho, 2008b: 23), or on the eve of any major anniversaries such as 4 June, the National Day, when some organisations experienced instances of their email accounts or phone lines being hacked into.[18] However, since 2012, crackdowns have become a more permanent feature of migrant NGOs' existence, and have lost their circular character. They can vary from tacit pressure on organisations, normally exerted through bureaucratic means or attacks on the premises of the organisations or activists, to concentrated overt crackdowns, such as outright arrests and sentencing.

MWU[19] is one of the Shenzhen-based NGOs which has experienced milder forms of harassment throughout its existence. The NGO was originally set up in Hong Kong by a group of academics, but quickly set up a branch in Shenzhen, which employs migrant worker women only. The formation of the NGO was inspired by the 'Chicco factory fire' accident in 1993,[20] which exposed the scale of exploitative working conditions in China at the time. The NGO initially had good relations with one of the Shenzhen hospitals, where they mostly did some counselling work and ran support groups for injured workers. At that time, they also developed a relationship with ACWF. However, in 2000, the local government started to perceive MWU as a threat, because they were seen as setting an example for the formation of other labour NGOs, and ACWF ended their support for the NGO. Throughout its existence, MWU has experienced crackdowns a number of times: all were conducted in a tacit manner. In one such clampdown the business licence under which the NGO was registered was found to be 'faulty', and the NGO came under fire. Mostly, however, the officials abstained from direct or far-reaching crackdowns on MWU, because of its registration in Hong Kong.[21]

A migrant worker-turned-NGO activist who has experienced much greater levels of harassment and outright crackdowns on his previous organisations is UA's founder, Mr Zhao. Mr Zhao's first experience with labour activism was setting up a trade union in a factory in Dongguan in the 1990s, which ended up with him losing his job.[22] In 2004, he established an organisation that aimed at providing legal education and training to migrant workers, mediating labour disputes and even attempting some advocacy with government officials. Even though the migrants who joined and built the organisation contributed material resources, time and commitment, Mr Zhao had to take out a bank loan to fund his organisation. The organisation aimed to be transparent, open and publicise widely (*gongkai*): the workers who joined the organisation held banners at political events in Beijing and Shenzhen to attract government officials' attention and openly publicised their programme online. The organisation grew to approximately 400 members in 2006, including migrant workers and even some officials, civil servants and lawyers from the Labour Bureau, and it became a form of *de facto* independent trade union, as Mr Zhao himself emphasised. The organisation was involved in advocacy efforts to change some arbitration regulations in 2006,[23] and published a petition online to collect public signatures. However, after articles about the NGO's work appeared in the foreign media, the government cracked down on the organisation; 100 police officers were dispatched to shut down four out of five of the organisation's offices. Mr Zhao noted:

> This is what the Chinese government hates the most: an organisation which has so many members, so many workers' support: this kind of activism is a real taboo![24]

Mr Zhao was deserted by the other workers and had to fend for himself:

> Because many migrant workers do not understand the government, when there is a crackdown they are all terrified. They became so terrified, that they even stopped contacting me ... They are scared that they will not survive materially or that they will not be employed in any factory after that. Just the day before, we had 400 members, and the next day: nobody.[25]

The information on the closure of the organisation was publicised widely; even the government's website and the MOCA website gave information about the crackdown. It was the first case of outlawing a migrant worker organisation since the post-Tiananmen crackdown: the government usually dealt with migrant worker NGOs by sending warning messages, exerting indirect pressure on landlords renting out properties, sending thugs to beat up the activists, issuing penalties or deploying other sabotage methods.

Yet, since 2012, repression has become a continuous feature of migrant NGOs' existence. Paradoxically, the 2012 Shenzhen crackdown came soon after the government of Guangdong put in place the 'more relaxed' regulations in January 2012, which simplified the formal registration procedures for NGOs. Shortly after the law was passed, an unexpected crackdown on seven labour NGOs in Shenzhen took place (by the end of 2012, a total of twelve out of fifteen Shenzhen labour NGOs had been subjected to harassment).[26] First, the water and electricity supplies to the offices of some labour NGOs in Shenzhen were cut off, and then the landlords were pressured to force the organisations out of their premises. The clampdown affected the outreach and effectiveness of NGOs' activism. One NGO which suffered in this crackdown, Shenzhen-based ET, has been operating from an undisclosed location since the crackdown, maintaining only part of its activities and eventually changing its name. During the litigation process for one of the migrant workers they helped in the court, ET employees overheard in court that their organisation's case was labelled as 'special' (*teji*), which means that it was treated as classified.[27] In order to find an effective way to decrease the risk to the NGO activists, the organisation eventually split into four small, separate NGOs in 2015, each specialising in a different area.[28]

The reasons for the 2012 Shenzhen crackdown were not clear. Some NGO activists suspected that it might have been a consequence of the tense power struggle between the reformist and conservative wings within the provincial-level government for succession after Wang Yang was promoted to the Politburo Standing Committee of the CCP.[29] Indeed, in the following years it became evident that the Xi Jinping administration takes much stricter steps on civic activism than the preceding one. In the Guangzhou crackdown of 2015–2016 eventually four of the Panyu Migrant Workers Centre's employees were arrested, put on trial and sentenced to suspended prison terms in September 2016. Even more severe punishment was meted out on the charges of 'subverting state power' in July 2017 to Liu Shaoming, a veteran of the 1989 Tiananmen protests and the founder of labour NGO, Volunteers for Workers' Rights,[30] which explicitly linked pro-democracy and labour demands. Liu Shaoming was put on trial without access to a lawyer and sentenced to four and a half years in prison. Before and during these events, there were also crackdowns on organisations in other parts of China. SFI, based in Yongkang (Zhejiang province), had its premises vandalised by 'unknown burglars' and, as with the Panyu Centre founder, the leader was physically abused by undercover police.[31] BWH, an organisation which has long had exemplary relations with local government, had to move its office to an undisclosed location, with its countrywide labour NGO training events shut down in Shenzhen in 2014.[32] The latest crackdown on five labour activists took place in January 2019 in Guangdong and Hunan provinces. The activists were held in detention without access to a lawyer for fifteen long months until April 2020, when they were put into a closed-door trial and received suspended prison sentences for crimes of 'picking quarrels and provoking trouble' and 'gathering a crowd to disturb social order'.

Though the past patterns of crackdowns point to the dominance of local-level governments as driving agents behind repression on migrant NGOs, under the Xi Jinping administration NGO activists and founders increasingly believe in the growing engagement of the central government in such repression, due to its countrywide character and severity. As seems to have been the case in 2012, the behaviour of local cadres was triggered by the cyclical changes of their leadership, rather than the particular behaviour of NGOs;

however, these factors no longer explain the sustained and severe character of the post-2012 crackdown. The extreme cases of confrontation with the state illustrated above show how organising 'rights protection type' and 'labour movement type' organisations in particular is a form of activist citizenship unwelcome to the state.

NGO–ACFTU relations and the rise of public procurement: between co-optation and confrontation

Another important state actor with which some NGOs interact is ACFTU. The position of ACFTU vis-à-vis employers has been notoriously weak and unrepresentative of migrant workers' interests. As local governments have their own stake in local businesses and seek to prevent labour (and wider civic) activism, it is difficult to see it as truly representing workers. Additionally, a branch of ACFTU established in a given enterprise owes its subsistence to that very enterprise's profits (by law, 2 per cent of company profits and 0.5 per cent of workers' wages are forwarded to a trade union branch affiliated with that company), which means that ACFTU hardly sees its interest in opposing employers. In fact, it often happens that the head of the ACFTU branch in the enterprise is actually the employer, or even a Party official, which presents an obvious conflict of interest (Pringle, 2011). The way ACFTU extends its membership base is not via recruiting, approaching and organising workers, but rather through setting up branches within enterprises in a top-down manner (Pringle, 2011: 110). Many workers are not even aware that they are members of their enterprise's branch of ACFTU, or have a cynical approach to it (Lee, 2007: 57–61). As a result, ACFTU is often uninterested in the enforcement of labour laws and collective agreements, and does not allow for workers' participation in politics, leaving no other recourse for migrant workers than strike action or autonomous bargaining (Friedman, 2014: 5).

It is worth mentioning that there have been some promising experiments undertaken in some ACFTU branches in Zhejiang and Guangdong in the last decade, including the introduction of direct elections of union chairs. These were initiated mainly because of pressure from migrant workers themselves following incidents such as the 'Foxconn suicides' and 'Honda strikes' cases (Chan, 2012b: 320–321; Pringle, 2011). The reforms to conduct direct elections in factories were pushed throughout the province by the Guangdong trade union, and in Shenzhen specifically they were introduced in 163 factories.[33] MWU NGO gave me an example of one of these factories, a subsidiary of Ricoh (the Japanese electronics manufacturer), where free and press-observed elections indeed took place in 2012. MWU talked to the workers several months after the elections, and found that the workers felt that despite the reforms, relations in the factory had not changed.[34] A representative of Shenzhen-based ET was also sceptical about the impact of the reforms: she saw the move more as a way of appeasing and pacifying the workers, rather than an authentic attempt to support workers' welfare and rights.[35]

While most NGOs view ACFTU as a paralysed and 'whitewash' institution, the establishment of a relationship with an ACFTU branch is always a desirable option for NGOs, who also see this as a way to stabilise their relationship with the state. Usually, the relationship with a branch of ACFTU serves a similar purpose to a good relationship with the local government; that is, it allows a greater scope for the NGO's activities and increases the number of migrants they can safely reach out to. Sometimes it also provides a source of funding. The establishment of such relations is not universal, however. Below I discuss the establishment of relations between ACFTU local branches and only five NGOs in my study which have ever established a relationship with ACFTU: NBW, JM, NHC, SC and UA.

For NBW, despite their belief that ACFTU still needs to improve representation of migrant workers and to provide a platform for dialogue, their limited relationship with the ACFTU local branch proved to be a security vent in an occasionally troubled relationship with the local government. They also received some funding through the local branch of ACFTU for their cultural activities.[36] Similarly, the relationship between the Shiyan-based JM and its local trade union branch is sporadic and usually limited to some financial support for printing legal guides and magazines created by JM and then distributed to migrants.

An example of an NGO that has a deeper relationship with the local branch of ACFTU is NHC, which came into cooperation with the official trade unions for similar reasons. Their relationship with the Zhejiang Federation of Trade Unions (ZFTU), which started in 2010, changed a lot in terms of the NGO's capacities. In particular, it opened up possibilities to more regularly access both tangible (financial and technical) and intangible resources (training and access to relevant government agencies). When NHC began running their cultural activities in 2007–2008, they had no premises and tended to organise gatherings and performances for migrants outdoors. However, such occupation of public spaces became a concern for the local authorities, and was met with repeated obstruction from city security guards (*chengguan*). In 2010, after negotiations between the NGO founder and the ZFTU, the union branch provided a two-storey building for migrant workers' activities, which addressed the conflictual relationship between the NGO and city authorities. In addition, the union has provided NHC with financial support for their cultural activities, especially during festivals such as Labour Day and Women's Day. It is also through this connection that NHC established a relationship with the local government and received some government funding for their training programmes. Nevertheless, the decision to begin cooperating with the ZFTU was met with resistance on the part of some migrant workers and soul-searching on the part of the NGO's founders. Some occasional supervision of the NGO's activities is carried out by the ZFTU. They were made aware that the government does not approve of contacts with foreigners, for example. As an interviewee from the NGO told me, 'there are some people in the [local] government who think that having relations with foreign people can cause social instability'.[37]

The formation of ACFTU–NGO links seemed to be a popular trend across China in the mid-2000s, when ACFTU pushed a countrywide campaign to include larger numbers of migrant workers in its membership base (Sun Chunlan, quoted in CECOC, 2006). In this process, ACFTU strove to co-opt labour organisations, and as some activists noted, learn from them. In 2010, while reflecting on the partnership with NHC, the vice-chairman of the ZFTU stated that each level of ACFTU should pay more attention to labour NGOs and strive to form partnerships with them. In such partnerships, the union should assume the role of a 'married woman's family'-like institution (*niangjia*) for NGOs (Cheng, 2010: 54), which clearly shows that ACFTU emulates the Confucian father–son rhetoric promoted by the state (with a particular gendered language being used, which feminises and further subordinates the NGO). Indeed, while the relationship has proven beneficial to NHC, it is also of great help to the ZFTU. NHC, unlike BWH, JM or UA, did not negotiate their right to mediate workplace conflicts on behalf of migrant workers. In order to enable access to lawyers for migrant workers, the NGO is encouraged to forward these cases to the ZFTU branch. Lacking recognition among migrant workers, the union is content to boost their numbers through NHC's popularity among migrant workers. There is a particular balance in that relationship: in exchange for non-interference in workplace conflicts (rights-defence activities), the ZFTU gives the NGO material support and tacit consent to undertake cultural activities. While such governmental co-optation strategies decrease the independence of NGOs, they facilitate rather than disable their cultural, integrational and identity-building activities, which can have a powerful effect on the remaking of citizenship identities, as I discuss in detail in Chapter 6.

The example of NHC is indicative of a wider local government strategy of social service procurement from NGOs (*goumai fuwu*), which was already taking place under the Hu-Wen administration. However, since 2013 the government has promoted this strategy with renewed energy (Howell, 2015; Fulda, 2013), clearly motivated by the desire to redirect NGOs towards domestic funding, a push accompanied by the crackdown on labour NGOs:

> The state is now doing the so-called 'co-optation'. After inflicting this great pressure on labour NGOs, these NGOs will now need to rethink their strategy and eventually cooperate with the government. So, there might be more and more government procurement initiatives emerging in the years to come, because many officials in the government say that people should also participate in social governance. But right now, there are still so few government procurement projects going on. In the labour field, the space [for public procurement] is very small, but in terms of the floating population family, it is growing.[38]

Public procurement is part of a wider change in the legal environment signified by the 2016 Charity Law and 2017 Overseas NGOs Management Law. As discussed earlier, these new laws close off access to domestic funding for 'more politically sensitive' organisations, such as labour NGOs, while at the same time preventing their access to overseas funding, further squeezing their capacity to organise. Parallel to this marginalisation of labour NGOs is the growth of government-sponsored social work organisations and labour aid centres (*laodong zhan*), particularly in Shenzhen, which compete for space with labour NGOs (see Halegua, 2016). These organisations tend to be the first choice for government funding. In this new environment, organisations often face the choice of either continuing the more contentious type of activism, such as rights defence or collective bargaining, and take the risk of disappearing due to lack of access to funding, or they must redirect their activities into more acceptable areas, where they can access domestic sources of funding. ET, located in Shenzhen, and SC, located in Beijing, can be seen as two additional examples of the latter trend.

ET used to be a vocal and prominent NGO in the PRD, engaged primarily with rights-defence activism (see Chapter 5) up until it suffered under the 2012 crackdown, which forced it to operate from an undisclosed location. Eventually, the activists working in the NGO decided to split up in 2015 and formed four smaller NGOs. While the 'rights-protection' daughter organisation of ET continues to deal with court representation (through public interest lawyers or government lawyers) and provide law training (albeit on a smaller scale than before), which prevents it from accessing domestic funds, the other three branches have adjusted their activities to be more acceptable to government. These three daughter organisations seek to adjust and rebrand their activities so that they can secure domestic funding: apart from the previous rights consciousness activism (see Chapter 4 for details), they are now also providing summer camps for migrant worker children, a cultural centre focusing on community integration and organisation for the empowerment of women. As family and migrant children is an area of activism where it is easier to procure domestic funds, and my ET interviewee admitted that the survival of the organisations depends on this transition, it is obvious that a substantial shift has taken place in terms of the NGO's activities. From being one of the most vocal and labour movement-orientated NGOs in Shenzhen, it is now turning to community building and educational areas. However, despite this move, it might still be extremely difficult for the ET daughter organisations to secure Shenzhen government funding, because unlike in Beijing or Zhejiang procurement in Shenzhen is not contracted through ACFTU, but rather through the Bureau of Civil Affairs, further marginalising labour organisations. As all my interviewees in Shenzhen told me, this type of funding is given almost exclusively to big (so-called 'class 5A') organisations with established relations with the government, which none of these NGOs possess.[39]

SC is another organisation which turned to fundraising from public procurement projects. The NGO was set up in Beijing in 2010 by a social worker, who had previously worked with FJ in Guangzhou. SC focuses on a very narrow area of health and safety and occupational health accident-prevention training among migrant workers on construction sites. The NGO also conducts advocacy work with the government: it seeks to expose cases of lax implementation of laws and proposes reforms based on other countries' experience (especially Germany). Concomitantly, it strives for change at the enterprise level, by providing training for construction site management in the hope of introducing a cross-industry Convention of Production (following the ILO standards), which would make companies' recruitment and supply chains more transparent. The NGO hopes that all these activities will create a systemic improvement in migrant workers' conditions in the construction industry, particularly in relation to law implementation. As the training and advocacy activities the organisation undertakes follow the central government's own desire to improve the level of law enforcement, and SC restricts its activities to the health and safety sector, they have received public funding since 2013 through both the Beijing Tongzhou district trade unions and local government:

> In 2012, when we started to implement our training, we didn't have the government's support and we approached enterprises directly by ourselves. We started with the Beijing IKEA factory, as they were relatively willing to improve [their health and safety training]; we created a template for training [courses], which then became quite famous across the industry … Finally, the trade unions learned about us, and they started to support us financially in 2013. We also hoped to develop a relationship with the government: yes, we want to protect our independence, but we also needed to have some interaction because on the one hand we want to show the government that our grassroots model can be effective, and on the other, the government's support will allow us to expand and grow. After we received support from the local trade union and the government, it became much easier to approach enterprises.[40]

The NGO receives RMB 10,000–50,000 (USD 6,600–33,000) every year in funding from the local union. However, the founder admitted that the legal constraints preventing NGOs from expanding their activities across the country impede the growth and effectiveness of their services (SC is formally registered under MOCA). Also, while the government's procurement through trade unions has increased in Beijing in recent years, it has focused on areas such as mental health, migrant children's education and after-school care. In contrast, Shenzhen's trade unions tend to do the work themselves, and it is other government agencies (such as the MOCA branches), rather than ACFTU, that procure services from NGOs. In both cases, the focus of NGOs' work should be migrant family, rather than labour issues. SC circumvents these constraints by registering as a community-support NGO under MOCA in Shenzhen, and by presenting their work in largely service-orientated terms to local government, as occupational safety training providers:

> We are the first NGO which can enter companies in this manner. This is because many companies are not open to NGOs, and also do not understand what we are doing. So, in order to open this space for our work, we must use this angle of occupational safety. Once we are in, now the question is how to make our model sustainable, how to lead to a policy change, establish lobbying in enterprises, build social support for our work, create pressure on enterprises and spread corporate social responsibility (CSR) measures in the construction industry, and in the future, also in the electronics industry.[41]

As the example above illustrates, although the organisation has been involved closely with local trade unions and the government, it uses the room for activism provided by these relationships to promote wider change in the conditions of work of migrant workers, including changes in the industry rules as well as advocating with the government to change their attitudes towards labour NGOs. Therefore, the NGO's relationship with the unions and the government is treated instrumentally, as a means to a greater end, in line with the strategy of 'resistance through accommodation'.

And what happens to organisations which do not abide by the rules of accessing government procurement, and refuse to change their focus to such 'less sensitive' work? The story of UA can serve as an interesting case. Despite his history of confrontational encounters with state authorities, the founder of UA had also had some positive experiences of cooperation with ACFTU. In the years 2007–2008, the central government started paying increased attention to labour disputes and it was at that time that it gave more explicit permission to ACFTU to increase its participation in the resolution of labour disputes. It was in this political climate that Shenzhen's Bao'an district branch of ACFTU turned to UA for assistance.

> When they [the Bao'an branch of ACFTU] came in contact with us in 2007, they were just learning from us all along. They learned the law from us, they learned how to provide services to migrant workers. Gradually they joined us during labour disputes as observers.[42]

UA received some financial support from ACFTU in exchange for its cooperation. In the end, though, the relationship was interrupted by the local government, which opposed ACFTU's financing of UA. The officials invoked national policy as the reason for that decision, since only organisations registered as non-profits under MOCA were allowed to receive government funding. UA was never granted formal NPO status, despite its founder's repeated applications. This situation exemplifies the arbitrary and localised application of central regulations: NHC was never officially registered either, yet it receives funding from ACFTU without obstacles from local government.

Moreover, UA has been trying to engage with ACFTU even after it was repeatedly harassed and stigmatised by the local government. In June 2016, the NGO was helping workers from Shenzhen's Guang Xie Electronics company to successfully resolve the case of collective bargaining regarding relocation, social insurance, housing fund arrears, illegally low wages, wage arrears and non-payment of overtime. The NGO provided training in collective bargaining: they helped to elect workers' representatives, trained workers how to negotiate with management, and explained the proceedings and legal grounds of the case. As workers were negotiating with management, the Shenzhen Longhua district trade unions learned about the case and intervened, promising successful resolution if workers refrained from turning to UA. In January 2017, the national trade unions' newspaper praised the ACFTU Longhua branch as an exceptional example of successful 'proactive' intervention, completely ignoring the role of UA in the negotiations. However, Mr Zhao declared his satisfaction with the outcome, despite his organisation's name being omitted in the press:

> Although our victory was taken away from us, we are really happy with the outcome. Why? Because the trade unions started to truly protect workers' rights. Although we could not contact workers' representatives afterwards, we knew from other workers that the

> union eventually helped them to secure compensation, so they really helped the workers ... I even wrote on my Weibo blog that I fully welcome this intervention of the unions. Because to see the trade unions really defending workers' rights under our national system ... it is really something that we are looking forward to seeing more of. Because relying on grassroots force [*minjian liliang*] is not enough: we are too small, too weak, we don't have the resources, and we can help too few people. If the unions get involved, they can resolve many large-scale issues. So, if only the unions engaged as they did in this case, we would gladly withdraw and make space for the unions to deal with those cases.[43]

We can see the shift in ACFTU's approach to labour NGOs under Xi Jinping: as both cases of cooperation between NHC and UA and their local branches of ACFTU in the 2000s show the benefits for both partners, and sometimes especially for ACFTU, the latest case clearly points to growing competition between the two types of organisation. Indeed, one donor of these labour NGOs, whom I talked to after the 2015 crackdowns, believed that the crackdown itself was a result of the pressure exerted by ACFTU on central government.[44] The workers' preference to approach labour NGOs rather than ACFTU with cases of collective bargaining and workplace mediation exposes the official unions' weak reputation as a form of workers' representation. It only seems logical that this situation has led ACFTU to increasingly perceive labour NGOs as a form of political competition. This competition is clear in the case of organisations such as UA and ET's 'rights defence' daughter organisation, which refused to stop working in the areas which ACFTU perceives as falling only under the party-state remit. It is certainly not the case with service providing organisations such as NHC and SC, which work in an area regarded as 'less politically sensitive', currently the only area for relatively unobstructed organisation by migrant NGOs.

Such a turn to partnership with ACFTU and other state agencies in search of funding begs the question of the actual impact of this transition on the needs of migrant workers and the current citizenship formulation around them. Are these partnerships leaving migrant workers without any effective form of representation? Or perhaps, on the contrary, does this transition signal a surprisingly effective avenue for NGOs to improve the position of migrant workers in China? How does the increasing trend of public procurement influence migrant NGOs' capacity to challenge the citizenship framework which marginalises the migrant workers group? From the examples above, it appears that while the organisations selling their services to the state must circumscribe their activities accordingly, they can still find some space for stretching the fabric of citizenship in China: perhaps less effective in some aspects than the work of more contentious organisations, but possibly more effective in others. First, the engagement with state agencies, and particularly ACFTU, allows for a steady source of income which can allow NGOs to undertake cultural activities which are transformative of the less contentious aspects of citizenship, such as citizenship discourse. As I discuss in Chapter 6, these kinds of activities may truly impact the way in which the general public views migrant workers, changing their position in the hierarchical citizenship structure, but they can also help by shaping migrants' self-perception as equal citizens. Second, these NGOs might have better access to policy-makers and advocacy groups, and in the long run succeed in changing some industry standards, regulations and law implementation practices, which can positively impact migrants' civil rights. However, the larger picture shows that when NGOs change their pattern of organising in the way which goes with, rather than against, this new legal environment for NGOs, they may indeed jeopardise the main impact on citizenship which is produced by the act of organising itself: creating greater political space for a diverse range of civic actors. This is because, while they may convince some state agencies of the usefulness of the more conciliatory types of migrant NGOs, this might entrench the trend among prospective activists of avoiding the truly problematic aspects of migrants' citizenship in China. In the long term, this can prevent the formation of NGOs which target any instances of labour rights violations other than those relating to the relatively politically correct occupational health issues (as I discuss in detail in Chapter 5).

The above sections have illustrated how the state constrains and enables migrant workers' acts of organising. The cases we have looked at show that state–society relations depend on the particular circumstances and local specificities, although this has been changing, with a flattening power of the central state in recent years. Still, citizenship remains largely shaped through relations between particular NGOs and state agencies, and is often relational and localised rather than defined by the law. It is through such relational forms that NGOs employ a strategy of 'resistance through accommodation' to advance their claims, which has potential to challenge the current citizenship formulation in China without necessarily confronting the state. In this way, the transformation of the citizenship discourse and citizenship regime is both an end product of and a channel for improving the well-being of migrant workers. To further understand just how risky and courageous setting up and operating migrant worker NGOs can be, a full appreciation of the interests behind the crackdowns on NGO activism and the unwelcoming attitudes of ACFTU is needed. State–business relations show how the local state's negative attitudes towards the act of organising stem not only from political reasons, but also those of an economic nature.

NGOs in confrontation with the state–business nexus

In response to the growing workers' insurgency in the 2000s, the Hu-Wen administration introduced a set of measures to address the social problems which resulted from the dismantling of the 'iron rice bowl' welfare system. It initiated unprecedented levels of expenditure on social security and more protective labour laws with minimum wage requirements (Friedman, 2014: 11; Lee, 2007: 18). However, the introduction of these new laws has proven insufficient in addressing labour conflict in China. Due to the centrally designated development model, which encourages local governments to prioritise economic growth over social welfare, local governments seek to attract and retain businesses, even if these evade labour regulations. Moreover, local business owners and officials often have close relationships or family ties in China, which creates a fertile ground for selective law implementation. Since economic investments are the main source of local government income, the local state has vested interests in protecting the interests of businesses from workers' insurgency. The profit-orientated state–business nexus, particularly in the export-orientated zones, relies for its profits on the maintenance of a docile and easily controlled labour force, and NGOs pose a threat to the maintenance of this status quo.

Hubei-based JM, which mainly represents migrants working on construction sites and in mines, came across many instances of illegal malpractices, such as poor health and safety standards, non-payment of social insurance contributions by employers, lack of contracts, forfeiting of wages or exploitative overtime conditions. According to the founder of JM, Mr Xie, the greatest obstacle to effectively claiming migrant workers' rights in court comes from the 'blood relationship' (*xueyuan guanxi*)[45] between the so-called 'dispatch agencies' (*laodong paiqian*) and the government on one hand, and between business owners and the government on the other. 'Dispatch agencies' evolved from some labour bureaus of the pre-reform and early reform eras, and they are closely linked to the party-state. In some industries, such as construction, they are the predominant type of intermediaries who employ migrant workers. The close links between businesses, dispatch agencies and the government mean that migrant workers, and labour NGOs, run into trouble when they expose or question the unlawful practices of these agencies (such as non-payment of social insurance or non-signing of legal contracts, for instance).[46] Direct relations between business owners and local government are another problem. As Mr Xie told me, it is these relationships that make many migrant workers' cases hopeless:

> As long as the government does not have vested interests in the construction project, there is no problem for us to mediate on behalf of migrant workers and to succeed.[47]

Global pressure does not reach these domestic enterprises, and the only way such instances can be exposed is through NGOs' advocacy or by individual or collective actions by workers with or without the help of NGOs, such as microblogging, filing lawsuits and striking.

To illustrate just how close the relationship between ACFTU, the government and business is, the experiences of UA's founder can serve as an example. While employed in a Dongguan factory in the 1990s, Mr Zhao set up a trade union branch which received authorisation from ACFTU as an official branch – a rather exceptional development at the time. The branch advocated for the payment of deferred wages, the improvement of food quality in the factory's canteens, and permission for workers to leave the factory compound. The organisation printed leaflets and put up slogans in the canteen to publicise its role to workers in the factory. One day somebody put up slogans calling for better quality meals under the threat of burning the factory down, and the branch came under false accusations from the factory boss that it was responsible for this action. The local government officials backed the factory boss, and the branch was ordered to close. The local Party chairman then approached Mr Zhao and offered some sort of truce:

> He told me two things that I will never forget. Firstly, he told me that as the head of the local government he is also the head of the trade union. Secondly, he announced that I was now formally fired from the factory. To that I thought: 'You don't need to come and announce all this. You are the local government's chairman, you are also the trade union's chairman, I get that, but have you also turned into the factory boss's lapdog [*zougou*]?'[48]

After boasting about his influence in the whole of Dongguan, the official offered Mr Zhao an opportunity of a transfer to another factory of Mr Zhao's choice, one 'with better working conditions' – a typical co-opting technique used towards labour activists. Mr Zhao agreed to the proposal, and while he promised not to set up a branch of ACFTU again, he openly told the official that he did not see anything wrong in helping workers and trying to address conflicts of interests with company bosses. Hearing that, the official revoked his offer, saying: 'well, if you insist on saying things like this, I clearly cannot help you'.[49]

As the above examples illustrate, the close links between ACFTU, local government and businesses are still a crucial reason behind NGOs' inability to address workplace problems, and as a distinct type of relational citizenship practice in China, they fuel labour abuse. To be truly able to respect labour rights, there is a need to expose the business–state nexus, which helps entrench the abusive practices in enterprises. As NGOs organise under these conditions and undertake activities which threaten to expose these relations, they challenge these exploitative aspects of relational citizenship practice in China. While such exposing is greatly limited by the lack of freedom of information in China, and due to the dangers that doing so poses for the activists, very few NGOs are able or willing to address the issue, putting great limitations on their ability to transform these structural factors that affect migrants' citizenship rights.

Conclusion

As migrant workers set out to form and operate a labour NGO in China, they must navigate many obstacles to organising put on them by the repressive environment for civic organising in China. This environment is only partially determined by the central state's legal framework on labour, internal migration and the functioning of NGOs in China: it also largely depends on the NGOs' own fragmented and multilayered relationships with the local state, and the availability of funding. It is often through the relational negotiation of the scope of activism with different agents of the local state that citizenship is reshaped through the act of organising. It is frequently the NGOs, and not the state, who initiate change in state–society relations by transforming the local state's approach to the work of migrant NGOs, by setting up mediation committees and negotiating with the local state the possibility of becoming citizen representatives in courts. While the state is often the crucial actor who extends the space for NGOs' involvement (Hsu J., 2017) or invites migrant NGOs to a 'dance' (Howell, 2015), many of the examples of organisations in this chapter show that they play a much more active role in state–society relations, shaping new practices of citizenship among civic organisations and using the laws to their advantage. The state was not the initiator of the work of BWH or SC: it responded to it by granting permission. JM would not be able to represent migrants in court, had Mr Xie not fought long and hard with the local state for permission. While it was the state who agreed to some of these activities eventually, the NGOs were the catalysts, who strived to change the state's attitude and who eventually negotiated these new ways of citizen engagement in the public life of China.

However, it is important to understand when and how this transformation is possible and how to make an act of organising successful. In order to organise an NGO, and therefore to perform other acts of citizenship, activists must often resort to the strategy of 'resistance through accommodation', which employs the state-abiding channels, such as the law and Communist slogans, to conduct activities which question and challenge the existing formulation of citizenship in China. But 'resistance through accommodation' is a fine balancing act between bringing change and surviving. Those

NGOs which cross the permissible lines of 'accommodation' suffer, which may be detrimental to citizenship transformation in the long run, as it breaks up organisations and removes the activists' ability to organise. On the other hand, NGOs which simply accommodate to the state's language and channels, without attempting to change any of the aspects of citizenship, do not have transformative qualities, and might even help to maintain the status quo. Even those NGOs who get the balance right might face an unexpected crackdown when they lose the relationships forged within the local state, or stumble upon clashing interests of various state agencies and levels. In any case, the 'resistance through accommodation' strategy proves that in authoritarian states like China, it might be more productive to use the state-provided framework to stretch the existing rules and transform citizenship from within the system than to perform acts of citizenship in opposition to the state or by breaking the laws, which much of the acts of citizenship framework postulates.

Notes

1 These are: 1998 Regulations on the Registration and Management of Social Organisations, 1999 Public Welfare Donations Law, 2010 Notice of the State Administration of Foreign Exchange on Issues concerning the Administration of Foreign Exchange Donated to or by Domestic Institutions, 2016 Charity Law and 2017 Overseas NGOs Management Law.

2 Throughout this chapter I will refer to these organisations that have significantly benefited from the revised legal framework concerning civil society organisations (CSOs) under Xi Jinping as a 'less sensitive' type of NGO. These NGOs are the ones which are singled out in the 2016 Charity Law and the 2016 revisions to the Regulations on the Registration and Management of Social Organisations as those which can directly register under MOCA, without the need to find a 'parent organisation'. These CSOs are: industry associations, chambers of commerce, and those working in the areas of science and technology, poverty alleviation, support for the elderly and orphans, disaster relief, medical aid, education and community service provision.

3 The controversy around the two representatives of the Red Cross in China, Guo Meimei and Lu Meimei, who defrauded money and posted

pictures of their luxury lifestyles on the internet in 2011, has led to a dramatic decline in charitable donations (China Development Brief, 2013).

4 See later in this chapter for details.

5 See Appendix 4 Table A4.1 for details.

6 Interviews no. 5 and no. 23.

7 Interview no. 6.

8 Interview no. 31.

9 For an in-depth study of the bureaucratic conflicts between these different horizontal agencies and how this impacted labour NGOs see Fu (2017). Jennifer Hsu's (2017) study highlights how migrant NGO–state partnerships are forged with different vertical levels of the state (central, municipal, neighbourhood).

10 *Guanxixue* is an established part of the social science inquiry into Chinese society and politics. *Guanxi* can be best defined as 'dyadic relationships that are based implicitly (rather than explicitly) on mutual interests and benefits' (Yang, 1994: 1).

11 I worked as an intern at BWH for three months, and this is where I conducted the bulk of the participant observation for this study (see Appendix 3).

12 Interview no. 32.

13 Participant observation, BWH, 2 March 2012.

14 This reaction illustrates the importance of 'saving China's face' in conversations with foreigners. However, many interviewees I spoke to decided to subdue their cultural inclination to 'save face' and told me openly that they would share 'shameful' details with me for the sake of research accuracy.

15 For a more detailed discussion on how the relationships between Public and State Security agents and NGOs shape NGO activism see Fu (2017) and Franceschini and Nesossi (2018).

16 Interview no. 20.

17 Interview no. 18.

18 Interviews no. 17 and no. 19.

19 MWU is one of the five organisations studied which was not set up by migrant workers. However, the Shenzhen office employs only migrant workers and is run by them, so I include it in the analysis.

20 'The Chicco factory fire', which is also referred to as 'the 1993 Zhili fire' took place in a Hong Kong-owned factory in Shenzhen, which subcontracted to an Italian label called Chicco. The fire, which consumed the factory and caused the deaths of eight-seven young female migrant workers and left another forty-seven disabled, became symbolic of the lack of health and safety, the exploitative working conditions and

near-slavery living conditions of migrant workers in many Chinese factories at the time. The event reverberated wide and loud in the international media, particularly in Hong Kong, and in China as well. One of the women who survived the fire later set up a labour NGO in Chongqing. Hong Kong advocacy groups felt especially responsible for the event as the factory was owned by a Hong Kong businessman, and consequently a lot of advocacy and social responsibility campaigns, which to this day press for the improvement of working conditions in China, started in the wake of this particular event (Interviews no. 5 and no. 17).

21 Interview no. 17.
22 The story is discussed further in the next section of this chapter.
23 See Chapter 6 for more details.
24 Interview no. 18.
25 Interview no. 18.
26 Interview no. 18.
27 Interview no. 19.
28 Interview no. 46.
29 Interview no. 17. Wang Yang, a provincial CCP secretary for Guangdong in the years 2007–2012, was regarded as an allegedly more liberally minded official. Under his leadership Guangdong was the province with the most permissive environment for the formation of civic organisations in China. After 2012 he was promoted and became a member of the CCP Politburo Standing Committee and the chairman of the People's Political Consultative Conference, which puts into question his presumed 'liberalism'.
30 These are real names of the organisation and the activist.
31 Interview no. 31.
32 Interviews no. 26 and no. 38. See Chapter 4 for discussion of these events.
33 Interview no. 17.
34 Interview no. 17.
35 Interview no. 19.
36 Interview no. 5.
37 Interview no. 9.
38 Interview no. 43.
39 Interview no. 46.
40 Interview no. 43.
41 Interview no 43.
42 Interview no. 18.
43 Interview no. 42.
44 Interview no. 39.

45 This is the term used by the founder of JM in a follow-up interview conducted via social media (Interview no. 48) on 24 April 2012, in Chinese. The notion is interesting here, as it relates to 'kin relations', and depicts ruling clan relations in pre-modern China. The head of JM is thus emphasising how the family links within the Party (nepotism) extend to businesses (which are often owned by Party officials or their families), thereby creating an almost 'feudal-like' system of workers' exploitation under capitalism.
46 Interview no. 3.
47 Interview no. 50, conducted via social media with JM on 23 January 2013.
48 Interview no. 18.
49 Interview no. 18.

3

Networking under the constraints of the state and the market

By April 2012 I had already worked in the BWH underground office for a couple of months. The office was located underneath the very heart of the capital, in the space under Beijing's booming Wangfujing market street. By then I felt increasingly tired of the artificial lights, humming air conditioners, and the tiny space of the three shoebox-sized office rooms. I frequently wondered how my co-workers could have spent years in that place. It was on one of those days in April when a bewildered man walked into the office. He had the appearance of a construction site worker, with his skin smeared in places, and clothes badly worn, but it was his feet that caught everybody's attention. The man had two plastic carrier bags wrapped around his ankles, kept in place with industrial tape. Underneath the condensation collecting on the inside of the bags we could see that his feet were red and swollen. The NGO founder, Mr Song, immediately asked him to sit on the chair. Since Mr Song had no place to live but his office, all his clothes were kept underneath the sofa bed squeezed in one of the office rooms. He called for his co-workers to bring a bowl of warm water and his own spare pair of shoes. He then touched the man's laboured feet, took off the bags and placed them in the bowl. Throughout the whole scene, the man was silent, and didn't say a word, just watching Mr Song unwrapping the bags. My co-workers looked at each other in shock, but Mr Song didn't mind them, and kept on cleaning the man's feet, then put on them his own clean socks and shoes and asked if the man was hungry and thirsty. After the man finished his meal, he left as quietly as he came, unwilling to utter a word.

This biblical scene left me confused. I was not sure if Mr Song was indeed living up to his deep-rooted commitment to serve the people, as he often emphasised in conversations with me, or if he was pulling one of his skilful commercial stunts, trying to impress me so that I would pass on the good word to the foreign donors about his selfless commitment to the working people. Struggling between the feelings of cynicism and awe, I then started to realise that perhaps his real intentions were not all that important. After all, he ended up helping a human being, and even if it was a trick to impress me, intended to gain future publicity, by doing the act, he managed to change a small part of somebody's life for the better.

Through the rest of my stay with BWH I would notice many meetings with foreign donors, migrant workers and other NGOs in the vaults of the office – the monotony sometimes interrupted by conferences organised by the NGO in nearby hotels. In front of foreign donors, my co-workers advertised the organisation's work ardently, making promises of how many migrants they could reach, and presenting ambitious plans for the organisation's future activities. I was perplexed by the very same feeling: are these attempts to impress intended purely to garner funds, or do they reflect a real commitment to bettering migrant workers' lives? As the literature on NGOs in China points to the impact of commercialisation and goal displacement on NGOs due to their preoccupation with fundraising (Hildebrandt, 2013; Lee and Shen, 2011), I was wondering how BWH manages to find its way through this labyrinth of pressures, from both the government and the funders, to actually end up doing what they say they are committed to do.

This chapter is an investigation into how NGOs' acts of networking with foreign donors,[1] other NGOs and migrant workers can be transformative of citizenship. While their relationship with the state is a recurrent theme in the literature on NGOs, their relationships with funders are much less well researched. But the discussion of these relationships is essential to fully account for civic organising in China as a site of citizenship transformation. This chapter shows how the ability to challenge the existing citizenship make-up through networking is heavily circumscribed by the divergent goals of foreign donors and NGOs and the competition between NGOs for resources. Yet, it also reveals how the act of networking can dramatically question and reshape the prescriptive citizenship practices imposed by the state, because it allows for the formation of networks both within the cities, between labour NGOs across China and across national boundaries, making activism around the purpose of civic organising crucial for citizenship transformation.

The formation of networks: challenging the taboo?

Citizenship practices in China are governed by both the laws (which shape citizenship status) and the unwritten rules, stemming from social, cultural and political practices (citizenship discourse and practice). The laws which prescribe NGOs' behaviour and establish mechanisms of state control over NGOs' ability to network are based on a range of legislation, as discussed in the previous chapter. The 2017 Overseas Management Law is especially relevant as it delineates the type of relations that NGOs are allowed to enter into with FAs. According to this new legislation, INGOs are now only allowed to engage in certain areas of social development (labour is not allowed, for instance), they are required to register with a sponsoring unit, only allowed to interact with domestic NGOs under the strict scrutiny of the Public Security Bureau, and cannot independently recruit their domestic staff in China. Therefore, the law not only limits overseas NGOs' freedom of operation in China, but also the ability of domestic NGOs to freely approach funders.

Yet, similarly to the case of NGO–state relations, the state governance of NGO–INGO relations in China has also been exerted through informal relationships with the local state. These informal relationships have been an equally important mechanism through which the state has prescribed permissible citizenship practice. Long before the 2017 Overseas NGOs law was passed, the state had used these informal channels to inform NGOs that networking with foreign donors and other NGOs is an undesirable activity. The main state actors who regularly issue informal warnings to NGOs are State Security agents, who regularly meet the activists to remind them of the informal or extra-legal boundaries of acceptable behaviour. They pay special attention to contacts with 'foreigners' (including Hong Kong-based INGOs), 'advising' the activists in an atmosphere of mutual understanding (Franceschini and Nesossi, 2018), which clearly testifies to the strength and self-evident nature of the unwritten rules of permissible citizen behaviour. Such informal communication entrenches the citizenship practices of atomisation and individualisation by treating the networking between NGOs and FAs, and mutual networking between NGOs, as generally 'troublesome'. Such mechanisms of entrenching acceptable citizenship practice can also be understood to constitute the state's 'governmentality' technology (Foucault, 1991: 100), because it results in internalisation of these unwritten rules, from self-labelling of the 'undesired' civic behaviours as 'politically sensitive' by NGOs, to creating a culture of self-imposed vigilance, self-censorship and lack of transparency in communications.

NGOs' relations with the state are therefore an important factor in establishing relations with foreign donors, though not one which can be easily mapped. NGOs which care about maintaining a stable and generally non-obstructive relationship with the local government are faced with the dilemma of how to procure funding without upsetting the state. The strategies these NGOs design to do so vary depending on their geographical location, relationship with the government actors and the type of activities they carry out. The first – and the smallest group of NGOs in this study – those which have very close links to the government (such as LHC),[2] generally do not apply for foreign funding from foundations and INGOs, because they usually have no problem receiving funding through the government-sponsored channels (LHC receives government funding through the Public Interest Lottery and IOs, for instance). For reasons of diplomatic conduct, IOs such as the United Nations (UN) (with its agencies such as the UN Development Programme (UNDP) and the ILO in particular), some countries' embassies, and to an extent the European Commission (EC) also tend to sponsor organisations such as LHC, which have closer links to the government, rather than unregistered grassroots NGOs.[3] Until 2014 these organisations used to be the main donors implementing large-scale development projects in China. When sponsoring projects, they are usually provided with a list of organisations that they are allowed to interact with, most of which tend to be GONGOs or NGOs closely connected to state agencies (such as LHC, which implemented a project in the area of 'good governance' run by UNDP and co-founded by the EC).[4] While the IOs and embassies tend to be restrained in their support for grassroots labour NGOs and look for more government-approved channels of distributing funds,[5] some embassies and the EC do happen to sponsor more 'authentic' grassroots NGOs as well. Through its many programmes supporting governance reforms and civil society in China, some of which have continued after major developmental funding was phased out in 2014, the EC strives to sponsor grassroots NGOs, although they usually rely on INGOs to find suitable organisations, so the EC itself rarely deals directly with applications from grassroots NGOs.[6]

As to the rest of the NGOs in this study, their relations with the state are not close enough to help them secure permanent access to governmental funds or major funding from IOs. These NGOs tend to apply for foreign funding mostly because there are no domestic funds designated for labour issues (as discussed in the previous chapter), and those small pools of domestic funding available in areas such as community development, urban integration or migrant workers' family and education are usually difficult to access for small NGOs, and cannot match the size of foreign funds.[7] These NGOs choose various other strategies for procuring funds. The choice of strategies does not necessarily correspond directly to the particular relationship that the NGO has with the state.

As discussed in the previous chapters, some NGOs turn to the new government procurement possibilities, but the importance of those should not be exaggerated. As presented in Chapter 2, the examples of SC and ET, the two organisations which have recently turned to procurement opportunities, indicate that these NGOs are still largely relying on foreign funds. Apart from NHC with its close relations to ZFTU, no other NGO in this study at the time of the fieldwork was relying on domestic funding only. This is because domestic funding is inadequate and still difficult to access, and even those NGOs which are increasingly relying on domestic funding, such as SC, see domestic procurement projects as lacking funds and transparency, and fear the withdrawal of foreign funders.[8] Even those NGOs which have worked out positive relations with the local state and sought not to upset the government still overwhelmingly relied on foreign funds at the time of the fieldwork, as the example of BWH and its branches in Shenyang, Shenzhen and Shanghai indicate: in 2012 alone, 98 per cent of the NGO's income came from FAs. However, these organisations that do have a good relationship with the local state agency or a municipal government official also tend to be self-vigilant as to their permissible language and activities, and they are under greater influence from the governmentality mechanisms, despite their reliance on foreign funds.

Some other NGOs, who have a weak relationship with the local state, or don't have one at all, might also fear state repression if they apply for foreign funding: NBW and AC are examples of that behaviour. NBW seeks self-reliance as much as possible (they collect funds through playing concerts, individual donations from migrant worker entrepreneurs or selling their albums and DVDs). They insist strongly on their self-sufficiency and independence from foreign sources. However, at the time of the fieldwork they still received funding from a Hong Kong-based INGO (FA 6) and justify this by insisting that these funds are 'domestic'.[9] The crucial factor here is probably the fact that Hong Kong-based INGOs are the key source of funds for labour NGOs.[10] It is also easier to approach these INGOs due to cultural and language proximity, and they provide the most long-term and sustainable source of funding.[11] On the other hand, AC was mostly funded from domestic sources because it works in the area of migrant children's education, where more domestic funds are available. In 2012 MVD and JM[12] both lacked an established relationship with local government, and were keen to receive funds from abroad, but had none of the necessary skills to approach foreign funders. Usually, fundraising is such an intensive activity for an NGO to undertake, that it must have one person employed solely for procurement purposes, who is usually able to converse in English (this is the case of BWH, for instance).

Additional constraints to foreign fund procurement have been experienced by those NGOs which operate inland, because most FAs are located in Beijing and Hong Kong. Some NGOs and FAs admit that Beijing has a large number of NGOs mainly because of the easier access to funding and because FAs which grant funding usually look for Beijing-based organisations or those which have their headquarters in Beijing.[13] Similarly, at the time of my fieldwork, Guangdong-based NGOs had more opportunities to network with FAs and better access to funding from Hong Kong. Beijing and Guangdong boast a vibrant labour NGO community, because some of the NGOs set up in the 1990s (as discussed in the introduction) created an inspirational and nurturing ground for the organisations which evolved in the 2000s. Those working further inland, such as SFI (in Yongkang, in Zhejiang province) and JM (in Shiyan, in

Hubei province), had much more constrained access to foreign funds due to their location. Both of these NGOs learned about such funding opportunities while attending capacity-building events in Beijing that were organised by BWH – in other words through 'translocal networks' between NGOs.

Finally, those NGOs which have long experienced conflicted relationships with the local state, particularly the rights-defence and labour movement-orientated NGOs located in the PRD, but also other rights-defence NGOs inland (e.g. Zhejiang-based SFI), rely almost exclusively on foreign funds. Their sources of funds vary: many labour movement-orientated NGOs in Guangzhou are sponsored by Hong Kong INGOs which provide regular training to the organisations they sponsor. An important source of funding for many more contentious types of migrant NGOs is China Labour Bulletin,[14] a Hong Kong-based NGO set up by Han Dongfan, an important figure in the Tiananmen movement. While such INGOs provide funding for more contentious activities, such as strike support or collective bargaining, they themselves are blacklisted in China, and NGOs which receive funding from them tend to be under particular pressure from the state agencies to give up their funds or find themselves further repressed. Some others of these 'more contentious' NGOs receive funding from British, German and American INGOs. This is probably the reason why foreign funding has been such a controversial issue for the Chinese government: it enables the functioning of organisations undesirable to the state. Moreover, these organisations tend to come together, particularly under difficult situations, which is also discouraged by the government. During the 2012 Shenzhen crackdown, the event had a positive and arguably strengthening effect on the inter-NGO networks.[15] A similar reaction among PRD-based labour movement NGOs also took place after the 2015 arrests of the Panyu Centre activists.[16]

Although NGOs often carefully calculate their involvement with foreign funders due to fear of the government's adverse reaction, these NGOs can also use their foreign links to prevent crackdowns or as leverage when they feel threatened by the government. BWH is an example of an organisation which, while maintaining a non-obstructive relationship with the local government, uses its foreign connections as a preventive measure; the office of the NGO is adorned with pictures showing foreign dignitaries (including high-profile politicians, such as Angela Merkel) and ambassadors shaking hands with the NGO's founder. A China-based scholar from the Beijing-based Communication University of China who is well acquainted with the organisation explained to me that such behaviour from NGOs is strategic and aimed at making sure the government will not touch the organisation and to ensure its relative safety. He told me that 'because of these [prominent] contacts a lot of "political issues" are prevented'.[17] Of course, this self-promotion also helps the NGO appear as a reliable and trustworthy partner to potential funders and migrant workers alike. Foreign networks can also be used during crackdowns to put pressure on the Chinese government. During the 2012 crackdown in Shenzhen the NGOs affected mobilised their networks, particularly in Hong Kong, to gain wider publicity about the way they were treated. Thanks to their networks outside of China, the foreign media echoed the events around the world. Additionally, a hundred prominent international scholars on China and labour issues have signed an online letter addressed to the Guangdong government defending these organisations (SACOM, 2012). These actions were repeated when Panyu activists and other NGO activists were detained in 2015, and again when five prominent labour activists were detained in 2019. This shows the ability of NGOs to mobilise actors on different scales, which creates new 'glocal' forms of shaping citizenship in China.

Inter-organisational and FA–NGO networking has been experiencing unprecedented obstacles from the withdrawal of larger foreign funding since the early 2010s, and particularly since the introduction of the 2017 Overseas Management Law. The major funding that supported much of the labour-related activism in China was phased out in 2014: for instance, the EuropeAid-funded projects which had channelled large funds since the 1980s to aid China's development terminated in that year.[18] Alongside the withdrawal of EU funding, the UN is also phasing out many projects in democratic governance and poverty reduction from China, as China is no longer regarded as a 'developing' country by many governments.[19] Similarly, while many foreign foundations continue to work in areas such as poverty reduction, AIDS and education, the number of those working in the areas of rights, including labour rights, had already been decreasing rapidly, even before the Overseas NGOs Management Law was discussed. This is part of a global trend of decreasing funding in labour rights activism, presumably because the outcomes in this sector are difficult to measure.[20] On top of that, the 2017 Overseas NGOs Management Law reshaped completely the foreign funding environment in China, resulting in the initial exit of foreign organisations from China: in March 2017 only 30 out of 7,000 INGOs managed to register with MOCA (Shi-Kupfer and Lang, 2017). As of 2020, some of the INGOs which have supported labour NGOs in this study are continuing to function in China, and their offices are still open. However, they must navigate the new environment carefully and are only able to support NGOs that work in government-accepted areas, which, in a similar way to the process of pivoting towards public procurement discussed in the previous chapter, influences the ability of migrant NGOs to continue reshaping the most contentious parts of structural citizenship in China. NGOs which used to address such contentious parts of structural citizenship are faced with literally no access to funding (see Franceschini and Nesossi, 2018), which combined with state repression, spells a prospect of the likely disappearance of these NGOs.

We can see that the challenges to the formation of networks are indeed great, and they have become even greater in recent years: not only networking with FAs but also inter-NGO networking is discouraged and is not part of the permissible citizenship practices in China, which are now institutionalised through a prohibitive legal framework. Two factors appear to be most prominent in NGOs' propensity to network: their relationship with the government and their geographical location. A good relationship with the government has allowed for the formation of more flexible international and translocal networks, while being located in a donor-rich environment, such as the PRD or Beijing, enables better access to funds, even in the difficult post-2017 environment. The act of entering into inter-NGO networks might be seen as an act of citizenship as it reworks the citizenship practices based on isolationism, competition and atomisation of civil society. But the act of networking is undertaken through a careful balancing of the NGO's own relationship with the state (relational negotiation of citizenship) rather than outright opposition to it, even if the act of networking, especially with FAs, challenges the prescribed forms of citizenship practices. While for

NGOs the act of networking relies on a strenuous balancing between FAs and the state, it can bring great potential for NGOs, not only financially but also in many intangible ways.

The exchange of ideas through networks: the reshaping of selves

While access to financial resources is important, access to non-tangible resources can be equally crucial for NGOs' ability to remake citizenship, as it opens avenues for the formation of a new civic consciousness. The reshaping of the civic identities of NGO activists takes place through networking with other NGOs and FAs in perhaps surprising ways. One way in which networking reshapes self-awareness of one's own role in society and leads to the formation of civic consciousness among NGOs often starts in the very moment when an NGO has to explain its work to foreign donors. In conversation with me, the founder of BWH, Mr Song, stated that before he learned about the possibility of applying for funding from foreign donors, and before he learned how to present his work in an application, he had not been aware that the organisation he had set up was actually an 'NGO'; he thought of it as just a telephone line giving advice to fellow migrant workers.[21] Moreover, as a result of BWH's engagement with foreign donors, the NGO founder realised the importance of sharing knowledge and experience with other activists, which led him to initiate countrywide networking events with other labour activists and donors.[22] These platforms give NGOs a chance to present their work to potential funders, thereby creating a greater awareness of their role in society. These events have also helped to forge a sense of fraternity and common interest among NGOs, shaping civic consciousness.

In March 2012, I took part in the most important conference organised by BWH annually, entitled 'Capacity Building Training for Labour NGOs in China'. The event brings together migrant worker NGOs from across the country, as well as academics, IOs, INGOs and representatives of foreign embassies. Apparently, in the past, the organisation had also invited some ACFTU representatives, but there were none involved in the event in 2012. The conference entailed a series of presentations by NGOs, donors, academics and

ILO representatives: each NGO presented their work, sharing their practices and then inviting questions and exchanging views on what could be improved in their work. Apart from the talk by an ILO representative, one by an INGO supporting an NGO, and one by an academic, the entire event was dominated by the NGOs presenting their work. The event had a very pragmatic character, focused on fund procurement and networking. It was particularly useful for NGOs coming from remote places, as it enabled these normally solitary organisations to meet other NGOs and foreign donors. Since the horizontal networks between labour NGOs in China, as mentioned earlier, are underdeveloped or even non-existent, such events are important ways of breaking the prescribed citizenship practices, which prioritise mass organisations or GONGOs under strict state monitoring as the forerunners of civic organising in China. Meetings like this allow for more spontaneous grassroots interactions and exchanges with FAs, which are normally discouraged by the state.

It is important to discuss further the role of the adoption of 'Western values' in this process. The fear of NGOs' adoption and then promotion of so-called 'Western values' has been one of the main reasons behind the state's opposition to NGOs networking with FAs and restrictive legislation in recent years. However, from my observations of such networks,[23] one cannot simply understand the shaping of civic consciousness of NGOs as a result of exposure to and adoption of 'Western concepts'. Similarly, in terms of ideology, I did not observe the replacement of previously held beliefs with the values promoted by Western donors, but rather a process of mutual learning and knowledge exchange. As some research has pointed out before, mutual benefit is emblematic of networking (Keck and Sikkink, 1998: 4). Indeed, I found a great amount of enthusiasm and willingness on the part of FAs to learn from NGOs; it was the NGOs who tended to transfer knowledge and experience to the FAs, while apart from technical and financial issues related to bookkeeping and financial transparency, FAs would not impose their viewpoints or values on domestic organisations. The process of boundary-crossing was therefore two-sided and clearly mutually beneficial. It also enabled NGOs to shape the networks rather than simply remain the passive recipients of previously formed mechanisms.

Indeed, if domestic NGOs turn radical, it is not because of foreign influence: they had usually had this attitude long before they met the donors. As discussed in the previous chapter, JM is an example of an inland organisation which does not receive any funding from abroad, yet its founder is as critical of the state and the capital as many of the foreign-sponsored NGOs in Guangdong province. Moreover, these organisations' leaders have their own strong views and are almost impossible for the INGOs to control, as a representative from one of the most important funding organisations in Hong Kong, FA 15, highlighted in an interview:

> We have a pretty hands-on approach to our partners on the mainland, meaning that we don't necessarily just sit back and say 'Ok, you promised to handle this many cases of employment discrimination, you can do so and so, and we're then going to check if you kept your targets.' No, our relationship continues [beyond that]; we have a much more hands-on and involved strategy. But at the same time, these organisations are all very different and by no means can you control them. Because they do what they want, they develop their own relationships, they strategise about their own situations … Because we had a lot of partners who had the most constructive and shockingly close relations with government, and with some of them we wonder what kind of deals must they have made with the local government to stay above water. But we don't know this.[24]

Moreover, the same INGO representative points to the domestic sources of militancy of many migrant workers who lead strikes and protests, and who are not NGO staff and have no support from NGOs or foreign donors:

> When the strikers start demanding things such as worker unions' elections … it is very easy to explain it in a way as 'this foreign intervention' or 'you must be helping foreign forces'. And some of these people [striking worker activists]: they have relations with foreign funders, but others absolutely do not. For example, if you look at the Walmart activists [the interviewee refers to Walmart strikes in China which took place in 2015 and 2016], some of them explicitly have relations with foreign NGOs, but some of them absolutely do not. They are just … real labour militants interested in labour history and even the Communist Party history. A labour organiser I talked to was a proper communist in the sense that he said 'I read early labour history, and they were all just militant workers. A hundred years ago, the Communist Party were people like me, organising workers in strikes. And this is what they should be doing.'[25]

Indeed, in most cases I observed during the fieldwork, FAs seemed passive rather than active recipients of NGOs' ideas and self-promotion activities, not in the least interested in spreading 'subversive ideas'. In conversations with me, many FAs themselves emphasised that they prefer to sponsor NGOs which have a constructive relationship with the state. Indeed, one of the most important funders of BWH, a German INGO (FA 5 in the study), stopped sponsoring the organisation after its branch in Shenzhen experienced a deterioration in its relationship with the local government in 2014.[26] ILO representatives, similarly, saw the conflicted relations between the PRD labour NGOs and the local government as an obstacle to their activism, and a reason to withhold funding.[27]

An example of how the concrete set of so-called 'Western values' was approached in the context of FA–NGO relations can be observed in the event held on the premises of FA 13, an embassy in Beijing, which I observed in February 2012. FA 13 organises regular meetings between various businesses, NGOs and academics from China and abroad, and is an important space where such 'ideological' exchanges take place. In February 2012, the mission held a conference on trade relations with China, entitled 'The role of Government, Business, Media and NGOs in Creating an Attractive and Sustainable Business Environment'. The discussion was based around the particular set of CSR measures, Ruggie's Principles, which were designed by John Ruggie and accepted by the UN Human Rights Council in 2008. Ruggie's Principles emphasise the importance of the human rights aspect in workplaces (that is, the design of appropriate policies, corporate responsibility to avoid infringement of workers' rights, and access to judicial and non-judicial remedy for workers). The event was attended by representatives of several labour NGOs from across China, business representatives of transnational corporations (TNCs), domestic private companies and well-known Chinese academics writing on labour issues in China. During the conference, a labour NGO representative from Guangdong, a European CEO and five Chinese entrepreneurs running private enterprises in China held an extended discussion regarding the concept of 'human rights' as part of Ruggie's Principles. The concept of human rights, used sparingly by FAs in China as it is regarded as 'sensitive', and officially sidelined by the Chinese government as 'Western-centric', could have been perceived as provocative and imposing by some observers. However, the embassy did not present any official standing on the issue, apart from the opening note which outlined Ruggie's Principles, and the intention was to create a platform for discussion between the speakers and the audience. Indeed, in the Q&A session, it was the Guangdong labour NGO representative who called for clarification of the meaning of 'human rights' embedded in Ruggie's Principles, so that it could be more easily adopted by companies and more understandable for labour NGOs on the ground.

This exchange clearly illustrated the negotiated character of ideas which are perceived as 'sensitive' by the state, rather than straight top-down imposition of their meaning by FAs. In fact, when asked directly about the possible agenda of foreign funders in sponsoring labour NGOs in China, Mr Song from BWH responded:

> [In order to apply for the funding] I need to draw up a plan saying how many people I want to help and that I want to help them to 'integrate into the city', then draw up a budget, explain how we will spend it (for example on manuals, books etc.); they [the donors] very gladly support me. It may be that the reason for this is to support the development of civil society or human rights in China, but they don't say it.[28]

This quote and the discussion presented above point to a pragmatic, negotiated and eventually 'indigenised' approach to the adoption of ideas that could be perceived as 'Western'. As to the process of 'reshaping of the selves' through events like the one above, my observation is that it is more important for NGOs to network with business representatives and potential donors during such events than to 'soak up the foreign ideas'. Such interactions have a highly pragmatic aim of learning the know-how (such as the transnational language of self-promotion) and creating opportunities to receive more funds. Therefore, networking should not be understood as transformative of citizenship discourse because it introduces 'Western' ideas of citizenship and rights. Rather, the transformation of civic actors' identities takes place through the discovery of their own role within the society and in the wider global context.

Through accessing training opportunities, participating in open dialogue with like-minded individuals and entering transnational networks, NGOs reinvent their identities and change the self-perception of their place as civic actors within the Chinese development project, both as migrant workers-turned-activists and as NGOs. This changed self-perception influences NGOs to then create their own networking events, to which they invite other NGOs' employees, migrant workers, academics and FAs, in this way forging a new idea of civic activism in China. The 'glocal' perspective, forged through networking, shapes the self-identity of NGO activists as global citizens. Interestingly, even those NGOs which do not receive direct financial help from FAs can access such intangible resources by participating in events involving foreign donors organised by other NGOs in their network.

Another example of how NGOs' civic identity is shaped through networking can be traced in their adoption of an idea of 'transnational labour solidarity'. For instance, BWH adorns its premises with pictures taken with migrant workers, including one presenting the NGO's founder in an embrace with American workers of African American origin. The picture was taken during Mr Song's trip to a construction site in the United States at the invitation of one of the NGO's former foreign donors. The picture alludes to the idea of transnational working-class solidarity, shared by the NGO staff. Among many conversations we had during my three-month-long internship with BWH, curiosity about the conditions of workers in Europe was a common topic of conversation initiated by the NGO staff.

Other organisations, such as NHC, NBW, FJ, MWU, UA and ET also have a strong sense of transnational labour solidarity. This is visible in NBW's 2009 theatrical play entitled 'Our World, Our Dream' for instance, in the dialogue between two workers:

> Have you read the papers recently? The Europeans are turning anarchist. Last year the Greek people supported anarchism [*wuzhengfu zhuyi*] and there were hundreds of strikes in France. Some held banners stating 'Capitalism has decayed'!
>
> Wherever there is oppression, there is resistance, isn't it? Don't you find it strange that the crisis has lasted for so many years, yet the capitalist spirit is still haunting us? ... It seems now that college graduates all over the world cannot find a job. What to do?
>
> Wait, doesn't it sound just like this slogan 'One world, one dream'?!'[29] [the audience laughs]

And in another part of the play, the actor says:

> 'We hope that our country can show the rest of the world's workers the hope of socialism. Workers of the world, unite!'

This idea of transnational workers' solidarity is strong not only among those NGOs who are sponsored by FAs, but also, like NBW, those who have been supported mostly through domestic funds, again showing the active role of NGOs in forging their own ideas, rather than simply internalising those passed down to them by FAs. The Marxist ideas of international class solidarity can have indigenous historical roots, and are not necessarily adopted by NGOs as a result of their contact with foreign donors. These ideas shape the global citizenship outlook of NGOs, as they lead them to recognise the struggle of migrant workers as part of a global problem. This reinvents their own positioning as civic agents in China: they employ a language which resonates with global and not only national discourses, and see their own identity as that of global citizens.

This indigenisation of transnational ideas in a local context can be seen not only with regard to the notion of 'human rights' or 'labour solidarity', but also in relation to the very idea of 'civil society'. In this book, I depart from the long-suffering Habermasian understanding of civil society as a space autonomous from the state (Habermas, 1989: 31–43, 231),[30] and instead understand it as a space of interactions between NGOs and both the state and the market actors through horizontal linkages (Salmenkari, 2013: 684). In this conceptualisation, civil society is a 'third space' where individual and collective action takes place (Somers, 2008: 19–20), but where the boundaries between civil society, the state and the market are fluid and permeable, and therefore changeable (Janoski, 1998: 12–17).

It is instructive to show, however, how the concept of civil society is understood by migrant worker NGOs and what role this idea plays in their activism and self-identity. When tracing the use of the concept by some migrant NGOs, it appears to be used sometimes as an ideal future state of state–society relations in China. The NGOs which understand and use the concept in this way have been consciously aiming their activism towards the formation of 'civil society' in China. Because they seek to engage migrant workers in the formation of such a civil society, they clearly challenge the dominant citizenship discourses around *suzhi*, which normally reserve political participation and civic action for elites and Party officials only. Indeed, NGOs' engagement with the concept of civil society directly challenges the citizenship discourse and practices, which, as described in Chapter 1, reject the notion of 'civil society' as a foreign-instilled concept.

Some NGOs openly and consistently promote the idea of 'building civil society'. It is often through participation in networks and organisation of an NGO that the actors become aware of their role as participants in civil society. As mentioned before, it was through the contact with INGOs and other NGOs that the founder of BWH understood his own identity as that of a civic activist and his organisation as a civil society actor.[31] The organisation uses the phrase 'civil society' regularly in its annual training sessions organised in Beijing. However, while the organisation consciously promotes the idea of 'civil society', it does so carefully, so as not to antagonise the state in the process. Indeed, outside of the networks and meetings with foreign funders, the NGO used to rely on a concept of 'public interest' (*gongyi*) more frequently. The NGO covered the walls of its premises with *gongyi* calligraphy and even presented one such painting to myself on my departure from the organisation. However, when resorting to the *gongyi* concept, the NGOs embraced it in the meaning of '*quanmin gongyi*' (everyone's public interest), and to frame labour NGOs' activism more specifically, they used the phrase *gongyi weiquan* (defending rights for the public interest). Both these notions convey the meaning of grassroots, bottom-up participation in public governance and tie it to the 'rights-defence' discourse, so they differ from the state-prescribed *gongmin cishan*, which conveys the meaning of 'rich people's' philanthropy, rather than grassroots participation in governance (see Wu, 2017). As the *gongyi* concept is much more acceptable, embracing the label with *quanmin* or *weiquan* add-ons by NGOs is an interesting example of the NGO engaging in a 'resistance through accommodation' strategy: of promoting some form of grassroots civil society but using state-approved language.

Another example of how BWH in particular treads this line carefully is the continuous emphasis on how the 'openness about their activities', so important to greater public engagement and networking, is also aimed at maintaining friendly relations with the government. Mr Song maintains that the transparency in their contacts with state agents is crucial for their long-term success, despite the fact that they occasionally use the now-unwelcomed phraseology in their activities.[32]

UA also understands the issue of openness (*kaifang*) about its activities as essential for the building of a transparent and strong civil society. UA's predecessor organisation (as discussed in the previous chapter) used to publish all its activities and its collective self-assembly mission online. As the organisation's leader told me, it was so open that even FAs believed it was a government-run organisation.[33] Mr Zhao continued these efforts to build a transparent civil society through his later organisation, UA, and he did that through networking and training activities co-organised through academic institutions and with the input from FAs, such as the course on 'Civil society capacity building' at Sun Yat-sen University in Guangzhou, which he attended in the past. His attitude to transparency as a fundamental element of building civil society is very clear-cut:

> I am often asked: 'Can we use your real name?' I answer: 'Yes, you can!' I say: 'I should take responsibility for my words and actions' ... We should promote transparency [*touming*] and public openness [*gongkai*] in society. I often say, maybe our work is not done in the best way possible, but I do hope that it is done in the most transparent way.
>
> In my opinion, an NGO's role is not only to help one social group, but rather society at large. We call it civil society [*gongmin shehui*]. ... The public interest organisations [*gongyi jigou*] should take some responsibility for it and should play a role in the development of this society. If you do things in a stealthy way [*toutoumomo*], you might still help some people ... but it is hard to help to push society forward. Because in the workers' society [*gongren shehui*] we all need to stand up and state our position clearly and in a loud voice [*dazhangqigu*]. This is what Chinese people lack the most; a lot of people just do things in a stealthy way, secretly and quietly – such an attitude will not inspire any change [*qidi*[34]].[35]

The commitment to transparency as a responsibility and a building block of civil society indicates the production of new civic consciousness. This civic consciousness challenges the existing citizenship formulation as it promotes engagement in public life and a certain type of values within that engagement, such as openness (*gongkai*) and transparency (*touming*). Here, promotion of such civil society not only encourages activism, it also encourages everyday ethical acts which contribute to building open public debate, which can further change attitudes to migrants and their citizenship.

The interactions with foreign donors and like-minded domestic NGOs lead to changes in the self-perception of NGOs and the reconfiguration of the civic activism of NGOs in China, and ultimately shape the representations and claims of migrant workers associated with these NGOs. However, as discussed above, this process is not a case of simply adopting foreign values. Through exposure to transnational ideas via networking with donors, NGOs attain transnational ideas, which they then adopt in their own activism in an indigenised manner. These ideas constitute very important material which helps to create new forms and ideas of citizenship in China. NGOs further transfer these ideas to migrant workers, who are exposed to glocal imaginations and beliefs through visiting NGO premises and participating in their events, potentially creating new civic consciousness in the wider group of migrant workers. These shared values also help to build the common citizenship identity of NGOs: as labour activists, global citizens and civil society actors.

Goals: displacement woes or just pragmatism?

However, not all NGOs' interactions with donors can be seen as helping to address problems associated with differentiated or limited citizenship. One of the consequences of struggling for funds is the dependence of NGOs on the donors and their agendas, which can lead to instances of 'goals displacement'. Goals displacement has a direct impact on NGOs' willingness or ability to negotiate new citizenship for migrant workers. This is, however, difficult to measure. Some NGOs simply employ the language and goals of the donors as lip service to procure funding, and end up doing what they intend nevertheless, as the comment from the FA 15 representative in the previous section indicated. However, there is a well-founded worry that with the growing scarcity of funding, particularly since the 2017 Overseas NGOs law, these woes might prove well justified.

To further explore whether NGOs do indeed end up displacing their chosen activism with that preferred by the donor, it is instructive to analyse how NGOs use the ideas and language preferred by the donor in their self-promotion activities during fund-procurement events. By revealing the politics and purpose behind that language, some light can be shed on the motivations of NGOs and the actual degree of goals displacement. Several months of working in BWH allowed me to observe how this language is used in NGOs' contacts with FAs, and how these interactions with the donors affected their actual activism.

In meetings with donors, BWH primarily advertised their work as being focused on alleviating the problem of wage arrears frequently faced by migrant workers in Beijing. The typical meeting would start with the NGO presenting the challenges that migrant workers face in their daily life and work. To do so, they used evocative images presenting the harsh conditions of migrant workers' lives in order to elicit an emotional response from the potential donor. Indeed, the majority of NGOs represent migrant workers as a 'weak and underprivileged group' (*ruoshi qunti*) in front of the donors and government bodies, as part of the universally recognised language of poverty alleviation. In China, the label of *ruoshi qunti* is reserved for underprivileged groups in society in order to advocate for their cases, and indeed the use of this label by migrant NGOs helps to convey the requests for justice, visibility and funding for NGOs.[36] This, of course, is problematic in terms of migrants' empowerment as it presents migrant workers as weak and in need of rescue by others, which maintains the dominant citizenship discourse of migrants as below and behind, and the practice of elites as the only agents able to rescue the group. However, it is important to bear in mind the pragmatic reasons for using this label: BWH used the 'weak and underprivileged' narrative in order to help secure funding from organisations which primarily focus on questions of poverty and development, rather than labour, which explains this particular pitching of the issue. Indeed, the NGO also showed images presenting workers as resisting citizens, such as the picture of a migrant woman climbing a construction crane in protest over deferred wages in the middle of winter; or that of construction workers protesting over deferred wages. Therefore, the NGO presented a dual narrative of migrants' desperation and resistance. However, the final message was that the NGO's work not only allows them to address the poverty of migrant workers, but also to stop them committing such acts of resistance, therefore aiding the state's 'social stability' project.

Such presentation of the NGO's work catered for donors' sensibilities and accommodated to the state's priority of 'maintaining social stability' (*weiwen*). However, while doing so, they also fulfil their own aim of expressing disagreement with social injustice and trying to remedy the migrant workers' situation. Therefore, BWH is an example of an organisation which adopts the strategy of 'resistance through accommodation' in their relations with both the state and the market. In the case of NGO–donor relations, the NGO uses the self-marketisation element of securing funds (accommodation) in conjunction with promotion of the social inclusion of migrant workers (resistance to the prevalent treatment of migrants), but it also maintains some aspects of the prescribed citizenship practice, such as the need for the group to be 'rescued' by elites. These strategies enable the NGO to present its own activities as empowering migrant workers' groups in language that is intelligible to foreign donors, while making these activities state-abiding, by the use of catch-phrases such as 'integration into the city' or 'maintaining stability'.

However, the effects of these efforts are highly beneficial to the organisation itself. BWH has received support from a vast array of FAs: in 2012 they were in receipt of funding from nineteen foreign donors in total, including embassies, the ILO, the World Bank and most of the INGOs which provide funding for labour NGOs in China. Remarkably, it is these relationships with high-ranking foreign politicians and ambassadors, paired with the organisation's willingness and active efforts to maintain a good relationship with the local government, that feed its success and protect it from government crackdowns. Of course, a careful avoidance of too strong an emphasis on rights other than the 'legal labour rights (*hefa quanyi*) of migrant workers' is also a strategy the NGO adopts to appeal to the state actors. However, while it allows the NGO to survive and thrive, the effect is mixed in terms of 'challenging citizenship', as it preserves rather than questions dominant citizenship practices and discourse.

While the importance of marketisation (procuring funds from donors and businesses) for labour NGOs has been mainly criticised as detrimental to their integrity and authenticity (Howell, 2012; Lee and Shen, 2011: 180), I argue that it should not always be seen in this light. I use the term 'resistance through accommodation' strategy here to highlight how these seemingly accommodating attitudes, just as is the case with the NGOs' relationship with the government, should not be seen as a sign of donor control over NGOs, but rather as a way to eventually meet the aim of aiding migrant workers and enhancing the position of NGOs, which are both essential parts of the transformation of migrants' citizenship in China. The relationships between NGOs and FAs are mutually beneficial, as they allow both actors to learn from each other. Moreover, while networking shapes the identities of NGOs, and consequently the migrant workers they come in contact with, the process of exchange of ideas is far from a one-sided imposition, as the examples of NGO's discursive strategies illustrate. The NGOs are far from acquiescent actors in their relations with donors: as is the case in their relations with the state, they use donor-enticing language in order to eventually project their own beliefs and exert their own actions on the subject.

However, some NGOs' activism may well fall into the category of goals displacement. Some cases of NGOs' engagement with corporations and businesses for the purpose of fund procurement can indeed lead to them abandoning their authentic effort to change migrants' conditions. Engagement with labour NGOs is a growing trend among the transnational corporations in China, intended to boost their CSR credentials; it is therefore especially important to discuss. These partnerships usually take the form of NGO-run grievance hotlines set within the factories subcontracting for the TNC. According to MWU, such hotlines are becoming a popular source of funding for many labour NGOs in the PRD, who receive funding in exchange for monitoring the observance of labour law, forwarding workers' grievances and facilitating dialogue between workers and management.[37] These cases can be seen as providing some form of empowerment to migrant workers in these factories, as they give them an opportunity to voice their dissatisfaction and find an amicable resolution, but at the same time, NGOs which receive funding from TNCs that they are supposed to monitor indicates collusion of interests, similar to that which takes place between ACFTU and employers.

This controversial impact of NGOs' reliance on corporate funding became clear to me in the case of the Shenzhen branch of BWH. The NGO is cooperating with an Irish international company specialising in development of products and sourcing manufacturers for giants such as Apple. In 2012, the TNC commissioned BWH to activate a complaint hotline for migrant workers. The hotline is advertised through posters in factories and dormitories, and workers are supposed to contact the hotline with grievances and concerns. The NGO then reports these grievances back to the company management, which designs ways to address any pressing issues related to working conditions. The NGO also organises regular round tables between the enterprise management and bottom-line managers (who are usually migrant workers themselves). In January 2013, I conducted a participant observation study during one of these meetings. In the meeting, the line managers were asked to share their experience of working on the factory floor. However, they were silent most of the time, and clearly reluctant to publicly voice their opinions, perhaps given the presence of a foreign CEO in the meeting. This situation hardly indicated an empowering or transformative practice, but rather one which maintains the status quo.

The dependence of NGOs on corporate funding is likely to deepen currently due to the new legislation which prevents migrant NGOs from accessing foreign funding, and it might even become the main source of foreign funding. Indeed, other studies (see Franceschini and Nesossi, 2018) and my own interviews indicate clearly that this is a rising trend among migrant NGOs, for whom engagement with the corporate sector has become the only avenue to procure foreign funding. Despite the TNCs' lofty CSR rhetoric, such engagement might result in instances where NGOs become instruments in the employers' agenda instead of remaining agents able to defend migrant workers' interests.

There is also a reverse trend of goals displacement, or 'mission creep' (Noakes, 2018: 10), happening among foreign funders in China, and it long precedes the 2017 Overseas NGOs Management Law. It relates to the way FAs have been presenting their work in order to appeal to government and convince it of their amicable intentions (Noakes, 2018: 10). Some NGOs in the study saw this as lack of true commitment to support rights-based activism in China among FAs:

> You will see that the majority of international actors who have offices in China are doing poverty, AIDS, education … you can see that none of them, or not many of them, talk about rights. It is not about 'how can I help you?' Even the UN and ILO offices don't talk about rights. [Maybe] it is good that some international actors have increasingly good contact with government officials [like the International Confederation of Free Trade Unions (ICFTU)'s relationship with ACFTU], maybe

> it will change the government. But [these increased contacts] are not about change in the structure. We still don't touch the core problem, that is [the problem] of people [not having the right to be] organised, openly talk to each other about their issues, and to be able to voice their problems out. There is no such platform. I can help you because you are poor, so I can send you money, medicine, food to help you. But why don't we talk about why this area is so poor; because the development on the coast is too high, and they are abusing the inner China people. It is the inequality of rights distribution! But no one touches it! Not even the UN![38]

The NGO highlights here that in order to address poverty and social inequality, material and economic aid is not sufficient; only with a greater change in structural citizenship can the inequality be addressed. However, there is no real interest in supporting rights defence as a core issue of development among international funders in China, despite their lofty assurances, which makes migrant NGOs' ability to procure funds for this transformative type of activism all the more difficult.

Conclusion

As the discussion above illustrates, the act of networking is important for an understanding of the ways in which labour NGOs shape various aspects of citizenship in China. Even though the reliance on funding from FAs might take over the NGO's agenda, networking can become an act of citizenship because it contests the prescribed citizenship practices of civic disengagement, the atomisation of NGOs and the prohibition on their contacts with FAs. Through conducting networking between themselves and with other actors, NGOs seek to reshape the rules governing citizenship practice in China, by making cooperation between civic actors more transparent and robust. The glocal imagination and perspectives that these NGOs gain and then bestow back upon migrant workers, and the fraternity which is shaped between NGOs through networks, transform both NGOs' and workers' identities, helping to shape new civic consciousness and civic values.

The issues of power relations between donors and NGOs and goals displacement have great impact on the degree to which NGOs can introduce these new citizenship practices and identities. The fieldwork findings indicate that the goals displacement problem is not a straightforward trend occurring whenever NGOs engage with foreign donors. When it comes to donors' ideational influences, the top-down transmission of Western concepts to NGOs is clearly not the case. The exchange of ideas and values between NGOs and foreign donors should rather be seen as a multidirectional process remoulding both NGOs and FAs. The exchange that takes place through networks produces some surprising identities for NGOs: they often indigenise and localise global concepts, but mostly use them pragmatically. Among these concepts, NGOs adopt their own versions of ideas such as 'transnational labour solidarity' and 'civil society' to shape new civic identities in the global, not only national perspective.

However, notwithstanding the ability of some NGOs to forge networks with FAs without seemingly upsetting the state, many of these relationships are coming, or have already come, to an end. As state regulations are tightened, with the notable case of the Overseas NGOs law, the redirecting of government funding towards other types of NGOs and the withdrawal of foreign funds in the area of labour rights, many NGOs which participated in my study fear tough days ahead, and some of them have already suffered closure, all painting a rather gloomy picture of the coming times. This creates the conditions for future goals displacement through deepening of reliance on corporate funding and the replacement of NGOs undertaking more contentious activism with those who can pitch their activism within the narrow area sponsored by the state and those FAs who can still operate in China under the new laws.

Notes

1 By 'foreign donors' I mean actors such as INGOs, including those from Hong Kong, Taiwan and Macau, foreign governments and IOs, and foreign businesses. I use the name foreign actors (FAs) when discussing them in this book.

2 LHC is not a migrant-established or migrant-run organisation (see Table A4.1 in Appendix 4).

3 Interviews no. 15, no. 16 and no. 22.

4 Interviews no. 15, no. 16, no. 22 and no. 27.
5 This is a finding from my research that has been previously mentioned in some other publications, for instance Fulda (2013).
6 Interviews no. 28, no. 29, no. 31, no. 33 and no. 36.
7 Interviews no. 43 and no. 46.
8 Interview no. 43.
9 Interview no. 5.
10 One Hong Kong-based organisation, FA 6, has sponsored over thirty labour NGOs in its history (Interview no. 14).
11 Interview no. 14. However, Hong Kong foundations themselves are widely supported by foreign funds, which problematizes the rigidity of the divide between domestic and international spaces.
12 Since then, JM has developed a relationship with the local branch of ACFTU, which provides some limited funding.
13 Interview no. 15.
14 This is the real name of the organisation.
15 Interviews no. 17, no. 18 and no. 19.
16 Interviews no. 39 and no. 42. Also see Franceschini and Nesossi (2018).
17 Interview no. 6.
18 Interviews no. 16, no. 27, no. 28 and no. 29.
19 Interviews no. 13 and no. 22.
20 Interview no 17.
21 Interview no. 4.
22 Such openness of the organisation to learn and share was also mentioned as the very reason for the organisation's success according to an ILO representative (Interview no. 23).
23 I conducted participant observation in about fifteen such meetings between BWH, a number of FAs (various countries' embassies, IOs such as the ILO, EU and World Bank, INGOs (mainly European) and, more rarely, banks and research institutions) and other NGOs in their offices. I also took part in three meetings organised for various NGOs by two different embassies in Beijing.
24 Interview no. 39.
25 Interview no. 39.
26 Interviews no. 26 and no. 32.
27 Interview no. 24.
28 Interview no. 4.
29 This was the leading slogan of the 2008 Beijing Olympics.
30 There is a problem with this understanding of the civil society concept: it relies on the adoption of a single tradition of theorising civil society, which overlooks the richness and complexity of the European-originating theories of civil society (Hudson, 2003: 9). Salmenkari argues that

civil society had been defined before in ways which easily respond to different forms of civil society found in a Chinese context and does not have to rely on the idea of autonomy from the state (Salmenkari, 2013).

31 Interview no. 4.

32 Interview no. 4.

33 Interview no. 18.

34 Literally: '... will not inspire enlightenment'.

35 Interview no. 18. I nonetheless decided to anonymise the identity of the interviewer due to severe crackdowns that his organisation experienced after the interview.

36 Also see Gleiss (2015) for further analysis of the use of this rhetoric.

37 Interview no. 17.

38 Interview no. 17.

Part III

Labour

4

Weiquan activism and its limits

Given the centrality of labour in migrant worker NGOs' work, why not simply understand their involvement in countering social injustice as labour activism? Indeed, a great proportion of the existing studies would label these organisations' work as part of a wider labour movement, primarily linked to the rise of working-class consciousness among migrant workers (Sun, 2014; Chan, 2012a; Friedman and Lee, 2010; Chen and Yang, 2017; Froissart, 2018; Xu Y., 2013). But isn't the history of the working class a history of citizenship rights formation? If so, what is the difference between citizenship activism and labour activism, and why does it matter?

This chapter and the next aim to address these questions by analysing the centrality of citizenship in the struggle for migrant workers' labour rights. They do so by focusing on two controversial aspects in the discussion of the relationship between citizenship and labour in China: the role of legal versus extra-legal forms of activism; and the centrality of labour versus citizenship claims. Indeed, on the one hand, the studies on legal action-type migrant worker NGOs often insist that their work cannot be transformative because it reproduces and strengthens the state's legalism regime, entrenching rather than transforming the status quo (Franceschini, 2014; Froissart, 2014). On the other hand, many labour-orientated studies turn away from citizenship as an unimportant, fancy, post-structuralist idea which does not reflect the true essence of migrant workers' struggle (Chan, 2012b). While the current literature on migrant worker activism in China presents migrant workers as active agents of change, it is mainly preoccupied with their struggle for labour rights, either by employing legal mechanisms or by undertaking collective action (strikes), rather than with their struggle for other-than-labour rights of citizenship. This literature frames the question of migrant worker activism as labour activism rather than citizenship activism.

The stories of how NGOs perform acts of citizenship around labour help us reconcile labour and citizenship as two sides of the same coin. By positioning these claims within the wider claims that NGOs put forward in this book, labour emerges as just one – even if the most prominent – aspect of these NGOs' activism. In this chapter, I focus on acts which engage with state-prescribed legal channels, as opposed to those acts which go beyond the law, and relate to the building of working-class identity discussed in Chapters 5 and 6. I discuss to what degree these acts can be understood as acts of citizenship, that is to what degree they can challenge existing citizenship formulation. Against the idea that sees law-abiding acts as preserving the status-quo, I employ the notion of 'resistance through accommodation' to present acts which can have a transformative impact despite their conciliatory character. The first of these acts which employs this strategy is 'defending', borrowed from the phrase of 'defending rights' (*weiquan*), the self-proclaimed *raison d'être* for the majority of NGOs in this chapter. While this is also the area most widely criticised in the literature on NGOs (varying from criticism of the source of legitimacy for NGOs to represent migrants, their accountability to the wider migrant worker group and the portrayal of NGOs as co-opted to state interests), it is indeed also the type of activism in which most NGOs see their greatest service to the migrant community. The second act I discuss is that of 'educating'. In this chapter, I focus on how this act is performed with the use of mainstream legal channels, such as education in law, training in legal proceeding in courts and preventative health and safety training. By pointing to the acts around the site of labour which are conducted through state-prescribed channels, I show the potential for citizenship transformation despite their embeddedness in the law.

Labour laws as instruments of workplace resistance

The debate on the legal action type of activism versus extra-legal activism has been prominent in the existing studies on migrant workers' resistance in China. Much of this debate has focused on the role of collective action and strikes as opposed to labour laws in bringing social change. As already discussed in Chapter 2, the law is an important tool of state control over society, and because of that, its use to defend migrant workers' rights can be seen as entrenching authoritarianism and state control rather than challenging it (Froissart, 2014; Friedman and Lee, 2010; Lee and Shen, 2011; Hui, 2016). In contrast, strikes and collective action are perceived as the only truly transformative form of activism (Butollo and ten Brink, 2012; Chan, 2012a, 2012b; Froissart, 2018). The focus on strikes as a primary instrument of labour activism in China has been particularly promoted by scholars associated with the Critical Legal School,[1] who see legal institutions as a way for the state to exert control over society through the dissemination of the 'rule by law' rhetoric to legitimise themselves and to channel social grievances away from the ruling class. Critical Legal School scholars reject the possibility of emancipation and empowerment through legalistic means, and see strikes as the only avenue that can emancipate the working class.

This debate on the role of law versus extra-legal activism in bringing change is intertwined with the debate on whether the migrant's activism is citizenship- or class- orientated. For instance, Lee argues that the workers' predominant framing of workplace mistreatment as 'breaking the law', and their use of largely legal means to fight it, makes labour activism a form of citizenship movement, as it indicates the rise of active citizenship (Lee, 2007). However, while Lee's findings resonate largely with my own, her understanding of citizenship is quite narrow: it treats active citizenship solely as a growing consciousness of labour rights among migrant workers. This has resulted in some criticism of Lee's argument, with scholars who argue that the workers' movement is predominantly a class movement, not a citizenship movement, because migrant workers see the law as already inadequate to respond to their grievances and instead choose to take on collective bargaining and strikes as the primary tool for the negotiation of their rights (Chan, 2012b). This point leads us to the apparent dissonance in the literature concerning the drivers and consequences of labour activism. Is it performed within the legalism framework or is it taking extra-legal measures? Does it indicate a growing class or citizenship consciousness? As I show in this chapter, such dissonance stems mainly from Lee's understanding of citizenship in liberal terms, as law consciousness. Yet, if we employ a wider definition of what constitutes citizenship-centred activism, it is clear that class and citizenship claims, as well as legal and extra-legal activism, can actually go hand in hand and all contribute to the process of citizenship transformation. To further investigate how this happens, I first turn to the role of law in this process of citizenship contestation.

The labour, welfare, pension and insurance laws introduced since the early 2000s are important parts of creating, at least theoretically, the legal means for workers' greater empowerment.[2] Many of these laws were introduced as a consequence of China's accession to the World Trade Organization in 2001. As part of the membership requirements, factories in China were put under a legal obligation to guarantee basic benefits for all workers, including migrants, such as pension funds, medical insurance and workplace accident insurance. However, these legal changes have been resisted by factory owners, and scarcely implemented (Cai, 2008: 68). The 2008 groundbreaking Labour Contract Law introduced further packages of rights and benefits for all workers. A special contribution of the Labour Contract Law was further formalisation of employment by making labour contracts compulsory. Formalisation of labour contracts is crucial for migrant workers. An employment contract enables legal proceedings in the case of employers withholding wages or occupational accidents. It also constitutes one of several documents that prove migrant workers' residence in the cities, opening access to many of the rights reserved to urban-*hukou* holders after a certain length of employment is proven. Yet, the extension of some of these rights to migrant workers changed little in their daily lives, as the market pressure for cheap labour means that migrants' income remains low, which is the main reason for their poor economic situation (Cai, 2008: 68).

Due to changing demographics among the first and second generations of migrant workers, who are now approaching their retirement age, many have realised that they would not be given due insurance protection in illness and old age. As a result, legal protection around social insurance, including pension funds, became especially important for migrant workers in the 2010s. The reforms around social welfare provision for migrant workers started in 2006, when the government introduced changes in the policy of insurance compensation, which equalised the insurance policies to allow for rural-*hukou* holders to be compensated at the same rate as urban-*hukou* holders (Wang, 2010: 93). The Social Insurance Law of 2011 was a further step towards the provision of universal social insurance to migrant workers in the cities. Drafted with extensive consultation with foreign delegations, especially European Union and Australian government experts,[3] the reform was intended to codify the obligation of enterprises and employees to make contributions into the pension, unemployment, healthcare and housing funds in order to ensure the equal coverage of workers and retirees, regardless of their *hukou*, across China. According to this law, the social insurance benefits are accumulated in personal accounts for each employee, and can be transferred to a new workplace when the worker moves to a new place of residence. However, the system has been scarcely implemented, as the welfare system is fragmented, and localities do not share information on insurance contributions adequately. Indeed, the central and local governments have transferred a large portion of this burden onto the individual workers rather than companies in order to ensure contributions are made (China Labour Bulletin, 2017). The 2014 Yu Yuan strike was caused by migrant workers' rage at the tacit permission given to companies by the government not to contribute adequately to the insurance scheme.

The labour law system has therefore been weakly implemented, and circumvented by both businesses and local authorities. Much of the literature attributes this to the inherent contradiction between the central government's imperative of law implementation and local government's priority of capital accumulation (Lee, 2007:18; Hsu J., 2017: 63).[4] As a result, the implementation of labour laws is often stalled at the local level as the Labour Bureaus (*laodongju*), which are responsible for the enforcement of labour law, are both employer-preferential and marginalised by local government, which gives priority to Economic and Commercial Bureaus instead (Lee, 2007: 20). In recent years, through a range of legislation, other agencies of the government, particularly the Public Security Bureau, have also garnered more influence over labour conflict, as the recent changes in NGO laws discussed in Chapter 2 illustrate. Despite their scarce implementation, labour laws are seen as the primary channel through which migrant workers (and other plaintiffs) can address grievances, and one which acquiesces to, rather than challenges, the state (Lee, 2007; Gallagher, 2006; Enjuto Martinez, 2016). However, as much as the workers are disillusioned by the ineffectiveness and corruption of the legal channels in China, they tend to look up to the legal system as the last resort before going on open strike. The workers do not demand rights beyond the current law, but rather protest 'against those who break the [existing] law', which, in Lee's opinion, proves the effectiveness of the government's management of social conflict through law (Lee, 2007).

However, not everybody agrees that engagement with the law by migrant workers means that they do not challenge the established legal system. Some scholars see the potential of the law to 'cut both ways', and to have the empowering effect of producing citizenship consciousness and new citizenship practices among the marginalised rural and migrant population (Brandtstadter, 2011; Jakimów, 2017). Indeed, the official bolstering of the 'rule of law' has indeed been internalised and acted upon by social actors (migrant workers, lawyers and NGOs) around China in ways not desired by the state.[5] These actors use the concept of 'defending rights' (*weiquan*) to justify their civic activism and to build new civic consciousness. They adopt the *weiquan* language in order to conform to the state's official rhetoric but also to utilise the space the concept allows to challenge the ways migrant workers are treated or understood, a challenge which often ends up running counter to the central and/or local government's consent (Benney, 2013: 8). However, it is worth noting that although the *weiquan* rhetoric was promoted by the Hu-Wen administration in the mid-2000s, it was progressively delegitimised in the early 2010s and replaced with the 'maintaining stability' (*weiwen*) (Benney, 2013: 46–48; Benney, 2016: 394) and 'national security' rhetoric (Fu and Distelhorst, 2017) ever since. As the economy has slowed down and wages have risen, making Chinese factories less attractive to foreign investors, both local and central governments have found any form of obstructing production and pressure to raise wages, including indirect action to train migrant workers in law, harmful to China's economic development. Indeed, the Xi administration has criticised the 2008 Labour Contract Law as overly supportive of workers, and harmful to employers' interests, and it is considering revisions to the law (Gallagher, 2017). Under this new, more hostile climate for *weiquan* activism, the attempts to train and empower migrant workers in law discussed in this chapter can be seen as a form of activism challenging the current citizenship make-up.

Labour law as an inspiration

While legalism has been increasingly serving as an instrument of control, it has also become an inspiration for a generation of migrant workers who have hoped that it can deliver justice. Several migrants-turned-NGO activists in this study self-trained in law, seeing it as an empowering mechanism. In the process, they became 'barefoot lawyers' keen to spread law-consciousness to other migrant workers. The story of the founder of Shiyan-based NGO, JM, Mr Xie, is instructive in this respect. Mr Xie was born in the countryside near Shiyan city in north-west Hubei province. Prior to setting up the NGO in Shiyan in 2008 (the first migrant NGO in Hubei province), Mr Xie had worked in many major Chinese metropolises, from Xinjiang to Shanxi to Guangdong, moving from city to city every few years for about seventeen years. He did some of the toughest and most hazardous jobs, such as working in coal mines, iron mines, factories, as a petty trader and a construction worker. Mr Xie suffered all the typical adversities of a migrant worker's life. He experienced both exploitation and violence at the hands of his bosses: his salary was withheld on several occasions and he was once beaten up by his employer to the point that he lost a tooth and received a 3 cm-deep cut wound to his abdomen. At this point he decided to self-train in relevant labour laws and two years later, in 2001, he made two claims against his employer in Guangdong for withholding his salary. This experience, he admits, drove him to take the 'amateur path of a law defender for the migrant workers' group' (the so-called 'barefoot lawyer').[6]

I met Mr Xie in 2012 during my fieldwork in Beijing; he appeared an energetic and strong-minded man with a great deal of passion for the organisation, and an even greater amount of anger. The insurmountably close links between businesses and the government, and his own experience of establishing an NGO in the face of stringent governmental regulations and discrimination against migrant workers were the key reasons for his frustration:

> Before I managed to open the office in Shiyan in 2011, I had already helped migrants for four years. I frequently visited them in factories and was very familiar with their working conditions and saw how poor they were: they had nothing. Through these years I was trying as much as I could to open the office and find the actual premises. I experienced a lot of hardship: I had no income, I went starving and I lost my hair because of the worry. I applied for the NGO to be registered and to open the office legally, but they [the government] replied, in just one sentence, that the NGO does not fulfil the requirements, so they rejected my application. I went to the department to talk with these people in person, but they were so discriminatory because I am a migrant worker.[7]

Like so many other NGOs in China, JM is registered as a business under the local SAIC bureau. This story reveals the great difficulties that migrant workers come across when they seek justice – and even greater when they try to help other workers to do so. Yet, what also emerges from Mr Xie's story is that while the laws concerning the formation of social organisations in China appear as limiting, other types of laws, particularly labour laws, are often perceived as the only possibility to carve a space in a violent world of social injustice, labour abuse, institutional discrimination and lack of material support. Law here serves as an inspiration providing a promise that even a greatly underprivileged person can engage with tools produced by the state to take charge of their own lives, and in this way become a more empowered citizen.

To further illustrate how the legal framework can create a channel for transforming civic consciousness about the remits of possible action, the story of Shenzhen-based UA's founder, Mr Zhao, is illustrative. After being sacked from his factory for trying to set up a local branch of the union,[8] Mr Zhao returned to his village in Hunan and struggled as a farmer and worker for some years. In the early 2000s he tried his luck again, this time in Shenzhen. After fighting for survival in a plethora of temporary jobs (*dagong*), he became a scooter delivery man and one day was injured in a traffic accident. Having suffered a serious injury, he was unable to work for several months and decided to undergo a long, costly and uncertain process of claiming compensation through legal means. Having undergone two operations on his arm in the meantime, he was short of funds, and with a family to support, he experienced first-hand the vulnerability of workers vis-à-vis businesses and the state:

> At that time, I did not understand the law at all, I did not understand what rights I had, I had no idea what to say in court, or what the order of the proceedings was ... and all the lawyers were so expensive: one hour-long legal advice cost 200 Yuan at the time[9] ... I did not have any contacts [*guanxi*] in court either.[10]

Though Mr Zhao lost the lawsuit eventually, neither the defeat nor near-bankruptcy diminished his faith in the law as a possible instrument of justice:

> If only I had known what the proceedings looked like, what I should have said and what evidence I needed, I could have won this case ... As I was running up and down the court, the Labour Bureau, the government building that year [2002], I met many, many other people in the same situation as me; they all lacked money for a lawyer. I looked at their documents ... and saw that their cases were dealt with badly ... So after I lost [in 2002], I put a lot of energy into the study of law, the judicial proceedings and litigation skills. Then I discovered that my skills and knowledge can help other unfortunate workers/ friends [*gongyou*] ... I already had the experience, the thinking and the framework of how to set up the organisation [referring to the 1990s' union experience discussed in an earlier chapter]; ... this lost lawsuit experience pushed me to give up everything else and put my all into setting up a workers' organisation. There were worries about the lack of funds, but I said to myself: there are so many of us migrant workers, hundreds of millions, this is a huge power we have. We can all create the platform ... [so that] we can learn about the law and help each other.[11]

This inspired Mr Zhao to form an organisation which, up to 2010, focused exclusively on providing legal advice for migrant workers, directing cases to volunteer or public-interest lawyers and self-arbitrating in selected districts of Shenzhen. After that time, the NGO directed its work almost exclusively towards collective bargaining cases, as will be discussed in Chapter 5. Before we follow the story of why this happened, it is important to pause and observe the process of how such 'rights-defence' activism functions and whether indeed it can be conducive to the formation of civic consciousness among migrant workers.

Defending migrant workers' rights: NGOs as mediators, arbitrators and litigators

The 'defending rights' slogan, promoted under the Hu-Wen administration, was readily incorporated into migrant NGOs' language to signal their state-abiding and 'lawful' intentions, while often allowing for unexpected avenues for civic activism (Jakimów, 2017). 'Defending rights' is often evoked to depict the commitment of NGOs to using the existing laws in mediation between migrant workers and employers. The issues that the NGOs usually get involved in relate to two areas of labour disputes: deferred wages and unlawfully low wages, or compensation for injuries resulting from workplace accidents. Some of these organisations undertake individual and group labour dispute resolution via mediation, a preferred method according to the Labour Contract Law, while others provide assistance with arbitration and representation in litigation courts. As discussed in the introduction, the choice greatly depends on the location of the NGO. Serving as so-called 'civil representatives', who have a right to represent (*dailiquan*) migrant workers in litigation courts, is only allowed in a few cities in Guangdong province. Court representation is not allowed in Beijing or Zhejiang: I have only come across one organisation which was allowed to conduct mediation, but not court representation (Beijing Worker's Hotline (BWH)). Below I discuss both these areas and different forms of worker representation by NGOs. The discussion allows us to reflect on whether and how engagement with the existing law by NGOs can have a transformative impact on citizenship in China.

NGOs as mediators between employers and workers

BWH is an example of an NGO specialising in using labour law as an instrument to claim workers' deferred salaries through mediation with employers on behalf of the workers. Mediation is the most common and often preferred form of labour conflict resolution by both migrants and employers, and is also prescribed in the law as a compulsory first step in workplace conflict resolution (Lee, 2007: 177). Mediation is the main method used by BWH; in 2011 alone, 98 per cent of its cases were resolved through mediation. The NGO's involvement in mediation on construction sites was initially met with suspicion and investigation on the part of the local township government, but in the end the NGO was officially certified as a Labour Dispute Resolution Mediation Committee. Since the Mediation Committee was set up in 2004 and until May 2012, according to the organisation's own statistics, the NGO had benefited 27,588 migrant workers, mediating a total sum of RMB 91.884 million (USD 14.220 million) of wage arrears.[12]

At the time of the fieldwork the organisation was based in Beijing city centre and was approached by migrant workers through a hotline and visits in person to the NGO's premises. Out of the average three to four days per week I spent in the office during the almost three-month period of fieldwork, I witnessed around a hundred (individual or group) visits to the organisation's office, which is consistent with the organisation's own statistics. The greatest number of cases came from migrants working in Chaoyang and Daxing districts: both these districts have a large migrant worker population. The majority of migrant workers visiting the NGO during my stay with BWH came with the problem of deferred salaries. This is an endemic issue in Chinese factories and construction sites because of employers' reluctance to provide work contracts and because the workers are most commonly employed through dispatch agencies (*laodong paiqian*), so the employers' responsibility is diluted making it easier to avoid payments. On arrival at the BWH premises, workers were welcomed with a glass of water and then the NGO employee (often a lawyer attached to the organisation) interviewed them in a very informal setting; both would usually sit on a sofa or chairs around the table. Some workers' cases were dealt with immediately, while others would need to wait a few days or weeks for their case to be resolved because the NGO's lawyers would be unable to solve the issue over the phone and would need to visit the construction site or factory. While describing their cases, some workers would be very vocal and angry and would openly pour out their frustration, and from the conversations I witnessed they seemed comfortable with opening up to BWH's employees.[13]

In order to analyse the 'citizenship-shaping' element in the NGO's use of labour laws, it can be instructive to trace two cases of mediation over withheld salaries that the NGO tackled in 2011. Below are the transcripts from one of the BWH employees involved in the mediation of the case of thirty workers whose salaries were withheld to cover the cost of the company's own accounting mistake. The workers contacted BWH because they had no direct contact with the site manager as they were all employed by the intermediary agency:

> We arrived at the site on the 29th of August [2011] at 10 am, led by the help-seeking workers. We first went to the workers' barracks ... As we entered we were hit by a pungent odour; there was a pile of rubbish in one of the room's corners and a simple bed made out of scraps of wood next to it. A swarm of flies was flying around the room. I kept on asking myself: how come that people who withstand such living conditions cannot even have their meagre minimum pay safeguarded? ... In the tiny office we met the relevant managers ... The talks were difficult and we were stuck in a deadlock ... Finally, around 12 pm, we reached a substantive settlement. The employers agreed to the following two requests: first, the workers will be able to receive their wages directly from the project office, and not the distribution agency; second, in addition to the regular salary we also negotiated the extra sum of 7,600 yuan for the workers. Having heard the result of our negotiations wide smiles bloomed on more than thirty migrant faces. Our meticulous work in earnest was also acknowledged by the engineering project's leader. He said that if not for our intervention, they themselves would not know how to handle the dispute. After the mediation, the workers asked us to accompany them to the construction site canteen to take out boxed lunch ... While eating lunch we learned more about the hardship of the migrants' lives.[14]

From the above example, we can learn some basic features of how the NGO conducts mediation. First, we can see the self-identity of the organisation as sympathising with the migrant workers and taking pride in their own work and the final decision they reached with the employers. Even so, the organisation is clearly intending to play a neutral role in the conflict. The NGO staff mingled with the workers, investigated the workers' living conditions and raised important questions about justice in China. However, the role of the migrants themselves during the mediation is passive: the workers wait outside of the office for news on negotiations. The description lacks detailed accounting for how or why the site managers agreed to pay the salaries or why an extra amount of wages was included, which seems quite puzzling.

A perhaps more active role of a migrant worker's involvement in their case can be traced in another case mediated by BWH:

> Mr Li had worked in Beijing for over ten years and he had come to Beijing Workers' Hotline once before to seek help with retrieving his wage arrears. This time Mr Li was employed in a small clothing factory in the Chaoyang district of Beijing. He verbally agreed with the boss on the monthly salary of 4,500 yuan [about 696 USD]; however, at the end of the month he not only did not see his money, but was actually beaten up by the factory boss for asking about it ... The employer argued that the clothes sewn by the migrant were not up to standard, causing the factory some losses ... [After unsatisfactory phone mediation], we decided to conduct face-to-face negotiations. The volunteer lawyer Wang presided over the negotiations between Mr Li and the boss, which soon became a heated exchange of mutual accusations ... Lawyer Wang said to this: '... Please settle this in an amiable and polite manner.' The boss spoke first, describing the events, then our worker [*women gongyou*] corrected the parts he disagreed with. Finally, the boss agreed to pay the sum of 2,200 yuan to our worker (the boss had agreed to pay the worker only 500 yuan before our mediation). ... After being cheated by private small enterprise bosses, our brother Li [*Li dage*] decided to go to a regular factory in Chaoyang, where now he even gets some days off every month.[15]

In the above mediation, we can see a more active role being played by the migrant worker, who actively agrees or disagrees with the outcome of the mediation (the sum mediated over the phone was 1,000 yuan, to which the migrant worker disagreed, therefore BWH arranged for mediation in person). Also, Mr Li's familiarity with the NGO certainly leads to a greater confidence of the worker in his own ability to deal with the employer's unlawful behaviour by contacting the NGO again.

Despite their shortcomings (the sum refunded to the migrant worker is lower than legally mandated, or the workers themselves do not necessarily take part in the mediation), the mediations undertaken by BWH seem to be overall mutually satisfactory and successful. However, some problems emerge with regard to whether and how NGOs' engagement in mediation affects the established citizenship practices or discourse. We can see that the lack of the punitive aspect of law enforcement here means that there is little to stop the employers behaving similarly in the future. On the other hand, though, undertaking arbitration, the more transparent and punitive process of labour dispute resolution, is difficult for workers because of the inaccessibility of the arbitration and litigation process and the high costs of the procedure. The attitude of the Labour Bureau staff, complex procedures and a long resolution time of such disputes also discourage migrant workers from accessing the state-run agencies for both mediation and arbitration. Therefore, even if the mediation stage doesn't bring the desired effect for the workers, the method is preferred by the migrant workers to arbitration and litigation, as it is fast, more certain and less costly. Under these circumstances migrant workers feel more comfortable to settle the conflict through mediation with a sympathetic agent. The fact that the NGO's assistance enables the workers to feel that there are ways to resolve the social injustice, and informs the employers of the existence of an agent who defends migrant workers, reframes the victimhood narrative and 'weak group' identity of migrant workers. Additionally, the mediation itself is already an exceptional example of civic participation in law enforcement, which came to pass as a result of the NGO's negotiation with the state. This concession creates a new role for civil representatives – as ones who can represent migrant workers in legal disputes – creating a niche for citizen action within the legal regime and with concession from the state. Therefore, despite its limited empowering impact, the mere fact of claiming the right to mediation should also be regarded as an act transforming the citizenship regime.

In the following section I analyse whether another instrument of 'rights defence', litigation, is better suited to transform citizenship formulation than mediation. Litigation is rarely permitted to be undertaken by migrant worker NGOs, and the main two examples of NGOs who have undertaken such activism in my study are the Shiyan-based JM and Shenzhen-based UA.

NGOs as citizen representatives in litigation courts

In 2005, Mr Xie (the founder of JM) was the key figure in an unprecedented event in Shanxi province. There had been an accident in the coal mine and as a result seven people lost their lives, with one heavily injured. Mr Xie's home town friend (*laoxiang*) was working in that same mine, and he contacted Mr Xie for assistance. Mr Xie collected all the necessary evidence and designed a negotiation plan for the case to be represented in court. Due to his contribution, the local government, who indeed recognised the mine's employers as guilty of negligence, decided on the necessity of compensation for the dead workers' families. Despite not being yet able to represent migrant workers' families in court at the time, Mr Xie's intervention helped to negotiate a higher compensation than was normally paid in such cases: in lieu of the absence of the crime perpetrator, initially the government was to pay RMB 30,000 (USD 4,600) per family, but after Mr Xie's mediation they agreed to a much higher sum of RMB 200,000 (USD 31,000). This event set a nationwide precedent for the government's reaction to an accident in a private mine.

JM is an example of an organisation that was set up in inland China (where it is more demanding and difficult to set up a migrant worker NGO) and it focuses, as the case above illustrates, on a wide range of issues related to 'rights defence'. Apart from retrieving withheld salaries, JM helps workers claim compensation in cases of workplace injury or death (as well as other forms of economic compensation). According to the NGO's own figures, from its humble beginnings in 2008 up to January 2012 JM had helped mostly migrant workers in Shiyan (Hubei), but due to the wide networks among workers in China it also operates in Hebei, Jiangxi, Shandong, Henan and Inner Mongolia provinces. The NGO resolved a total of 329 cases during the first four years of its existence: 189 cases concerned retrieving wage arrears and insurance compensation, 136 cases involved compensation for workplace injuries, and the remaining four dealt with worker's death-related compensation for workers' families. According to the NGO's own figures, the total amount of money claimed by the NGO as of January 2012 was over RMB 11.787 million (over USD 1.824 million). One of the most prominent cases that JM has handled so far was the mediation in a Shanxi private mine, where they managed to negotiate compensation for a permanently paralysed miner of RMB 450,000 (USD 64,446) which, according to the NGO, was a record-breaking high at the time.

While most NGOs outside of Guangdong province do not represent migrant workers in court due to political sensitivities and restrictions posed by local officials or GONGOs, JM staff actually help to litigate migrant workers' disputes in court. Although the local branch of the Labour Bureau did not initially allow this in 2009, it finally agreed later that year for the NGO to represent migrants in court if it could personally secure consent for its role as an arbitrator from the local court.[16] The NGO's ability to arbitrate and even represent workers in the litigation process is quite unprecedented in China: the typical scenario among other labour NGOs (apart from those interviewed in Guangdong) is that they have to refer a migrant worker's case to the Labour Bureau and the government-dispatched lawyers for arbitration instead.

Being represented by a labour NGO in court greatly decreases the costs of legal proceedings for migrants, which allows a greater number of workers to claim justice if the mediation stage has been unsuccessful, impossible or unsatisfactory. Such an unprecedented level of juridical representation, in what Mr Xie called an 'entirely monopolised' profession of law, also gives the NGO a certain level of independence and empowerment. Mr Xie believes that 'each NGO should strive for the power of attorney – this is the best way for migrant workers to cut the costs of legal proceedings'.[17] We can see therefore that the way in which JM negotiated its ability to represent migrant workers is new and transformative of the established legal practices, and therefore changes the position of citizens in their access and ability to actively seek justice.

Before 2013, similarly to BWH and JM, the main area of UA's activities had been the mediation of labour disputes in workplaces and the representation of migrants in court.[18] UA helped to solve more than 1,300 cases in the years 2009–2013 (as of January 2013), which is over 300 cases annually. According to Mr Zhao, the NGO not only had the largest turnover among all the labour organisations in China, but it also tackled some of the most difficult cases.[19] The NGO used to represent migrants' cases in court in all districts of Shenzhen before 2008, but in 2008 the regulations in Bao'an district changed, and only professional lawyers were allowed to represent workers in courts in that district. In 2013, the organisation arbitrated disputes in the Longgang, Futian, Luohu and Nanshan districts of Shenzhen. Since 2007, UA has been charging workers for litigation cases which necessitate the involvement of a professional lawyer. For those workers who are particularly hard-pressed, and those who have been arrested or fired as a result of participation in strikes, the organisation doesn't charge any fees, even when a professional lawyer is involved (the lawyers the NGO cooperates with are public interest lawyers, who can be recruited either free of charge or for a lower than usual fee). If a UA employee represents the worker no fee is required. The legal advice is free; however, after receiving compensation, the workers are welcome to donate an amount of their own choosing to the organisation. The following description of the litigation process clearly illustrates the time and financial costs involved in the litigation process as well as the training in law provided to migrant workers alongside this process:

> The litigation process consists of three parts: first the arbitration, the trial of first instance and then of second instance. Depending on the case we usually have to go to court five or six times for each case ... For labour injury cases the process is much longer: sometimes we have to go twenty to twenty-five times ... Normally, the professional lawyer would charge you at least 500 yuan to accompany you to court to register, and for the hearing they would take 1,000–2,000 yuan. We ask migrants to pay half of that sum for our lawyers. We make sure that we don't ask workers to pay more for legal proceedings than the lowest possible salary of two months combined. Actually, we haven't changed our fees since 2005: the lowest salary then was 900–1,100 yuan, so we take 1,000–2,000 yuan for the entire case, while the lawyer would take a minimum of 3,000–5,000 yuan ... We take care of the registration for workers and the legal materials they [the workers] need to learn; we prepare and pay for it, so that the lawyer's charges are decreased.[20]

It becomes clear from the above example that NGOs' lower costs of access to arbitration have enabled many migrant workers to access justice more easily. It also emerges that the NGO helped migrant workers prepare for the process in court and trained them in some aspects of the law, which has a potentially empowering element. A question of rightfulness of taking payment for services, that is the professionalisation of NGOs, might be raised. If an NGO collects fees, can it still be seen as a civic organisation? Actually, some of the funders I interviewed, particularly FA 4 (a German foundation), expressed the opinion that every NGO should request a small payment after a case is successfully resolved, because this is the most viable source of income, giving the NGO more independence from funding bodies and enabling them to avoid reliance on project-based funding.[21]

In the context of the above cases of participation in arbitration and representation in litigation courts, how can we see 'defending' as an act of citizenship? As with mediation, it is the ability of NGOs to enable migrant workers' access to the channels of claiming justice that makes 'defending' an act enabling migrants to access their rights of citizenship – the access normally being removed from them due to low income and lack of familiarity with the process.[22] Thanks to these legal action NGOs, migrant workers learn about channels of claiming justice, and sometimes they learn about their rights alongside the process, something they would be reluctant or unable to do otherwise. As to the NGO employees, the use of legal channels here, rather than being simply the top-down imposition of a state-established mechanism, becomes a space of contestation where the new forms of civic participation are being worked out; these forms extend and transform existing legal practices and mechanisms, such as who is allowed to mediate and arbitrate on behalf of the workers.

However, since migrants' participation in the process makes them dependent on the NGOs involved, the NGO's arbitration, as described above, limits the possibility of turning migrants into 'active citizens'. The inclusive and non-discriminatory treatment of workers throughout the process – very different from the one they experience in contacts with the Labour Bureau, which tend to be arduous and humiliating (as exemplified by Lee, 2007: 173, 198) – helps build workers' self-esteem and in some cases the feeling of solidarity between NGOs and workers. In addition, the ability to see how the law can be applied and how their rights can be defended allows migrants to become aware of the mechanisms available to actively change their situation. Nonetheless, the mere process of mediation and arbitration largely enforces the state-designed framework of legalism as the 'rightful path' among many NGO employees (particularly BWH), and prevents migrants' own engagement with the law. While many NGOs see mediation and arbitration as very important for migrants' ability to claim compensation, they also see it as a temporary instrument and only a first step in the greater process of emancipation. In the next part I focus specifically on this aspect of migrant workers' empowerment and discuss whether and how NGOs' acts of 'educating' can transform citizenship in China.

Educating in the labour laws: doing the state's work or shaping active citizens?

SFI is based in Zhejiang province, in the town of Yongkang located in the industrial heartland of the Yangtze River Delta. It was established in 2009 by a charismatic migrant worker, Mr Wu, who helps injured workers claim compensation. Apart from Yongkang, the organisation also helps workers from across Zhejiang province, from cities with large populations of migrant workers such as Jinhua, Wuyi, Jinyun and Yiwu. The NGO founder's advocacy and assistance for migrant workers earned him some reputation with the factory bosses, who even tried to physically assault him.[23] Yongkang is a city of 600,000 inhabitants (among whom 100,000 are migrant workers). According to SFI, including the surrounding counties, there are about 600,000 migrant workers in the industrial hubs in the area. This collection of factories is a global centre for low-tech hardware manufacturing of carpentry products, glass, doors, electrical appliances and car parts – and because of the high number of injuries at work, it has earned itself the nickname of the 'Capital of Broken Fingers'. SFI provides legal advice, mediation and arbitration in cases of injury compensation, and to a lesser degree, unpaid salary arrears. Just during the period between summer 2011 and summer 2012, the organisation mediated in 145 cases and arbitrated seventy-six cases, winning a total of RMB 9.5 million (USD 1.47 million) in injury compensation and withheld wages (according to the organisation's own figures). The NGO pays visits to hospital wards, where the NGO staff distribute their manuals on occupational safety information and upholding rights. They distributed over 4,000 copies of the manuals in hospitals in that one year alone, and a further 8,000 in industrial zones and factories.

Apart from distributing manuals, the NGO also organises training courses, attended by hundreds of workers, which are held on the NGO's premises as well as in public squares and industrial zones. These training courses provide information on injuries, legal rights and exemplary compensation cases; they therefore have a potentially empowering character. Besides the training, the organisation also organises awareness-raising events in the city centre, which are supposed to bring wider public attention to the endemic problem of industrial injuries in the area.

IMH is another organisation providing training in laws. It was set up in 2012 in Foshan by a migrant worker who split from FJ, based in Guangzhou. The reason for the split was FJ's different focus (on rights defence, and increasingly collective bargaining cases) to that of IMH, which deals solely with industrial injury cases (the founder himself was injured, and in effect permanently disabled, and so were the majority of employees and volunteers in the organisation). At the time of the fieldwork, there were about a hundred workers coming to the office each month for legal advice. While the NGO did not represent migrants in arbitration cases, and directed such cases to the Labour Bureau instead, it engaged in mediation cases directly with the employers. However, as one of the NGO's migrant worker-turned-activists told me, the NGO helped the workers prepare both for their visit to the Labour Bureau and the court hearing:

> Others might not have the patience for migrant workers because of their unclear speech and inability to stand their case, but we have patience for them. We train them in how to interact with Labour Bureau officials and how to collect evidence for their cases.[24]

They believed that instead of arbitrating on behalf of migrants, such preparation is more empowering for the workers:

> Helping workers [*gongyou*] to go to court by themselves and resolve their own cases actually allows them to go through the experience by themselves and realise that they have the capacity not only to manage their own problem, but also to spread the experience and help other workers go to court by themselves. I also was like this; at the beginning I didn't understand anything, but once I went through the process, I learned from it, only then I was able to help others.[25]

Instead of arbitration, the NGO provided legal advice on compensation, legal training (once a month for thirty to sixty workers), court hearing simulations, cultural and outdoor activities, psychological support groups and training for disabled workers on how to work with their disability. These instances of migrant training reveal that empowerment is not only about learning technical details of law, but can also take psychological form.[26]

ET is a Shenzhen-based organisation which was originally set up in 2003 by a male migrant from Hubei. Since 2007 it has been run by three migrant women and one man, from various provinces across China, and later also by social work professionals, graduate lawyers and volunteer migrant workers. The NGO suffered in the 2012 crackdown in Shenzhen, and it eventually split in 2015 into four separate organisations, each concerned with a different area of migrant worker activism (as discussed in Chapter 2).[27] ET was originally established as a women-orientated organisation, like many other labour NGOs in Guangdong, because of the comparatively greater number of female workers in Shenzhen (Pun, 2005: 40). The original founder of the NGO decided to set up the organisation in the wake of his own experience with occupational illness, and since then the NGO has mostly targeted workplace injury and occupational illness-related cases. In 2013, ET still represented migrant cases in court (*daili*) or cooperated with volunteer public-interest lawyers who did not charge for their services. At the time, their ability to self-litigate depended on permission from a particular judge. However, the NGO was particularly committed to transferring the skills of litigation to the workers themselves:

> Our eventual aim of helping workers [*gongyou*] with the court cases is to enable them to have the ability, through their own hard work, to stand up by themselves. So, we will train them on the order of the proceedings, let them observe another worker's trials, so that they can see that it is all really quite simple. Through this kind of training we actually enable them to have courage to go to the court by themselves. Unless there is a worker [*gongyou*] who is really unable to go to the court; for example, his (her) speech is unclear, he (she) has problem with writing, or the case involves multiple infringement of rights, then we would step in and help … We hope that this way we can make a collective change.[28]

This clearly shows the ET's commitment, similarly to IMH, not only to represent, but also to educate and empower workers to be able to stand up for themselves and become self-sufficient.

Some NGOs come up with imaginative ways of providing law education. For instance, BWH handed out decks of playing cards to propagate information about the Labour Contract Law: each

Figure 4.1 Labour Contract Law deck of cards.

card in the deck contains an illustration of and specific information about an important article of the law, with an explanation about when the article would apply (see Figure 4.1).

The organisation also produces manuals with comics and illustrations aimed at newcomers to the city as well as the migrant workers visiting their office. Every Wednesday BWH employees go to Beijing Railway Station, to meet incoming migrants and distribute booklets on how to protect their legal rights and how to integrate in the city. BWH's Shenzhen and Shenyang branches distribute the booklets in factories and at construction sites to help workers to contact appropriate organisations and services for legal advice. The booklets contain a variety of information: from 'integration to the city' to contact numbers of appropriate state-run agencies (such as the Labour Bureau) and various migrant worker NGOs.[29]

The organisation claims that the main reason behind these awareness-raising activities is to empower migrants to be able to claim and protect their own rights. However, through my three-month-long stay in the organisation I didn't witness any legal training for migrant workers; there was one legal training course in the office, but that was conducted for the volunteer lawyers. While the NGO does conduct legal training for migrants, these courses seem to be rather sparse in number and outreach. Having observed conversations between migrants and NGO staff in the office, I witnessed lawyers' to-the-point explanation of what can be done in a particular case. I did not witness much direct coaching or training of migrants in the law.[30] Despite the best efforts of the pro bono lawyers, they mostly appeared unconcerned with actually making sure that migrant workers learn about the law, or that this would lead to their self-empowerment. Here is one observation I noted down during one of the first days of my fieldwork in BWH:

> A migrant worker from Henan comes to the office. It seems like his matter is not urgent or new, as after being welcomed with a compulsory glass of lukewarm water he is met with rather slow answer from the staff. GL finally gives him a form to fill up and explains quickly what is to be filled: the amount of salary forfeited, among them. Yet, this seems not to be enough to a weary Mr Jin [the migrant's name], as he sits heavily on the chair and stares blankly at the form. Ten minutes go by and he still has not filled a single bracket. The staff does not seem to care. When he speaks ... his voice is loud and coarse, like that of a person who spends a lot of time surrounded by noise and who smokes two packs of cigarettes a day ... They [the staff] want to take a photo of me and him together; the migrant, once again, responds passively, without showing any engagement with the situation. I feel awkward knowing that this is probably going to serve the NGO's self-promotion activities.[31]

The above case exemplifies how the staff might be unable or unwilling to make sure that the worker understood every detail of the case or that he is indeed 'empowered' by the legal knowledge they convey. The staff seems more concerned about taking photographs to support their self-promotion, rather than sitting down immediately to work on the worker's case. This must be frustrating or even intimidating to some visitors, rather than empowering.

Apart from the lack of staff attention to effectively bestowing legal knowledge, there are also limits to empowerment through legal training that pertain to the law itself. Migrant workers might perceive the law as ineffective, and the NGO activism might not change these perceptions easily. In Huang Wenhai's (2017) documentary about the labour movement NGOs in the PRD entitled *We, the Workers*, in one scene we see an activist trying to distribute manuals on workers' rights to passing migrant workers in Shenzhen. The workers are not easily persuaded to engage, and once they do, a discussion starts about the uselessness of laws. Despite the activist's insistence on legal knowledge as something that can benefit workers, and his attempts to convince migrants that even their engagement with the law can help to enforce the law in the long run, the migrant worker involved clearly remains sceptical. Actually, many NGO leaders themselves see the limitations and inadequacies of the law. They also feel frustrated with migrant workers' resistance towards understanding the legal proceedings, but at the same time share their concern over the ineffectiveness of the law:

> Sometimes to try reasoning with the workers is impossible ... I mean, their culture and education is fine, but ... they really lack any legal knowledge! He [the worker] really doesn't understand why the result of this case is bad [unsatisfactory]. It is us who did the things wrong. Arrrgh... It is the Chinese law, the judicial system's [fault]; the vast majority of unsatisfactory resolutions are not because the lawyer is bad ... They think that the court will read a chapter from the legal book, and just like that, will give you a verdict! But legal cases in China are not resolved this way! The resolution is not based on the law; it is based on judicial interpretation, in confidential meetings, based on internal memos [*tongzhi*], based on the leader's instruction, after the leader's phone call; this is how the legal case is resolved! These are the things you will not find in the legal books ... So a lot of the workers [*gongyou*] keep on thinking 'In the Labour Contract Law it all sounds so rosy, why then did you lose the lawsuit?' They don't believe you.[32]

This quotation indicates that there is a lack of trust in the NGO–worker relationship, and the law in general can also limit the effectiveness of labour law training. While the NGOs struggle to teach the laws, explain the legal proceedings, organise mock court trials, mediate and litigate in labour cases, migrant workers might choose to disengage from these attempts or even distrust the NGOs conducting the training. This also shows the limitations of the ability to transform citizenship through the state-prescribed legal channels.[33]

As we can see from the above analysis, the act of 'defending' is often accompanied by the act of 'educating' on laws and occupational safety standards. First, we can see that many NGOs are highly self-aware about the importance of training, education and workers' own involvement in the mediation and arbitration processes. Some

NGOs, both in Guangdong but also in Zhejiang and Beijing, do encourage workers to learn the proceedings and the law themselves in order to ultimately be able to represent not only their own interests in court, but also to help other workers. This education in the laws, procedures and legal language is therefore an essential part of the citizenship empowerment of migrant workers and the formation of 'active citizens'.

However, in order for the training to have a real element of citizenship empowerment, it seems that direct coaching in particular legal cases, rather than training in abstract legal articles, is a more effective method of passing down the legal consciousness and knowledge, particularly in cases where NGOs intend to seriously support migrant workers to win cases in court. But it is important to see labour law training as only one aspect of the 'empowerment' that NGOs provide through their educational activities. Often, without building a trusting and close relationship with migrant workers, the attempts to convey legal knowledge might be ineffective. As I discuss in the next chapter, training in labour law is not the only aspect of empowerment of migrant workers in relation to labour issues. It already emerges from the above case studies that the status of fellow migrants and a 'pass it on attitude' are essential to the process of remaking migrant workers from passive victims to active agents of change. In order to truly empower migrants to stand up for their rights or even to challenge wider social discrimination, it is essential to also provide education going beyond the laws, including issues such as labour exploitation, class solidarity, collective bargaining and labour activism, which further highlight the intrinsic link between citizenship and labour activism.

Conclusion

Much of the literature has been critical of the effectiveness of law education and 'defending rights' in the process of moulding migrant workers into active citizens. The studies concerning labour NGOs more directly vary in this respect, with some pointing to the ineffectiveness of mediation, litigation and law training to empower migrants (Froissart, 2014; Enjuto Martinez, 2016), and regarding other forms of activism around labour, such as strikes and collective bargaining, as more empowering and effective (Froissart, 2018). However, while the law and legal channels are indeed a state-prescribed outlet for channelling citizens' grievances, migrant NGOs' interaction with the law is far from acquiescent. The law is treated as a shield against arbitrariness and abuse by employers and the state alike, contrary to the Marxist Critical Legal School belief that subscription to 'rights talk' necessarily means acquiescence to the state. Mediating workers' disputes, representing migrants in courts and educating them in the laws all have the potential to bring immense change in migrants' citizenship rights and access to justice, sometimes against the will of the state–business nexus, even if they are performed within the established legal framework. Even those NGOs which focus on education in law within the prescribed framework still have a chance to endow workers with knowledge of the law, which can open up unforeseen avenues for their empowerment, as we have seen in the cases of NGO founders who applied their knowledge of relevant laws to fight for their rights. This double-edged and ambiguous role of the law will be even more visible among the acts discussed in the next chapter.

However, despite this potential for challenging the citizenship formulation, 'defending' and 'educating' can also do the opposite. While some NGOs indeed struggle to effectively educate migrants through interactive activities and training in self-representation, others neglect the importance of the actual knowledge that workers take away from the interaction with an NGO. The unquestioned application of laws and mediation on behalf of workers without their active participation might indeed contribute to keeping migrant workers as passive recipients of NGOs' services, maintaining their status as 'obedient citizens' (*shunmin*) rather than 'active citizens'. While these acts can bestow migrant workers with new citizenship consciousness and equip them to become active citizens, therefore transforming citizenship practices, their effectiveness is very difficult to establish. Therefore, the law remains an ambiguous tool in the process of citizenship transformation: it can bring greater empowerment to individual migrant workers when the migrants become involved in the process, yet it might also help maintain the existing power relations. It is therefore important to consider how NGOs go beyond labour laws as a tool of activist citizenship;

that is, when and how they put it into question, reshape it or even reject it.

Notes

1 See Peerenboom (2002: 164) for an explanation and critique of the applicability of Critical Legal School theory to the case of China.

2 Among these, most important are the 1995 Labour Law and the 2008 Labour Contract Law and also some lesser regulations, such as the Occupational Work and Safety Laws (2001 and 2002), the Prevention and Treatment of Occupational Disease Law (2001, updated in 2011), the Trade Unions Law (2001), the Labour Disputes Mediation and Arbitration Law (2008) and the Labour Promotion Law (2008).

3 Interviews no. 16 and no. 27, and personal communication with the Australian Embassy (28 February 2012).

4 However, I disagree with these interpretations. While the central government might indeed officially encourage legalistic responses to workplace conflicts, local governments remain subject to the pressure of meeting the economic development agenda set out by central government (see Qian and Weingast, 1997). It is rather that the central government manages the social costs of economic development by scapegoating local governments. This helps to uphold the regime's legitimacy, as the central government maintains the image of a Confucian fatherly figure upholding the law.

5 The basic distinction between 'rule by law' and the 'rule of law' is that in the case of the latter the state authorities themselves are bound by the law, whereas in the case of the former the state authorities use the law to solidify their power without necessarily abiding by it themselves. While the current party-state's rhetoric presents China as a country with 'rule of law', what is indeed meant by it, is rule by law, where the laws are used to remove whoever is perceived as a political threat to the ruling Party.

6 Interview no. 3.

7 Interview no. 3.

8 See Chapter 1.

9 According to Mr Zhao, at the time of these legal proceedings the average wage of migrant workers in Guangdong province was 800 yuan a month (around USD 124) (Interview no. 18).

10 Interview no. 18.

11 Interview no. 18.

12 For other figures on the NGO's performance, see Table A4.3 in Appendix 4. The calculation is based on the average exchange rate from 2011 according to the World Bank (6.4615/1 USD/RMB). Other calculations also use World Bank statistics.
13 See the next part of this chapter for more details.
14 From the BWH files (Case no. 214/2011), translated from the Chinese original by myself.
15 From the BWH files (Case no. 279/2011), translated from the Chinese original by myself.
16 Personal communication via social media (Interview no. 48) with the founder of JM on 24 April 2012, in Chinese.
17 Interview no. 48.
18 The organisation has moved to focus on collective bargaining cases since 2013, as described later in the chapter.
19 Interview no. 18.
20 Interview no. 18.
21 Interview no. 12.
22 A similar dilemma, that of the lack of material and social capital, related to social rights of citizenship, as preventing rightful access to civil rights of citizenship, was presented by T. H. Marshall in his watershed study on the development of rights of citizenship (Marshall, 1992 [1950]).
23 Personal communication with an FA 4 representative on 23 March 2012.
24 Interview no. 20.
25 Interview no. 20.
26 See the discussion in Chapter 7 on the mutual aid aspect of empowerment.
27 As discussed in previous chapters, this strategy helps organisations to survive the tough times of crackdowns and keep a low profile.
28 Interview no. 19.
29 For analysis of the language and information in the manuals, see Chapter 7.
30 Similar scepticism about the law training has been highlighted in other literature on the subject (Enjuto Martinez, 2016).
31 A field note, 17 February 2012, BWH premises, Beijing.
32 Interview no. 18.
33 I will say more on these limitations in the Conclusion.

5

Labour activism beyond the law

While the previous chapter reflected on the role of the state-approved channels of labour law in the process of citizenship transformation, this chapter looks at the acts of citizenship around labour which call the law into question or which put forward claims beyond legalism. These acts, however, should not be understood as 'illegal'. Some of them reach out beyond the law simply because they question the wider social order as the source of labour exploitation, rather than focus only on the law. Others try to shape the existing laws through methods which are legally allowed, but informally discouraged by the state. Yet others use channels which are outright taboo, yet which are not explicitly illegal, such as petitions, collective bargaining or strikes. These channels are used to put forward a request for change in the law as well as for wider social and political change. As will emerge through the chapter, the majority of NGOs performing these 'acts' continue to use the language of law in order to legitimise and sustain their activism, which further emphasises the ambiguous role of the law in the process of citizenship transformation in China. These acts are, however, different from those discussed in the previous chapter because they seek to go beyond the existing law and push for change in the rights of citizenship related to labour, such as through unionism and petitioning.

Below I discuss three acts that go beyond labour law: 'educating', 'advocating' and 'claiming'. The act of 'educating' discussed here aims at a different set of issues from the act of educating discussed in the previous chapter, as NGOs focus on informing migrants about sources of discrimination as stemming from their socio-economic position in China. By the act of 'advocating' I mean the attempts at intervention in the law-making process and the criticism of existing law and legal mechanisms. The final act of 'claiming' relates to migrant workers' assertion of the rights which are not enshrined in the law, such as effective bodies for political representation of migrant workers – that is, self-elected workers' representatives, the right to strike and the right to elect their union representatives. I conclude with a discussion of when these types of activities can become acts of citizenship, which responds to the criticism raised in the existing scholarship on NGOs and makes the relationship between labour and citizenship clear.

Educating beyond labour rights

While many NGOs undertake acts of educating, the content of their educational activities might vary widely. In the previous chapter, I discussed education in labour rights and in arbitration proceedings. Yet, there is another type of education that migrant NGOs provide, which goes beyond the existing laws or even calls them into question. Some NGOs discussed in this book actively seek to change workers' self-consciousness, by directly discussing the sources of their subjugated status in urban China, which they see as stemming from capitalist exploitation in the workplace and their second-class citizenship status. While I discuss the latter in Chapter 6, as they are related to the claims to space, here I focus on forms of education which seek to endow workers with a working-class consciousness. However, as a response to the citizenship versus class debate in the scholarship, it is important to emphasise that class-orientated and citizenship-orientated education are often intertwined in such educational activities.

The NGOs which seek to change migrants' self-consciousness in relation to their class status do so by providing opportunities for workers to reflect on their socio-economic condition. This is the type of training that is often treated as 'politically sensitive' by the state. Shenzhen-based NGO ET's experience in this regard is a case in point:

> The difference between us [and the government-run agencies] is that we not only [resolve individual legal cases], but we also discuss [with migrants] why they have such problems in the first place. They [the workers] think that the reason why they work so hard in the factories

> and still earn so little is because they haven't studied hard enough, because they didn't attend university, because of fate. We educate them that this is not their individual fault, but it is the whole social allocation of resources and the way the educational system works. We say a lot of things like that, so the government really hates our work.[1]

By pointing to collective, socio-economic reasons for workers' condition, the NGO clearly challenges the ideas contained in the *suzhi* and neoliberal citizen-subject discourses, which delegate the fault for someone's failure to their individual lack of 'quality' or 'entrepreneurship'. Within such educational activities, the NGO also discusses issues related directly to migrants' working conditions, such as the problem of low wages. ET educates migrants that wages are not fixed and that what the bosses offer is often unfair or below the minimum wage, and that the workers can and should actively negotiate their wages.

SC is a Beijing-based NGO, and as mentioned in Chapter 2 it receives government funds through the local branch of ACFTU. The NGO strives to educate migrants in occupational safety and explicitly focuses on training which aims at prevention of industrial accidents and occupational illnesses, rather than post-exposure hospitalisation assistance.[2] The organisation provides after-work training in the construction sites located in the rural–urban fringe of Beijing (*chengxiang jiehebu*). However, SC's training in laws and occupational safety often includes the type of training which goes beyond education on rights. Because of that, their training usually relies on workers' own experiences as a starting point for discussion; it is intended to empower workers by highlighting their pre-existing knowledge and skills and building on them:

> When it comes to law education and occupational safety education, we do not tell them that 'you are workers, you should be proud', because they will think it is a joke if their rights are not even protected. Instead, we explain what rights they have as citizens and as workers: social insurance rights, employment rights. We explain those in detail ... When we train migrant workers in health and safety, we do it every evening, after workers finish their work. We believe that the workers do not lack knowledge, because many of them have worked for a very long time, they have rich experience. If you explain the basics, such as that by law they have a right to an eight-hour working day, they will just laugh. So, we prefer that workers reflect on their

> own experience. Why do we always work longer than eight hours? 'Because the salary is too low, so we have to work overtime.' And then we can analyse: is the salary you receive a living salary, is it reasonable? We talk a lot about these kinds of issues in our occupational safety training.[3]

This form of training, similarly to that provided by SFI, intentionally links industrial accidents and occupational illness cases to the abuse of laws by employers and wider social problems such as low wages. The organisation informs workers that the problems with labour relations and occupational safety are structural, and insists that they do not result from workers' 'low awareness'. This training should therefore be seen as going beyond just focusing on what the letter of the law says, as they are intended to help migrant workers reflect on their wider life and social causes behind lax occupational safety and low wages.

UA also sees the importance of training and education beyond the labour laws, and when it was providing legal action-type services it used to include the discussion of migrant workers' social position, the sources of social inequality and ways to change it. When I interviewed Mr Zhao for the first time in 2013, he saw this training as fundamental and even more important than representation in court:

> In 1994, I came to think this way: the workers cannot just rely on themselves, or even on a few close people. They must rely on a wider group, they must unite and organise. Only in this way can we completely change the social disdain towards workers, the lack of respect ... Through these last years as I have been doing the 'rights defence', I wanted to ameliorate the workers' problems. But to ameliorate all the problems of migrant workers is very difficult. You help him once in court to fight for his rights, the next year he changes the factory, his rights are infringed again, you go to court to help him again ... how long are you going to keep doing this? ... So, we need to let migrants realise one thing: what is the source of power? The real power comes from themselves! In order to resolve the problems of China's labour, they need to learn to find the strength in themselves, and not rely on our labour organisations, lawyers, scholarly texts ... To put it in a scholarly way, there is a need for self-awareness (*ziwojuexing*), self-organising (*ziwozuzhi*) and solidarity (*ziwotuanjie*); there is a need for awakening [of migrant workers].[4]

Mr Zhao, therefore, clearly points to the need to raise self-awareness of the sources of abuse and inequality, and to do that through solidarity and self-organisation between workers. For that reason, UA has focused since the early 2010s on supporting and coaching migrant workers in collective bargaining and helping to mediate collective bargaining cases.[5] Also, training and education for migrant workers has become more pronounced in the NGO's agenda. Lastly, UA recognises the NGO-unfriendly environment in China and seeks to forge links with other workers' organisations in order to strengthen their position and to change public attitudes towards greater acceptance of civic engagement in public life.

In the above cases, we can see the drive of some NGOs, particularly those in the PRD, to educate workers in aspects that go beyond the law: the awareness of what is a fair wage, the importance of collective bargaining, self-awareness of being a group that is discriminated against and the importance of unionisation. We can see that some NGOs treat the law not as the ultimate goal, but as the means for greater empowerment. They do not simply regurgitate the law or blindly apply the state-designed channels, but reinterpret them to empower workers. We also see that these NGOs aim to empower migrant workers as both citizens (awareness of rights, awareness of the instruments with which to claim these rights and awareness of their own position in society) and as members of the working class (educating on wages, encouraging and supporting collective bargaining and workers' solidarity). It is clear from the NGOs' own experience that these two aspects of civic engagement go hand in hand: that greater awareness of one's rights and position in society can be mobilised into greater solidarity with one another. This solidarity is founded on workers' identity, but also the identity of migrants as second-class citizens. This double aspect of migrant workers' emancipation creates what I call the figure of 'worker-citizen', which derives from and is based on both the citizen's and worker's claims.[6]

Advocacy and petitioning: reshaping legal rights

The next act voiced around the site of labour but going beyond the law is the act of 'advocating'. Advocating is only conducted by some of the NGOs in the study, but it is a growing area of activism, which is often based on the organisations' experience of resolving cases in courts, their research and the desire for political involvement in the law-making process. It is a powerful and usually under-represented aspect of migrant NGOs' activism, which directly relates to the remaking of the citizenship regime.

The founder of the Shiyan-based JM actively seeks to propose changes in labour laws and their implementation, but also advocates further changes, beyond the law, with the government. The NGO sees the current minimum pay system and the employer's social security contribution as lacking strong support mechanisms in law.[7] In addition, the existing law in this regard is not effectively implemented. JM's founder, Mr Xie, gave me an example of the state-owned enterprise (SOE) Gong Feng Automobiles factories in Shiyan, in which 50 per cent of employees are front-line migrant workers. Around 60 per cent of these employees are employed though dispatch agencies (*laodong paiqian*), which by law are required to pay migrant workers' monthly social security contributions. However, the agencies do not abide the law: they tend to postpone the payment of contributions or pay less than is required by the law. The law stipulates that an enterprise's contribution to the social security payment is determined on the basis of a yearly average salary in the given locality, and it should not be lower than 60 per cent of the average salary. However, this rule is interpreted by the dispatching agencies as permission to always pay the lowest possible contribution (60 per cent rather than 100 per cent): this harms the rights of workers by decreasing the pool of security contributions available to them in the long run. JM seeks to advocate with the local government to change the security payment rules and exert greater control over dispatch agencies:

> The law should be changed to resemble more closely the Western European countries' model or Japan's social security laws and there should be greater separation of powers between the dispatch labour agencies and the Labour Bureau for this to function properly.[8]

But Mr Xie sees much greater obstacles than just the law to his ability to change the unlawful treatment of migrant workers:

> One question remains: our country's government has been omnipotent from the beginning. It is the government which pays the bill. Hence all the employees of 'dispatch agencies' are in fact dispatched by the

> Labour Bureau: they are both policy-makers and policy-executors: they have permission from the Labour Bureau [to abuse the law]. Indeed, they [the dispatch agencies] have a 'blood relationship' with the government so they have the government's protection [to do so].[9]

We can see, therefore, that the dispatch agencies' evasion of social insurance contributions is possible on the one hand because of a certain interpretation of the law, and on the other because this behaviour's unlawful aspect is ignored or even covered up by the government. This point runs into the deeper critique of the political system, and particularly its authoritarian aspect in relation to the lack of separation of powers.

JM advises the government regularly on how to improve various social policies. In 2011 Mr Xie wrote information packages concerning fourteen cases that the NGO had dealt with, in the hope that these would help to clarify what needs to be improved in the workers' situations. He then forwarded these advocacy materials to representatives from the United Front (a grouping of the CCP and other main parties aligned with the CCP), the National People's Congress (NPC) and members of the Chinese People's Political Consultative Conference (CPPCC), who acknowledged their receipt. JM also submitted a report to the most important yearly session of the NPC and the CPPCC, at both central and local levels, called popularly *lianghui*. In the report, the NGO emphasised the lack of safety measures and the ineffectiveness of law implementation, as well as the problems with existing laws regarding the construction industry. The report goes into detail on five cases of workers who experienced injuries, describing the situation in their work teams and their struggle to claim justice. The final part of the report gives specific recommendations on how to tackle the problems. First, it criticises some parts of the labour laws in China, particularly the decentralised managerial responsibility, the arbitrarily set injury compensation which differs in each location, and the lack of punishment measures for employers who fail to pay insurance contributions. Then the report points out the exact legal loopholes, particularly article 60 of the 2004 Work Injury Insurance Regulation, which contains unclear formulations commonly interpreted by employers in a way which harms the rights of migrant workers and which consequently facilitates the large-scale abuse of workers' rights, as it enables enterprises to avoid paying social insurance contributions and the ensuing injury compensation. The report concludes in an evocative tone that: 'these individual enterprises and their lawyers show utter contempt for the fundamental human rights enshrined in the law of our country. By using the legal loopholes, they malevolently pervert the laws and avoid taking responsibility for their actions.' The report is concluded by proposals as to how these legal articles could be rewritten in order to address the loopholes and to provide migrant workers with rightful levels of social insurance and compensation.

Similarly, UA sees the social insurance scheme as a ripe field for workers' rights abuse. UA faces slightly different challenges when dealing with privately owned factories in the PRD than those faced by JM, which deals mostly with SOEs. However, what they have in common is the enterprises' evasion of social insurance contribution payments. While private enterprises in Shenzhen are obliged to pay insurance contributions into workers' accounts at the level of 10 per cent of the worker's salary, they often retain the insurance contribution. The enterprises also make it bureaucratically and technically difficult for workers to claim their insurance. Additionally, they put a tax on workers' contributions when they leave the factory, meaning that the workers can rarely, if ever, retrieve more than 40 per cent of their original insurance contributions and take them with them to another workplace. Not surprisingly, the workers feel it is completely pointless to concern themselves with social insurance in Shenzhen, so they are often left without any:

> The workers tend to ignore the pension insurance schemes and do not bother checking on their insurance situation ... As for health insurance, workers also think that 'all this doesn't concern me, I just want to collect my salary' ... They often don't view the situation as a form of rights infringement, but isn't [this] also a type of rights infringement!? ... This situation is specific to Shenzhen. Shenzhen is unlike most Chinese cities: it has a legislation-making power. So, the city sets policies which especially discriminate against migrant workers ... China is the kind of country where a particular policy often overrides the law.[10]

From this and the previous example of critique from NGOs, it is clear that while addressing aspects beyond the law which relate to the characteristics of the political regime (the lack of a clear separation of powers), these NGOs also seek to advocate for greater uniformity of employment laws across the country. Another interesting instance of how the act of 'advocating' aims at remaking not only rights of citizenship, but also citizenship practices, is the involvement of wider groups of migrant workers in the advocacy effort.

An example of one such action which sought to extend citizenship practices in China to include migrant workers, was the attempt by Mr Zhao's previous organisation (disbanded in 2006) to advocate with the government through a workers-supported petition.[11] In 2006 the association collected 10,000 signatures on its petition to the government to stop the change of law regarding arbitration rules. This change would mean that from 1 May 2008, the responsibility for paying the arbitration registration fee (of 4 per cent of the final compensation) would be borne solely by the worker (claimant).[12] UA saw this reform as harmful and unjust to migrants, as it would mean that many workers could not even begin the process of claiming justice if they had to pay part of the fee upfront. The association decided to put up a petition banner (*hengfu*) on the streets of Shenzhen requesting cancellation of the arbitration fee and encouraged workers to sign their name under the petition. After it had collected over 10,000 signatures it approached many representatives of the NPC (*renda daibiao*) from Shenzhen and the media asking for their petition to be presented in the NPC and in the media:

> But there was nobody who dared to report the case or present our petition to the lawmakers, not even the so-called migrant workers' representatives, who are just following the instructions [*qingshi*] (from the Party)] and do not represent us really.[13]

Indeed, after setting up the *de facto* trade union in 2004, Mr Zhao openly approached officials in the Shenzhen government hoping to register the organisation. Many of them praised him and his idea, but when it came to official support they declined, saying that the policy doesn't allow it. The NGO had collected the signatures just before the *lianghui*. Having no support from the Shenzhen officials, the activists decided to enter the Shenzhen *lianghui* by themselves. As some 'society representative observers' are allowed to enter the *lianghui* each year, particularly on the local level, Mr Zhao borrowed the attendance certificate from a friend who was allowed to audit the *lianghui* and used it to enter the Shenzhen congress. He waited in the foyer for the appropriate representative to lobby the case, but the security guards, having some experience with petitioners, approached the activists and took them to a police station:

> The officers then inspected the banner/petition and exclaimed: 'This is a very dangerous thing! Is there anybody else with you? Do you have another banner like this?' I said: 'There is one more man with the smaller banner; he entered the assembly hall.' The policeman looked frightened to death. He immediately called the leader and reported the case, and then about fifty policemen turned up, those from the emergency unit. They went to the assembly hall, found our co-worker, brought him over and they detained us all in the police station.[14]

What saved Mr Zhao from more serious trouble turned out to be his relationship with a local official:

> In 2005 [a year before the petition took place], I wrote several times to the municipal Party secretary, Li Hongzhong, asking for support to recognise our organisation officially. I directly corresponded with Li Hongzhong and he recommended my organisation to the MOCA office in Shenzhen. Then I was one of the auditing society representatives in the *lianghui* in Shenzhen in 2005. I met with Li Hongzhong then and we had a picture taken together. As we went to the *lianghui* this time [2006] to petition, I brought this picture with me … After the police detained us I showed them the picture. The policeman did not believe the picture was real and called the Shenzhen Party Congress office to enquire if the event, as I described it, was true and the office confirmed my story. Then he spoke to his leader [*lingdao*], asked us to write a 'self-criticism statement' [*jiantao*] and then finally released us. Now, when I think back, I realise that what we did, entering Congress like this with the banners, was indeed a serious matter; we might have been sent down to be 're-educated through labour' [*laojiao*]. A lot of petitioners [*shangfang de ren*] have been treated this way before.[15]

Mr Zhao did not give up, however, and decided that perhaps they could finally succeed if they were only greater in number. He hoped that if the other labour organisations and public interest organisations all came together and presented a petition again the following year, with 100,000 rather than 10,000 signatures, their advocacy efforts could be rewarded. So, Mr Zhao's organisation opened up an online petition, and soon after, it was re-published by foreign media. Even though many officials had known about the organisation before the event, they had been turning a blind eye to its activities despite the organisation's openness and widespread publicity. However, the involvement of a foreign media outlet changed the government's approach and Mr Zhao's organisation was disbanded in 2006. Even though the NGO did not succeed in their petitioning efforts, the law was eventually altered in October 2010 for Shenzhen and the arbitration fee was fixed at 10 yuan for the employer's registration, while workers were allowed to enter arbitrations free of charge. Some other places across Guangdong, for example Dongguan, still uphold the earlier rules of a 4 per cent arbitration registration fee. Another interviewee I spoke to in 2016 attributes this success to UA's efforts.[16]

ET has also been involved in advocacy efforts, particularly since 2013, with regard to the non-payment of pension insurance to migrant workers. The regulations expecting employers to pay towards the social security fund were put in place as early as 1999, and were then reinforced in the 2011 Social Security Law. However, the Shenzhen governments did not push for implementation of these regulations. As the situation became tense around 2013, because many workers nearing their retirement age had realised that the payments towards their pension fund were not being made, the government issued a directional instruction for arrears dating back to 1999 to be paid out by the employers, but it did not admit malpractice on the part of the businesses. ET contacted representatives in *lianghui*, the People's Congress and CPPCC, giving their suggestions on how to implement the social security system. These comments were passed higher up in 2015, but not in 2016 because the NPC representatives were concerned about the 'tense political situation' at the time. ET also supported the petitioning migrant workers when they went to the Social Insurance Bureau requesting for their back payments to be paid out. However, eventually in 2016 the local government warned the NGO not to get involved and discouraged the petitioning workers from accessing ET's help, calling it an 'illegal organisation'. This example illustrates that when an NGO supports active citizenship among migrant workers, the limitations put on it by the government can severely curtail its ability to mobilise and eventually support migrant workers. Even when organisations are hiding behind the individual migrant workers, which as Diana Fu argued allows them to 'mobilise workers without the masses' (Fu, 2017), the state can eventually learn about their engagement and stop it, as was the case with ET's efforts.

Once again, through the above examples we can clearly see that some NGOs are far from being passive enforcers of state-defined laws. As ardent users and practitioners of the law, they see the loopholes, constraints and limitations of the law and seek to actively change them. 'Advocacy' is a profound act of citizenship which not only targets the law itself, but also criticises many social and political practices and political institutions in the country. It therefore provides a critique which reaches beyond the law, but is embedded in the state-abiding language of law. The use of the 'legal rights discourse' in this context (the 'resistance through accommodation' strategy) is crucial for the ability of NGOs to transform the citizenship regime. Such transformation results from the direct involvement of NGOs and migrant workers in the lawmaking process, as illustrated by UA's petition or advocacy performed by other NGOs. It, once again, highlights the relationship between labour activism and activist citizenship as not that of two contradictory terms, but rather of two co-dependent phenomena.

Claiming rights beyond legalism: why acting collectively matters

The final act in relation to labour, and one which goes beyond the law, is that of 'claiming' new rights. The most prominent right discussed below that NGOs attempt to claim, is that of creating workers' own forms of representation in the workplace. They do this by creating workers' organisations, coaching workers' representatives and claiming rights to democratic union elections. Claiming this right is linked to both labour and citizenship, as it involves negotiation of new rights of citizenship through political engagement. If we consider migrant NGOs as a form of workers' 'own representation', the right to representation can be claimed through acts of organising as well (as presented in Chapter 2). However, the act of claiming the right to representation that I discuss here concerns the right of workers outside of these NGOs to vote for their own official ACFTU representatives, to create their own organisations, and sometimes to form independent trade unions.

Marxist scholars have been quite eagerly awaiting the appearance of demands for such forms of representation in China for decades, in the hope that it would signal the emergence of authentic class consciousness. However, for a long time it seemed that there was little evidence that workers are interested in requesting free elections of trade union representatives or even undertaking inter-factory action indicating rising class consciousness (Friedman and Lee, 2010: 520). However, the patterns and motivations behind strikes have been changing over the last decade. There has been a noted change from strikes demanding wage increases and better working conditions before 2007, to a growing number of strikes in which workers request democratic elections to the enterprise's trade unions (the 2007 Shenzhen crane operators and 2010 Foshan Honda strikes for instance) (Butollo and ten Brink, 2012; Chan, 2012b: 320–321). In recent years, there has been a new wave of strikes requesting the provision of forfeited social security payments from local governments (the 2014 Yu Yuan strike for instance) and the formation of independent trade unions (e.g. the 2018 Jasic dispute). Interestingly, the recent strikes, such as the Jasic dispute, were supported by Pekin and Tsinghua University students, who requested the release of workers arrested in the aftermath of the strike, which shows instances of inter-class and inter-provincial solidarity.

Indeed, strikes in China have been a major form of migrant workers' resistance. According to the China Labour Bulletin's Strike Map, in the years 2011–2018 an estimated 10,000 industrial actions were undertaken across China (China Labour Bulletin Strike Map, https://maps.clb.org.hk/strikes/en).[17] Despite the harsher measures taken against striking workers such as dismissals, police detention and arrests under Xi Jinping, there was a steep increase in strikes in the years 2014–2016 (see Figure 5.1). The protests have not only risen in number and size; they have also spread in terms of geographical outreach to many provinces along the coasts and deeper inland (see Figure 5.2). Interestingly, there has been a growing involvement of labour NGOs in supporting striking workers, particularly since 2010, which has prompted some observers to label these NGOs 'labour movement type' (see Chapter 2).

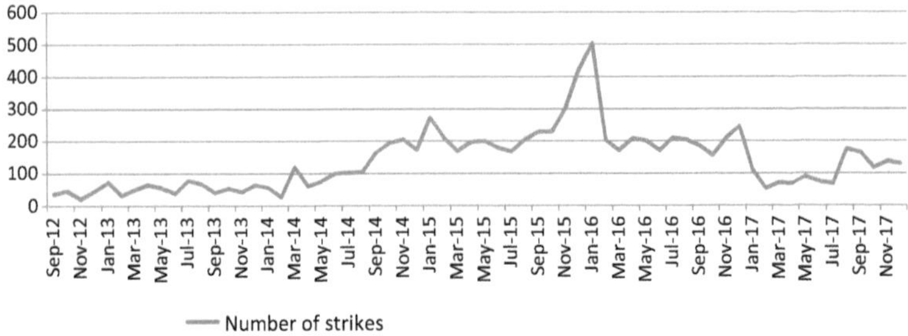

Figure 5.1 The number of recorded strikes in the years 2012–2017 (whole of China).

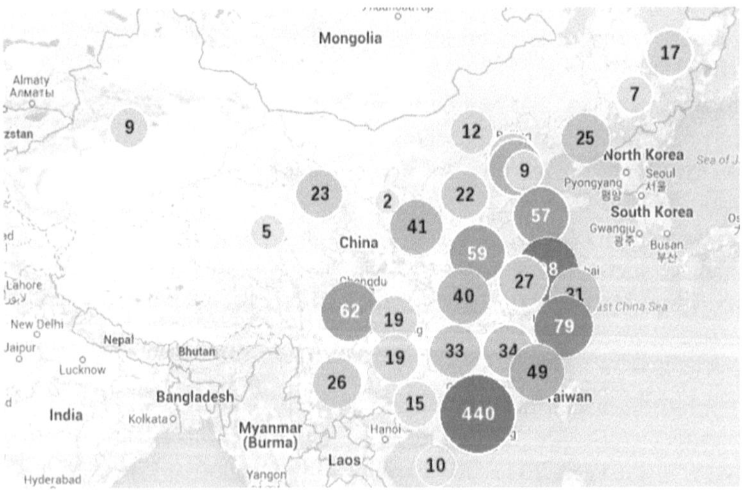

Figure 5.2 The geographical distribution of strikes 2011–2018 (showing number of strikes per location).

As strike support and independent trade unionism is one of the most 'politically sensitive' areas of migrant worker NGOs' activism, those NGOs which usually have close relations with the government avoid such activities. For instance, Hangzhou-based NGO, NHC, which has entered into a relationship with the ZFTU, is very careful not to step beyond 'permissible conduct'. The NGO does not support strikes, and if migrant workers approach the organisation for help or support, NHC only gives them legal advice, or redirects them to official trade unions or the Labour Bureau:

> ACFTU is able to organise and represent migrants better than we do, so our role is to help migrants get in touch with the trade union and seek their help.[18]

This behaviour partially confirms the general findings in the literature on labour NGOs as organisations which facilitate the state's 'regime of law', particularly in the context of strikes. In this respect, the NHC–state relationship adheres to the co-optation model and is mutually beneficial: the NGO dissipates 'social conflict' by directing migrant workers' grievances to the government, which can provide some limited legal representation and even welfare provision to migrant workers in exchange. This particular choice of engagement with the government is perhaps also encouraged by the more welfare-orientated policies of the Hangzhou government, which seek to appease workers' discontent by providing limited welfare to non-urban-*hukou* holders.

However, not all NGOs see the role of the government agencies as sufficient in terms of representation vis-à-vis employers. NBW sees the formation of 'self-representation' (independent trade unions and organisations) as the best channel to resolve the problems of exploitation of workers:

> The biggest problem for migrant workers now is the lack of migrant workers' own organisations in the city. The problem of the lack of fair dialogue with capitalists [*zifang*]... For example, in the case of Foxconn, which promised to increase workers' wages. But what they did in fact is they took all the regular allowances [*butie*] and added them on top of the salary, saying that they increased wages, [while] in the meantime the accommodation costs increased. This is a kind of problem for which there is no good mechanism to help workers to enter into dialogue with the employers. Actually, society [as a whole] does not have a reasonable mechanism of dialogue either. So, when such problems arise, the workers have to take extreme measures to resolve them ... The best way is to have real representation through their own trade union.[19] Although we have trade unions nowadays, they do not represent workers. Recently there have been many strikes in the south; their aim is to establish workers' own trade unions ... [This] requires a change in the government's policy regarding independent trade unions. The development of labour NGOs is an important factor and it might lead to independent unions.[20]

Throughout the interview, the NBW representative referred to his NGO as 'our trade union', which illustrates some migrant worker NGOs' own self-perception as *de facto* trade unions (though without the necessary attributes of unions, such as democratic elections). He also highlighted that the problem of representation and of ability to voice one's concerns is not only limited to migrant workers: rather, it is a wider problem of China's political system. This shows this act's profound link to the remaking of citizenship: the claim for representation is not solely linked to class consciousness, but is a wider claim to alter the system which denies workers' representation more widely, not only in the workplace. However, NGOs, once again, do not seek to do so in confrontation with the state, but rather simultaneously with state-led reforms:

> NGOs can also currently provide help to workers through the activities already promoted by NGOs ... but for NGOs, there is also a need to have their basic operational aspects protected. It is an experimental stage right now ... In an environment which cannot be changed, what we can continue doing is to slowly accumulate more and more power and slowly change [this environment] ... Because the big organisations have already solidified, there is a need for a bottom-up [*zixiaershang*] movement. If one conducts a violent revolution, then the status quo can be completely changed. [In our case] if we merely want to enhance the current order, then surely, we need to do it from the bottom-up. But the government also has to conduct their own conscious reform. It is not enough just for the workers to try changing the system.[21]

The NGO actively maintains the dialogue with the local government and ACFTU, and in this way seeks to change attitudes towards NGOs and towards greater empowerment of migrant workers, attempting to transform citizenship rights from within the system.

One such essential part of the process of claiming representation is by self-organisation of workers through collective bargaining. Collective bargaining is conducted by several Guangdong-based, so-called 'labour movement type' NGOs. In the sample of NGOs in this study, those who helped workers in collective bargaining were FJ, UA and ET.[22] It is important to emphasise that these NGOs have cut down on collective bargaining and strike-related activism since 2017, due to arrests and crackdowns on NGO activists.

The importance of collective bargaining as a transformative act of citizenship emerged in the conversation with the former head of

ET (who left the organisation in 2016). Interestingly, she did not see collective bargaining as an illegal or subversive act, but rather conceived of it as an act starting with everyday small collective negotiations, and by extending solidarity to other workers in small, non-confrontational disputes with employers:

> Workers should start practising collective bargaining from small things, such as, for example, provision of water tanks in their workplaces. It cultivates certain habits and style of dealing with issues. In the past experience of our organisation, in 2011, we helped collect signatures for a female migrant worker who wanted the company to put up a staff room where they can charge their phones, and it was successful. It is by such small collective experiences that they can then face bigger issues.[23]

This form of progressive education in collective bargaining skills indicates a desire on the part of NGOs to instil a collective civic action-consciousness among workers. This civic action is presented to migrant workers as entirely legal. Indeed, NGOs do much to calm workers' fears and explain that by undertaking collective bargaining, workers are not breaking the law.[24] Indeed, NGOs use the language of law and legality to convey the rightfulness of collective bargaining, and see it as a more effective and less risky action for workers than strikes:

> It is important to discuss with employers in a 'rational' way, because in the current climate acting chaotically will be squashed, especially if workers go on strikes and block roads: they might end up in jail. Confronting the government is useless: it is better to strategically negotiate with them. So, it is important to provide collective bargaining education: it helps protect the workers. With strikes, everybody wants the joint rights, but nobody wants to share responsibility [when things go awry]. With collective bargaining, everybody has a clear role to play, there is an organised structure, so it is a better long-term strategy than strikes.[25]

However, this does not change the fact that by training migrant workers in collective bargaining and aiding the process, NGOs play a role typically performed by trade unions. Indeed, either via pushing for institutionalisation of collective bargaining, or through helping to formulate workers' demands for free union elections or for independent trade unions, NGOs promote the institutionalisation of a more democratic trade union system. As I learned from funders familiar with the more 'militant' NGOs, which support strike action and collective bargaining, workers' claims for independent trade unions, which emerge through strikes, are almost always exclusively a result of these NGOs' intervention and coaching.[26]

Shenzhen-based UA is an example of an NGO which since 2010 has trained migrant workers in collective bargaining during strikes. In the beginning, after a few months of these activities, UA was approached by the Public Security personnel, who tried to dissuade it from supporting collective bargaining, and then even invited Mr Zhao to the police station where they argued with him angrily:

> They told me that these kinds of activities will not bring any benefit to us, to which I said that what we are doing does not violate the law, so why should I stop doing it?[27]

UA has continued to support striking workers, despite the government's monitoring and obstruction, using the liminal space between what is legal (legal advice) and what is considered a 'political taboo' (legal advice provided to striking workers). At the time around the year of the transition of power (2013) this was still possible:

> We have been doing this for over two years now. Even though our political regime stipulates that workers need permission for strikes, and even though the government does obstruct our activities in this area and monitors us, they have not suppressed us or clearly told us that we cannot help them. So, we use this space [*fanwei*] of their [government's] indecision.[28]

Mr Zhao sees the support for collective bargaining and strikes as important, because he believes that strikes not only lead to a better life for the workers, but also that the experience of striking can be ultimately transformed into independent workers' organisations. When discussing strikes, Mr Zhao also points to another side of the emancipation process that strikes can bring, that of looking for change beyond the law and seeing the insufficiency of the law:

> And what is the end product of strikes? The end product is that the workers unite and organise and that new workers' leaders will emerge from these strikes. By going through the strike process of fighting for a cause for many days together, they will feel real freedom and see that through united action they can solve their problems. Because

> even if you win your case in court, you surely won't be able to return to your factory. But after a strike, you don't have to leave your workplace! And also, if you win the lawsuit, this can only solve the problems within the framework of the law, for example [you can secure the minimal wage] ... But what if 1,500 yuan [the minimum wage] is still too low, what would you do then? ... A lot of problems cannot be resolved by the law: only if workers unite can they resolve these problems. If workers unite, they will not only address the labour issues, but also their social status, and social position in society; you can resolve it all if you unite.[29]

Once again, UA, similarly to NBW, sees claiming the right to representation as a crucial aspect of wider-than-labour claims, relating to the social status of migrant workers and their discrimination in popular discourse and social practices: all contingent on the citizenship formulation in China. This transformation is possible through collective acts of citizenship.

How can collective bargaining and strike support be regarded as acts of citizenship? The case of the April 2014 Yu Yuan shoe factory strike might serve as an example. According to UA's leader there were several elements combined together in the dispute, among which the social security issue was just a catalyst for the many issues causing workers' dissatisfaction with the factory. First, there was an issue of non-compliant labour contracts, which were not registered with the Labour Bureau. Although the 2008 Labour Contract Law deems all contracts signed by both sides as legal, local schools refused to accept migrant children as they regarded the non-registered contracts from the Yu Yuan factory as illegal. The problem of illegally low social security (pension) contributions made by the factory was another issue: when some workers nearing retirement discovered that the company wasn't paying the correct level of contributions towards their pensions, and treated them as 'temporary workers' despite them working in the factory for periods of twenty years or more, they started to spread the news about the company's misconduct through social media. The workers then started protesting (*kangyi*) in front of the Dongguan government office. The officials promised that the factory would deal with the case within the next nine days (by 14 April) and would pronounce their resolution on the factory gates. The workers then found the details of UA online and sought legal advice on further actions. At this point, the NGO's involvement exemplifies the typical way in which PRD-based NGOs train workers in collective bargaining:

> As we learned the details of their case, I realised that in order for the workers to come together, their demands must be adjusted, because the pension demand is something that only part of the workers would care about: the 18, 19, 20 year-olds don't care about such issues yet. Then I told the workers that there are two issues which can help them unite: one is the issue of raising their wages, and the other of the housing provident fund [*fanggong jijin*].[30] This housing provident fund is something that nobody pays attention to. A lot of migrants say 'I don't have Shenzhen *hukou*, I don't have Dongguan *hukou*, what use is this housing fund to me?' But in fact, you can take out the accumulated funds from the housing fund and build the house in your home town. They hadn't known that before. So, these two demands made everybody care to take action: old and young ... Then I explained how to make workers across all the factories unite. As each factory sets up QQ groups, the most active workers [*jiji fenzi* (activists)] then enter those groups, spread information about how to defend the workers' rights, how to go on strike: they clearly explained everything to the workers in those groups ... This way we built a communication platform and unified the workers' demands across factories. And then we waited for 14 April, but we knew already, from experience, that neither the Social Security Bureau, nor the factory management will willingly satisfy workers' demands. So, we told the workers: as you will have read the factory announcement, and once you know that the factory won't meet your demands, you should then go on strike straight away. We strategised for three main factories to start the strike, 30,000 people in total. And indeed, on the first day all three factories started striking, and on the second the rest: 60,000 people in total.[31]

While UA's role in the strike was important, as the organisation helped to make the action effective and highlighted the common ground for the workers, it was the migrant workers employed in the factory who had initiated the action originally. Although UA supported migrants' action and helped with cross-factory solidarity, the strike would most likely have happened with or without the NGO's support. However, the involvement of UA allowed the activist workers to emerge, and to learn the process of collective bargaining, which they then spread across the factory workers, shaping workers' legal and collective action consciousness.

However, the price of 'claiming the right to representation' can be very high for those who perform this act in China. The consequence of UA's involvement in this biggest ever migrant workers' strike in China came at a great personal cost: the activists were arrested, detained, threatened and their activities have been continuously obstructed ever since. After the April 2014 Yu Yuan strike, in conversation with the media, Mr Zhao revealed that the arrest of his colleague was really a 'lesson' meted out against UA, as the government believes their active advice to the workers contributed to the expansion of the strike. The UA leader was eventually detained in 2019 and sentenced in April 2020 to a suspended prison term.

While the majority of scholars see support for striking workers and their right to self-representation primarily as an example of growing class consciousness, UA further highlights the intrinsic link of labour claims to 'activist citizenship':

> Why would a person do public interest work? What is the aim of public interest work? Overall, it is to build a workers' society [*gongyou shehui*] ... A lot of organisations say they do 'rights defence'. If you ask them 'do you have any real aim behind that?' you will find not a single one which will dare tell you that they have 'a real aim'. They just answer 'we do not have any [political] aim, we only do the rights defence'. But if you think hard, what really is implicated in the 'rights defence'... which aspect of that is not related to politics!?[32] Politics has a wide meaning; actually, in our lives there is not one thing which is not related to politics! ... Our civic politics is about addressing the problems of people's livelihood, the question of our fundamental rights. I believe I can [have a right to] speak about this kind of politics in a loud voice [*dazhangqigu*]. A lot of people ask me: 'Do you have a political aim?' I say: 'Of course I have!' I am a man with a sense of social responsibility; you cannot say there is no political aim involved. I can only say that my aim is not to overturn the regime and build a new political regime; this is not my aim. My aim is to provide service to the lowest level [*diceng*] of society, the weak and vulnerable [*ruoshi qunti*]. And this service is necessarily linked to politics, isn't it? ... So, in this society, what exactly is not related to politics? I believe everything is; all you need to do is to clearly and openly say it, so that they [the government] understand what you are doing. If you do so, I believe there is no problem ... Only if you openly publicise and speak in a loud voice, only then can you really change other people's consciousness and viewpoints.[33]

In the conversation we had in 2016, after the Yu Yuan strikes, when reflecting on his engagement in the local elections in 2011, he further emphasises the intrinsic relationship between labour rights and citizenship rights, and the importance of claiming the right to representation as an essential pathway for effective labour activism:

> You asked why I stood in the elections to become People's Representative in the NPC ... It wasn't that I wanted to change the political system: this is very dangerous. I just said to the government: we are people from outside, we have no voice, we should have some role in the local policy-making too. Of course, I wouldn't really be able to contribute to the policy, but at least I could let my voice be heard. I thought to myself: if I am elected, I can help more people, help migrants access voting rights in the city. Only this way can I influence this local policy-making level, can change it. Because now it is only the local residents [*bendiren*] that count when the cake is divided: we migrants are always omitted, we just get some scraps ... So why are economic rights and political rights intertwined? Because if you don't have wider citizenship rights, you don't have that foundation: it is very hard to protect your labour rights. Why is it so easy to violate migrant workers' rights? Because migrants don't have their own representatives, nobody to put in a word for them, nobody in the government participating in the policy-making process.[34]

This quote clearly demonstrates how the activities of NGOs, particularly of UA, are a form of citizenship activism as they self-consciously build on the idea of the political (Mouffe, 1993): that is, of civic involvement in the active shaping of politics. While UA's aims are clearly linked to the migrant workers' grievances regarding labour, they are also linked to a wider aspect related to citizenship: the right to voice, self-assembly, representation and participation in politics. But in the case of UA and many others in this study, it is not just about making demands: the NGO is clearly *claiming* the right to participation in politics. The act of claiming is both transformative of structural citizenship and an act of establishing its performer as an activist citizen.

However, the cases discussed above illustrate that state–society relations in China primarily take the form of negotiation, and only secondarily that of conflict with the state. Neither NGO seeks to estrange or fight the state: they wish for the right to voice in discussion with the government. The ultimate claims they raise are for migrant workers to be allowed to participate in 'dividing the cake' decisions, to be heard and to be able to choose their representatives in local unions and state institutions. The participation of migrant workers in decision-making (which in itself transforms the citizenship regime and discourse) is essential, in the view of my interviewees, to change the condition of workers' exploitation and their treatment as second-class citizens in public discourse, society and the law.

Conclusion

Since as early as the 1990s, labour study scholars have discussed the evolving labour movement in China in terms of class self-consciousness building, and in Marxist terms of class struggle (Sun, 2014; Friedman and Lee, 2010; Chan, 2012b). Strikes, collective bargaining, legal proceedings, creation of NGOs and acts of workers' suicide have all been framed mainly in terms of working-class formation and labour activism. Yet, much of the struggle for a so-called labour movement can also be clearly seen as a struggle for citizenship rights. Indeed, citizenship scholars have been pointing to the inseparability of citizenship and labour, and some have indicated the bias pertinent to labour studies of interpreting citizenship claims as labour claims (Steadman-Jones, 1983; Somers, 2008, 1996). Indeed, the fieldwork above reveals a surprisingly close relationship between the notions of labour activism and activist citizenship. While labour- or class-based solidarity emerged as an important factor for many of the NGOs in this chapter, they also emphasise the importance of rights to voice, recognition and representation, all of which, while taking labour as a unified platform for these claims, go far beyond the issue of labour in their impact on structural citizenship. Labour activism should be seen as a type of citizenship activism which derives from a common class identity. Indeed, the notion of 'class' has often been historically a 'common master-narrative that can unite the … oppressed collectivities' in their search for recognition (Miller, 2004: 232–233), making the division between cultural and material false, as 'justice today requires both redistribution and recognition' (Fraser, 1995: 69). Indeed, I have illustrated in this chapter how the claims put forward around the common 'worker' identity go hand in hand with the formation of 'citizenship consciousness'.

Moreover, this chapter has extended the discussion about NGOs' relationship with labour law-based activism. We see here that NGOs' relationship with the law is far from acquiescing: they utilise and interpret the legal framework in ways unforeseen or even undesired by the state. They frequently criticise existing laws and their application, and express claims going beyond these laws. While some NGOs, particularly those outside of Guangdong and especially in Zhejiang and Beijing, tend to educate workers strictly within the legal frameworks, many more educate workers on aspects going beyond the law, such as unionism, collective bargaining, solidarity and sources of discrimination.

Yet, there is still more to the migrant NGOs' impact on citizenship than labour-focused activism. Even in this chapter we can see that NGOs deploy political and identity claims which go beyond class-based identity or material claims. Similarly, their struggle is not just orientated against the capitalist class, but also incorporates criticism of the legal and political regime and social attitudes towards migrant workers. As I will further expand in the next chapter, this extra-labour struggle takes space as its core. Spatial inequalities embedded in the citizenship discourse become a target of criticism. The discursive tools that NGOs deploy, of migrants as citizen and migrants as workers, emerge even more clearly in the context of space-related claims. At the same time, urban spaces play an important role as the incumbent space for activism: a space where the activism takes place, and a means through which it is conducted.

Notes

1 Interview no. 19.

2 Apart from SC and SFI, there is another NGO which deals with occupational health, the Beijing-based SWS. However, unlike most NGOs dealing with occupational safety, SWS deals mostly with post-exposure assistance with the costs of hospitalisation in the case of sufferers from pneumoconiosis. It mostly helps with the cost of hospitalisation from its own fund-raising, rather than undertaking legislative action against employers, working as a charity rather than a legal action NGO in this respect.

3 Interview no. 43.
4 Interview no. 18.
5 I will discuss these in the last section of this chapter.
6 See the next chapter for a further exploration of this theme.
7 Indeed, the weakness of the law with regard to social insurance contributions is widely criticised in the academic literature. Internal conflicts make the enforcement of the law quite impossible. According to the Regulations of the 1994 Administration of Labour in Foreign Invested Enterprises and the 1995 Labour Law, the social security scheme stipulates that the employer should contribute to the welfare funds on the employee's behalf. SOEs are not able, or not willing, to make such contributions and often expect workers to make the contributions themselves. Apparently, many employees in SOEs are forced to 'sell years of job tenure to an employing state enterprise in order to obtain such benefits' (Ho, 2003: 14–15). The situation in private enterprises is much worse (Ho, 2003: 15). The Social Insurance Law of 2011 (as discussed in Chapter 2) has not changed much in the implementation of the law, as recent strikes across China illustrate.
8 Interview no. 3.
9 Interview no. 3.
10 Interview no. 18.
11 See Chapter 3 for more details.
12 The existing policy stipulated that it was both the employer and the worker who shared the costs of the arbitration fee, and the fee was only 50 yuan regardless of the case.
13 Interview no. 18.
14 Interview no. 18.
15 Interview no. 18.
16 Interview no. 44.
17 China Labour Bulletin estimates that it only records a small sample of all strikes taking place in China (China Labour Bulletin Strike Map, https://maps.clb.org.hk/strikes/en).
18 Interview no. 9.
19 The NGOs avoid using the phrase 'independent trade unions' (*duli gonghui*); instead they prefer to call them 'own trade unions' (*ziji de gonghui*).
20 Interview no. 5.
21 Interview no. 5.
22 See Fu (2017) and Froissart (2018) for another study of labour movement-orientated NGOs, some of which are not included in this book.
23 Interview no. 46.

24 However, according to another study, due to the crackdown in the sector of movement-orientated labour NGOs under Xi Jinping, the NGOs undertaking collective bargaining are now warning migrant workers of the risk in undertaking this form of activism and using NGOs' assistance to do so (Franceschini and Nesossi, 2018).
25 Interview no. 46.
26 Interviews no. 31 and no. 39.
27 Interview no. 18.
28 Interview no. 18.
29 Interview no. 18.
30 There is equal contribution towards the fund: 50 per cent is paid by the employee and 50 per cent by the employer.
31 Interview no. 42.
32 UA's founder refers to the common dislike of 'discussing politics' as something related to the government and something 'sensitive' in Chinese society (and among NGOs).
33 Interview no. 18.
34 Interview no. 42.

Part IV

Space

6

The figure of the worker-citizen

The focus of the remaining two chapters is the type of activism which addresses temporality, marginality and exclusion of migrants' experience in their encounters with the city, and which transforms the spatial relationship between urban and rural that defines migrants' citizenship. While citizenship-altering activism performed around the issues of civic organising and labour is much talked about, the activism which takes space, and particularly urban space, as its core is often neglected. While human geographers have recently focused on spatial strategies of migrant workers' struggle for urban citizenship (see Swider, 2015; Kochan, 2019; Qian and Zhu, 2014; Qian and He, 2012; Ren, 2012), these observations have yet to transpire in political science's discussions of migrant workers' activism, which are dominated by the focus on labour and/or resistance to the state. This is important because the claim areas of civic organising and labour do not really address migrant workers' marginalisation within the cities and their figurative and legal exclusion from urban citizenship. Neither labour nor civic organising relate to the demands for both physical and figurative belonging to the city itself. Are there any claims put forward by migrant worker NGOs which delve into the key aspect of being granted space in the city or the right to decide about the city? Having been given no access to housing, and no prospect of being regarded as urban citizens, with their rural origins rendering them unfit to be regarded as proper Chinese citizens, what role do migrant organisations play in addressing this situation?

In this and the next chapter I answer these questions, by using a concept of 'space' as a common issue uniting these types of claims. I understand space and its conceptual relationship to the city in two ways: figurative and material. In the figurative, 'inner' sense, space pervades the dominant citizenship discourse, and is internalised by migrant workers. In the material, or 'outer' sense, space relates to the material expression of citizenship exclusion from the city's resources and rights of urban citizenship. This chapter is particularly concerned with the former meaning of space: the migrant workers' spatial exclusion embedded in citizenship discourse, and the NGOs' strategies for addressing this exclusion. As discussed in the introduction, the discursive exclusion of migrant workers from citizenship stems from the role that the rural–urban divide has historically played in the formation of modern citizenship in China. This discursive exclusion relies on the hierarchical character of the rural–urban divide, whereby the urban-*hukou* holder is regarded as a modern, civilised and therefore proper citizen, while the rural migrant is regarded as backward, uncivilised and in dire need of being transformed into a citizen through the flattening process of urbanisation (see Zhang, 2002; Jakimów, 2012). While material exclusion from the city is crucial in migrant workers' life chances, and will be discussed in Chapter 7, the discursive exclusion is equally important in the everyday experiences of migrant workers.

Just as the production of citizenship in China has relied on internalisation of this spatial dimension of citizenship discourse, the remaking of this discourse necessitates the reclaiming of rural and migrant identity as that of a 'citizen'. In this chapter, I discuss how migrant worker NGOs' attempts to shape migrants' identity in relation to the rural–urban divide can transform citizenship in China. I explore three acts related to this figuratively understood concept of space: voicing (migrants' experience of spatial exclusion), challenging (of the current citizenship discourse and regime) and constructing (the new identity for migrant workers). The act of 'voicing' reveals the relationship of citizenship to space, as the narratives which emerge through this act reveal how the citizenship marginalisation in urban China creates an experience of the city as 'spaces of exclusion'. The act of 'challenging' aims to target the rejection of migrant workers from figurative urban citizenship by disagreeing with the portrayal and treatment of migrant workers as non-citizens and reclaiming their figurative right to the city. The act of 'constructing' is expressed through educational and cultural activities which aim to create a new identity for migrant workers, that of 'worker-citizen'.

Voicing: the experiences of the subaltern

The crucial part of the NGOs' activism in this area is the act of making the experiences of marginalisation known and visible. Migrant worker art festivals, such as the one mentioned in the opening vignette of this book, is one way in which NGOs achieve this. While migrant workers' voices have become increasingly noticeable over the last decade in the mainstream media, the voicing performed by migrant workers and migrant-created organisations is of particular importance, as the head of NBW mentioned in the opening address of the first Migrant Workers' Festival organised in 2009:

> We often hear that it is the government's role to create a stage for people to perform and express themselves. But don't we have an ability to create such a stage ourselves? All of us here have this one very deep experience: that is, if we do not have our own stage on which we can perform, we don't have a place to express our own voice; we can then only ask to be allowed on other people's stages. But do we really have no culture? We do have our own culture! But our culture is not yet visible, it does not have its own stage, it does not have a recognisable style and has not yet found a space in which it can be displayed.

'Voicing' is, therefore, an act of creating the stage and making migrants' culture visible. In this book, I discuss cases where voicing is performed by both rural migrants who work for NGOs and by migrant workers who might be just loosely linked to them (as the NGOs' constituency or as volunteers). The act of voicing is performed through NGO-sponsored publications, and outlets created by migrants themselves as an effect of NGO-led training in various technologies and artistic activities. It is important to look at the content and form of what is being voiced to understand why and how it has the potential to challenge citizenship in China.

The migrants' experience of discursive and material exclusion from the city is expressed in 'dissociation from the city' and 'longing for home' narratives. Poetry is a very important channel through which migrant workers express such experiences. From the NGOs' founders, to the migrants who shared their poems with me in the offices of NGOs, to the many migrants who interact with NGOs in the PRD and Beijing, poetry is one of the favourite pastimes, which apart from fulfilling a therapeutic role, can also play a political one, as it highlights injustice and allows for a social dialogue. In a volume published by MWU, a migrant woman, Kang Yihong, expresses her experience of displacement from the city in the following words:

> I often say I arrived in a foreign land
> This foreign land is a workshop
> And a rented flat, place the size of two fingernails
> And just like the fingernail it pinches and pokes my flesh and my soul
> Daytime I spend in the workshop toiling, just like a buffalo ploughing and pulling in the field in my home village.[1]
> I am pulling using my whole life energy, pulling all along with no end
> And I am so cruel on myself, I often realise, that I
> Stand behind my back, and yell with them together at myself
> Deep into the night I come back to my rented flat, just like a wounded buffalo
> Hide beyond the field bounds chewing the cud suffering but happy
> Over and over again, as I chew this bitter grass, I arrive in my home village
> (Kang, 2010: 7)

We can see in the poem the feeling of alienation from the city and the living and working spaces, but we can also see how the spaces of rural and urban are experienced simultaneously in everyday experience. The rural and urban, the space of work and the space of living are all blurred into one oppressive and alienating feeling of bodily displacement from both spaces, while simultaneously living in both.[2] The poem also conveys the deep sense of loneliness and abandonment linked to the transient, uprooted, temporary and community-lacking experience of migrant labour. The *hukou* identity card, represented as 'a thin piece of paper' in this author's other poem, complicates this situation of displacement.

This displacement and the feeling of alienation from both rural and urban are also echoed in the narratives expressed through NBW's artistic activities and the forms of self-expression that the organisation promotes among migrant workers. The urban village where the NGO is based is located on the outskirts of Beijing city's prosperous Chaoyang district, near the sixth ring road. At the time of my visits, in 2012, it was home to nearly 10,000 migrant workers (and 1,400 local urban-*hukou* holders) working in the nearby factories manufacturing mainly furniture, doors and windows.[3] The outputs produced by NBW which enable 'voicing' include magazines for migrant children and workers, an arts troupe, a band, training for migrants in the use of new technologies (computers, phones and cameras), and the Museum of Migrant Workers' Art and History. Some of these channels serve as a medium for the NGO founders' own artistic expression of their experience of *dagong*, and others are aimed at enabling the wider migrant worker community to voice their experiences.

An example of the voicing of such emotions, and how the experience of spatial exclusion plays a central part in them, can be found in the 2010 theatrical play entitled *Life in the City*, based entirely on true migrant workers' stories which the NGO collected through the 2009 'Survey on Migrant Workers' Residential Status' conducted in four cities (Beijing, Shenzhen, Xi'an and Suzhou). In the play, two construction workers (played by artists from NBW's arts troupe) reflect on their spatial position within the city:

> Lao He: It does not matter how tall the buildings we construct are, we have nothing to do with them, as for all the houses we build, none belong to us! ...
>
> Da Hu: At least there are many famous places we can see in Beijing. Have you seen any?
>
> Lao He: I managed to take a day off once just to go to Tiananmen Square and take a good look at Chairman Mao.[4] But even before I had a chance to pay homage to Chairman Mao, I was circled by five people requesting my papers and questioning me. They scared and dumbfounded me: I did not dare to see Chairman Mao any more!
>
> Da Hu: We have two days off, what about hanging around, going to see the city?
>
> Lao He: ... Go by yourself, I don't want to. I feel like a fish out of water. In a big shopping mall, as soon as you enter, a salesgirl follows you everywhere ... like you are about to steal something. I also feel out of place on the bus, where everyone seems to dodge us as if we were squalid, fearing to touch us as if they would get dirty ... I'd rather admire the buildings we are raising up; this scenery makes me feel comfortable.

From this self-evident dialogue, we see the spatial oppression the migrants feel in the city they are actually building, and how this exclusion is linked to their citizenship status and the spatial imaginary embedded in it (of rural as backward, dirty and uncivilised). Even the seemingly universal cultural right of every Chinese citizen to access historical sites appears to be fraught with hostility and bodily humiliation, which builds boundaries between those who are deemed to be rightful citizens and those who are excluded as 'suspicious' and 'unfit'.

Many of the lyrics of songs written by the NGO members are also about spatial and bodily exclusion, and they reverberate with the narrative of a marginalised experience:

> Through the red-eyed women workers working overtime,
> Through the small street vendors ready to run when policemen come,
> Through the workers standing on the roof of high-rise buildings threatening to jump
> Through the small low houses rented to migrant workers outside the 5th Ring Road
> We have to take a second look at the city
> ('City Life' from the album *Our World Our Dream*)

In this song, the spatial marginalisation is expressed with reference to the embodied individual experience of interaction with the material city spaces: the worker threatens to jump from a skyscraper; a street peddler experiences threat in the public spaces of the city, and migrants are pushed to live beyond the city proper.

These aspects of the experience of life in temporary, precarious conditions of constant movement, squeezed living spaces and spatial exclusion from the city's housing and schooling reverberate especially strongly through the narratives of migrant workers' children. NBW creates space for migrant children's expression in the form of a monthly publication entitled *The Voice of the Transient*, which is solely devoted to first-person accounts of children's experiences of life in two urban villages. In one of the issues, a second-grade female student, whose parents are collectors of recycling materials, records her experience:

> I am with my parents who are working in Beijing ... My home is constantly on the move ... Dismantle and move, dismantle and move

> … it is all for the development of Beijing, for the prosperity of the big city. I am now used to the mobile home. I am willing to accept this if this means a contribution to the city.

An attachment to the city and the view of the city as a mobile home, where people flee the constant experience of demolition, is also present in the story of a 10 year-old girl called Yue, living at the fringes of Changping district:

> My mother took me to Beijing last year, when I was 9 years old … I live with my parents in Dongsanqi village. My parents rent a place for collecting recycling materials, and we actually live together with the garbage … The space we live in is so small … My mother gets up early every morning, at about 5 am, to go to collect iron, and comes back after 9–10 pm. My father collects wood and he leaves around 7–8 am. They work every day. I often wait for them at the village entrance hoping that they are on time for dinner … I heard that Dongsanqi village is to be removed. It sounded so sudden to me in the beginning. I was really worried that my parents would send me home. I feel very relieved that my parents will take me with them to another place and will look for another school for me.

A narrative of the transient experience of dislocation, the missing of school and the founding of one's worth on 'the contribution to the city' reverberates in the children's experiences. The narrative of the desire to contribute and to be a productive member of the urban community in order to belong is founded on the 'neoliberal citizen-subject' discourse, which serves to justify migrants' claims to belong to the city as long as they are economically 'useful'. The experience of school as a founding and rooting place in the city is present in almost all of the stories by migrant children. A place at school in the city is one of the social rights of urban citizenship that the rural children have restricted access to, particularly in Beijing.[5] In Beijing, local policies make access to education for migrant worker children particularly difficult. The price tag on access to good-quality schools, including primary schools, is prohibitively high for most migrants (Kwong, 2011: 874).[6] Migrant children are therefore forced to attend overpriced and underdeveloped private schools in urban villages, which are under continuous threat of demolition. The 2014 National New-type Urbanisation Plan did not change this situation, despite promising to enable school places for all children, whatever their place of origin (PRC Government, 2014; Liang, 2019).

A place at school is an aspect which binds children to the city and shapes their identity as 'Beijingers'. When asked about the children's attachment to the city, my interviewee from NBW said that children tend to identify with both: the city (of Beijing) and their (parents') home towns. They often see themselves as belonging to both places simultaneously,[7] similarly to the experience expressed in the poem by Kang Yihong quoted earlier. In one of the paintings on the wall surrounding NBW's compound, in rough-edged red-on-white strokes we can see the city at the bottom, the village at the top and the group of migrant workers (women, men and children) in between (see Figure 6.1). The spatio-temporal aspects of the experience of migrant workers' situation of 'fluidity' and 'temporality', embedded in the notion of 'transient population' (*liudong renkou*), is also represented here.

Despite being seen in a negative light, belonging to both urban and rural simultaneously opens space for a new reimagining of the spatio-temporal aspect of citizenship, because it questions the discursive incompatibility of urban and rural in the citizenship formulation in China. It is precisely this third space of non-belonging to either rural or urban, while simultaneously living in both, that opens up the possibility of negotiating a new identity which enables belonging to the city, and subsequently remakes migrants' position within the bifurcated citizenship discourse where rural and urban are necessarily opposite and exclusionary.

Moreover, while enabling migrants' artistic expression seems a low-impact form of activism, it has the power to bring a wider social and political change, as the story of Fan Yusu illustrates. Fan Yusu is a migrant woman, who has experienced all the typical adversity of a migrant life in Beijing, while suffering domestic violence and the hardship of life as a single mother. After joining the literary classes provided by NBW, she made a sweeping entry as China's hottest real-life novelist in 2017 with her blog posts describing life in Beijing from migrant perspectives. And although the blog was quickly censored, and the author, overwhelmed by fame, went temporarily into hiding, the cultural activities of a small NGO, which for years has nurtured talented migrants such as Fan Yusu, brought an unexpectedly broad impact. The blog was shared 100,000 times in just the first twenty-four hours of its post online, and it created a momentary glow of fraternity between migrant workers

Figure 6.1 'The third space' [the name of the NGO was removed from the plaque by the author].

and the urban middle class. This story shows how this small and insignificant NGO's mission has been somehow fulfilled: the people have heard the voice of the transient, and this act of voicing brought down the barriers between urban and rural citizens, creating a bond above the rural–urban divide.

Enabling the voicing of first-hand experiences is an act of citizenship as it allows migrant workers the right to voice injustice and contributes to the political debate in public space. Although the outputs produced by or with the help of NGOs present migrant workers as excluded, exploited and marginalised from the city due to their citizenship status (rural origin), they are simultaneously laced with calls for action to challenge the status quo. This latter narrative represents the transition from the act of voicing to the act of challenging, and will be discussed in the following section. The act of 'voicing' is the first step in the process of remaking the citizenship discourse, as it leads to questioning and challenging of the understanding of who is a citizen in China.

Challenging marginalisation: the migrant workers' culture

The process of formation of new identities which transgress the cultural ideas of migrant workers as non-citizens begins with the act of 'challenging', which targets existing representations of migrants in the mainstream culture. Some NGOs, such as Shenzhen-based ET for instance, highlight the reasons behind the discrimination against migrant workers and challenge some pre-conceived ideas related to the *suzhi* discourse, such as their 'backward' status and 'low quality'. In this way ET addresses the social injustice linked to the spatial hierarchical dimension of the rural–urban divide and the associated material and cultural alienation in the cities:

> We also provide some education, which does not necessarily relate to the migrant workers' legal rights. [We tell migrants things like:] 'Once you come to the city to *dagong*, you, in fact, acquire a new identity of a "worker", so you enjoy the citizen's right to work in the city. You will not always be able to claim this or that in the city and the social system [*shehui zhidu*] will tell you that your home is on the land, so when the time comes you should go back to your home village. But what the social system tells people is not right! Because when you go back to your village, will you still be able to live off cultivating your land? You will not! ... More so, the land you own today can be expropriated tomorrow. Returning to the countryside is not the way out for you! On the other hand, you think that you do not belong here [in the city], so you do not go fighting [for your

rights]. So finally, you end up having nothing! But you have contributed so much; if you do not discuss your rights, if you only watch your pay and your gain, do you think you get justice? Just look how many of the city products, goods, buildings are all made by us. Whenever you finish constructing a building or making a product you need to move again, while others can have what you made so cheaply. If other people can so easily access the goods you made, shouldn't you receive not only the material gains but also the inner satisfaction as well? You should receive the respect, but it seems you just serve other people!' This is how we discuss things. We don't give them answers or tell them what to do; we just discuss these issues.[8]

The rural–urban divide in the citizenship regime and discourse results in the idea that migrant workers do not belong to the city and that their place is in the countryside. Migrant workers' orientation towards the countryside has also been seen as further entrenched through their material attachment to rural land, a key factor which presumably stops migrant workers from taking part in collective forms of civic activism (Lee, 2007: 24). But the ET representative sees the material link with the countryside as flimsy, as even the right to land can be dispossessed. Moreover, owning land in the countryside does not provide a livelihood; this is the argument I came across over and over in my discussions with NGOs. Migrants do not belong to the city, but they acquire some right to figurative 'urban citizenship' if they become workers who contribute materially to the city. This approach to citizenship as a sort of commodity acquired through a particular material contribution leads to the understanding of citizenship as a contractualised commodity and results in a formation of neoliberal citizen-subjects (Ong, 2006). Yet, in the case of migrant workers, the belonging through this commoditised notion of citizenship (Somers, 2008: 3) is only temporary, as their right to belong to the city dissolves once they are no longer materially 'useful'. Once they have fulfilled their role as 'neoliberal subjects', they cease to be regarded as citizens, and have to move, for the condition of *dagong* is the only justification of their 'claim to the city'. ET highlights the injustice of such arrangements by challenging the idea of migrants' non-belonging to the city, their lack of rights to the fruits of their labour and the necessity of their 'return to the countryside' or further migration. They see the way out as being to fight for rights to their means of production, the right to the city itself and the new identity of the migrant workers group as 'deserving respect'. This attitude can be seen as both the socialist and the radical activist citizenship answer to their condition.

NBW and NHC, similarly to ET, seek to break the cycle of displacement discussed in the previous section. In December 2011, I observed a theatrical play by NHC under the overarching theme 'rethinking the culture of overtime, promoting harmonious treatment of workers' (*fansi jiaban wenhua, changdao hexie yonggong*)[9] (see Figure 6.2).

The play's main message was that in order to develop a sense of belonging in the city, migrant workers should engage more actively in the migrant community. Participating in the artistic activities of an NGO is an antidote to the hardship and routine of their lives. NHC and NBW both aim to address the detachment of migrant workers from both the rural and the urban by breaking the space-time attachment to the village (particularly the imagined 'future return' orientation) through enabling migrant workers to celebrate their present life in the city. Through artistic activities, often treated as

Figure 6.2 'Rethinking the culture of overtime, promoting harmonious treatment of workers'.

trivial and benign by the state, we can trace the narratives challenging the contemporary formulation of citizenship which underlies such feelings of alienation.

Another example of challenging the foundation of the current citizenship discourse, this time by critiquing the treatment of rural migrants in the city, is contained in similar theatrical plays put on by NBW. The NGO sees satire as an especially potent way to challenge the current treatment of migrant workers. Indeed, satire is an important tool of political resistance in an authoritarian context as it allows for indirect, and therefore safer, yet still poignant, criticism. The stories of migrant workers in the 2010 play *Life in the City* were selected precisely for their shocking yet borderline absurd quality to give voice to such a formulated critique, which can escape the constraints of political censorship. This is, for example, visible in the scene presenting the treatment of workers by a female Taiwanese factory owner,[10] who welcomes the new employees with the words:

> As most of you come from the countryside, be aware that all your old ways now need to be discarded while you are in the city. I do not want to see any of your rural rubbish around; if I see it, I will throw it away.

The scene clearly exposes the violence performed upon rural identities by critiquing how rural identity is forcefully 'modernised' through urban factory regimes.

In another scene, we see a property developer encouraging migrant workers to help him build a new housing estate for the rich returnee overseas Chinese and the local Beijing-*hukou* holders in the place of the urban village that the company is about to demolish. The angry response follows: 'So now, you want to demolish the migrant village beyond the 5th ring road as well? Is there a place in Beijing that has not been demolished yet?' In this scene, the play's stinging sarcasm is aimed at the capital-fuelled expansion of the fabric of the city through the extraction of migrant workers' labour with a simultaneous physical expropriation from the city.

Similarly, a scene portraying city guards chasing away peddling migrant workers mocks the exclusion of migrant workers through modernisation discourse, *hukou* legislation and the neoliberal project of turning Beijing into a 'global city' to impress 'foreigners', initiated before the Olympic Games of 2008:

> 'In my opinion, the reason for the existence of city guards is to provide jobs for the local *hukou* residents. [Says the street peddler] What is wrong with putting up a street stall? We are just self-employed [*zizhu chuangye*] in answer to the call of our government. Do you think that only if there is no grain of dirt in the city, that the city is now modern and internationalised, and only if the city follows global standards you can save face?'

The play further critiques the formation of 'global cities' in China through the exclusion of the 'unfit' and 'unmodern':

> 'Haven't you heard? They will clear up [*qingli*][11] Beijing for the sake of the Olympics!' [Here a female migrant enters the stage presenting a big sign with the characters '*qingli*' written on it] 'Wait! Please, everybody, pay attention to the key word here: "clear up" [*qingli*]. Have a look at this word, how "civilised" it is, how "humanistic" it is ... how sick it is!'

Here, we can see how the NGO challenges the powerful discourses of modernity and neoliberalism underlying the urbanisation policies in China. Overall, the play is intended to ridicule the presumed superiority of the urban lifestyle and the modernity project which is implemented through the 'discarding of bad rural habits' and 'cleaning the city of dirt'. These artistic forms of resistance challenge the role assigned to migrant workers in citizenship discourse by questioning the understanding of urbanisation as built upon processes of cultural flattening and spatial exclusion from the city.

On the other hand, the museum created by NBW challenges the portrayal of migrant workers as people without culture and in need of being 'civilised'. The museum is intended to present an alternative story of China's reform period, one which centres on migrant workers, and seeks to establish their 'rightful' place in urban China. This commitment is emphasised in the statement on its entrance wall:

> If we do not keep a record of our culture, then there is no record of our history. Without knowing our history, we will not be able to build the future.

The recording of history and culture is aimed at 'challenging' the most entrenched, denigrating images of migrants in popular discourse in China, which portray them as a group of 'low quality' (*suzhi di*) (Murphy, 2004: 14–15) and 'uncivilised' (*bu wenming de*) or 'uneducated/uncultured' (*meiyou wenhua de*) (Fang, 2011: 19) – or people 'without culture' (Woodman, 2017). The NGO sends a clear message that migrant workers actually do have their own 'culture', and it is only not perceived as such, because it lacks representation in the Chinese mainstream. They clearly oppose the *suzhi* discourse here by presenting migrants as culturally different, but equal citizens.

Spatial metaphors also abound in NBW's critique of the 'neoliberal citizenship' discourse. The NGO's reservation towards the narrative of migrants as valuable tools of economic growth is expressed, for instance, in the opening statement in the museum, which while employing the official Party language, is aimed at resisting the current treatment of migrant workers:

> Moving from the countryside to urban areas, migrant workers are the links and bridges [*chengxiang de niudai he qiaoliang*] between the two worlds, and as a new type of labour are the driving forces of China's social progress. They are actually holding up the whole nation [*zhonghua minzu de jiliang*].[12]

In this statement, the image of migrants as peripheral second-class citizens is challenged by putting migrants at the centre of the nation, as its 'backbone' (*jiliang*). Migrants are portrayed through spatial metaphor as bridges, who help to overcome the inequality between rural and urban China. They are therefore portrayed as essential, rather than marginal (as is the case in the official discourse) to the remaking of China towards a more equal and well-off society. As to the neoliberal discourse, NBW, similarly to ET, still refers to the 'due place' of migrants in society, given the contribution they make to national economic growth, but they take this neoliberal narrative a step further, by pointing to other aspects of migrants' contributions beyond their economic relevance. Migrants are not merely the engine of economic growth – once again they are the 'driving force', which 'holds the nation together', and the emphasis is not placed on economic growth, but on social coherence. This view reappears in the song lyrics, theatrical performance and the language the organisation uses to depict migrants.

In the above discussion, we can see that challenging the dominant discourses on migrant workers is aimed at the spatial categories embedded in the dominant citizenship discourse in China, presenting migrant workers as lacking culture, marginal to the nation, culturally 'below' and 'behind' the urban, and only afforded some notion of urban belonging when economically useful or when they 'move forward' towards the modern, urban identity. What NGOs' act of 'challenging' particularly signifies is the shift from treating migrant workers as culturally inferior (*suzhi* discourse), from the *hukou* stratification of society into rural versus urban (*bifurcated citizenship*), and from the commoditised understanding of migrant workers as citizens only if they remain disposable cheap labour (*neoliberal citizen-subjects* discourse).

Constructing 'worker-citizens': remaking the citizenship discourse

The next act, the act of 'constructing', moves beyond criticism of the existing order and seeks to create a new place in society for migrant workers. In order to see how the act of 'constructing' should be seen as transformative, it is first important to understand why and how migrant NGOs seek to reshape migrant workers' identity':[13]

> One of the main aims of our organisation is to develop workers' self-awareness. Migrant workers themselves know that they are labelled as 'workers', but deep inside they do not hold such an identity. They are confused. They know they are called 'workers' but in their head, they live in a separate world, a kind of fantasy that numbs them. They think that this *dagong* fantasy world is their temporary situation; they keep on dreaming that they will turn into a boss one day and they live by this dream. It is a kind of illusion; it does not help you resolve your immediate problems. It actually harms you. The reality is that they have meagre chances to move up the social ladder.[14]

As an antithesis to such a 'numbing illusion', NBW promotes the identity of 'new workers' (*xin gongren*). They call this identity 'new workers' in order to distinguish them from the Maoist-era urban workers (traditionally labelled 'working class' – *gongren jieji*), who were a privileged group in Maoist China (and still remain so, though their number decreased considerably after lay-offs in the SOEs in the 1990s) (Chen, 2010: 144–145). Migrant workers are not officially regarded as part of this formerly privileged group, and in contrast to the 'proper' city workers, they are regarded as 'peasant workers' (*nongmingong*). The label of 'new workers' aims both to question the importance of their rural origin by appealing to the merit of their work instead, and to justify their right to belong to the city as the 'old' working class did. Therefore, even if it is related to a 'worker' identity, it carries the undertones of citizenship claims as it seeks to redraft the spatial imaginary at the heart of citizenship formulation.

Such attempts to construct a new identity, and their connection to citizenship, emerge even more clearly when looking at the attitudes of NBW towards the label of 'peasant workers' (*nongmingong*), as evident in one of the NGO's plays:

> Dear friends, have a good look at this label *nongmingong*. This label marginalises [*bianyuan*] us. It is a modern product emphasising hierarchy. This label should have long been left in the pages of history. We do not like it, so please, don't call us this. You may ask, would it make your life better if you weren't called this? I am telling you here, that [by asking you not to use it] we are basically requesting some respect and equality.
>
> (*Our World, Our Dream*, play, 2009, NBW)

This quotation clearly shows that the NGO regards 'peasant worker' to be a hierarchical label, which entrenches citizenship inequality. Such negative attitudes towards the *nongmingong* label are common among migrant NGOs and the workers. My NBW interviewee regarded the label itself as derogatory and inaccurate (since many so-called 'peasant workers' 'have never actually worked in the fields').[15] Also, both NHC and NBW representatives confirmed that the majority of migrants dislike the label, which has even resulted in considerations by the Guangdong provincial government to abolish the label from its official vocabulary.[16]

However, while such rejection of the '*nongmingong*' label is a sign of resistance against the denigrating attitudes towards 'migrant workers' on the one hand, the NGOs' aversion to the label somehow succumbs to the spatio-temporal hierarchical imaginary discriminating against the rural as 'unfit'. This might be done unwittingly, yet it weakens attempts to remake the citizenship discourse. This conflict is well addressed by the interviewee from NHC:

> I think that these few words sound quite good. Actually, when you think about our lives and what they involve, they make this word sound quite powerful. Yes, there are people who take offence when you call them this name. But there are also some people who think quite independently about it. They think that it does not matter whether you call me a peasant worker [*nongmingong*] or new urban citizen [*xin shimin*]; it's all the same, what matters is what is behind the label, whether we have the same benefits [*liyi*]. In other words, it does not matter whether my *hukou* is a temporary resident or a permanent city resident; if the name on the card is different but all other things are the same, it doesn't really matter.[17]

While the NHC and NBW representatives have different views about the *nongmingong* label, both acknowledged that the material, legal and cultural marginalisation entrenched in the condition of 'peasant workers' is the major issue at play. Rather than rejecting the label, the NHC representative rejects the pejorative connotations linked to it, which seems like an actual attempt to erase the boundary between the rural and urban which is at the heart of the official citizenship discourse in China.

Notwithstanding their different views, both organisations seek not only to challenge the existing social image of migrants but also to replace it with a new, more empowering identity. NHC tends to call migrant workers 'worker-friends' (*gongyou*), 'new urban citizens' (*xin shimin*) and 'new Hangzhouers' (*xin Hangzhouren*). On the other hand, NBW prefers to use names such as 'new citizens' (*xin gongmin*), 'new workers' (*xin gongren*) or 'new labour' (*xin laodong*), 'contingent workers' (*dagongzhe*) or 'external workers' (*waigongrenyuan*). These new labels reveal a dual theme in the construction of the new identity: one centred on legal and spatial 'equality' with urban citizens (labels such as 'new urban citizen', 'new citizen' or 'new Hangzhouer'), and the other which constructs identity around vocational or class belonging ('new worker' or 'contingent worker'). This twin aspiration to be regarded as a worker and a citizen forms the foundation of the newly emerging identity of 'worker-citizen'. Worker-citizens are supposed to identify their interest as 'working people' and at the same time demand to be treated as rightful citizens equal to urban-*hukou* holders. This new identity creates a new spatio-temporal imaginary of migrant workers as having the right to belong to the city notwithstanding their rural origin.

Both NGOs seek to remake the hierarchical spatio-temporal citizenship discourse also by 'demanding respect' for migrant workers' culture. A central element of that culture is labour (and *dagong* more specifically), which they perceive as standing in opposition to the hypermodern and neoliberal values embedded in the urban citizenship discourse in China. The idea of 'respect for labour' is very important to NBW, who feel that the identity of 'worker' was devalued in public discourse in the reform period. The NGO's leading slogan, 'labour is the most glorious' (*laodong zui guangrong*),[18] is a paraphrase of Deng Xiaoping's slogan 'to get rich is glorious'. The intention of the founders of the museum of taking pride and assurance from 'the value of labour' is exemplified by making a tricycle recycling cart – an iconic symbol of migrants' everyday struggle – a centrepiece of the museum's exhibition (see Figure 6.3).

Figure 6.3 The tricycle cart. Left: in New Beijing Workers' museum. Right: as seen on the streets of Beijing, Haidian district in the spring of 2012.

But migrant workers' culture is clearly characterised by more than just 'the value of labour':

> Our culture is not a kind of mainstream culture, which is based on entertainment value. Our culture is a kind of culture of rights, culture of claims ... The values of us migrant workers are working people's values; our culture can also represent our claims ... When our claims are reiterated through the cultural channels and they are publicised, we are able to reach more and more people and allow them to reflect on these issues [we raise].[19]

NBW's understanding of migrant workers' culture as a form of rights activism illustrates the transformative aspect of the act of 'constructing' on citizenship practice. The NGO promotes the expression of migrant culture as a 'culture of claims' by training migrant workers in the use of artistic means (such as photography and film-making) to actively record and reflect on their everyday life.[20] The NGO's Weibo and Weixin accounts are regularly updated with pictures of work and life taken by migrant workers and migrant children. The act of 'constructing' is enabled, rather than directed by the NGO in this case.

Conclusion

We can see that the acts of 'voicing', 'challenging' and 'constructing' performed by some of the NGOs are linked together in an attempt to redraft the dominant citizenship discourse which deprives rural migrants of their voice, figuratively presents them as 'lower quality' citizens, or citizens only when they are economically productive, while excluding them from urban citizenship legally, spatially and economically. Among these acts, 'voicing' serves to open up space to express how such denigration of migrant workers results in their experience of suspension between, and in effect displacement from, both rural and urban. Acts of 'challenging', on the other hand, strive to reject the hierarchical spatio-temporal citizenship discourse and recast those elements in migrant workers' condition which are scorned into a productive and important contribution made by migrant workers as Chinese citizens. 'Constructing' takes this criticism one step further, by recasting these characteristics as part of a unique migrant workers' culture: a culture based on both 'value of labour' and on claims to be recognised as equal and rightful citizens. These acts, therefore, construct an identity of 'new worker-citizens'.

In the previous chapters, I explored this identity with reference to how the use of legal channels, such as labour laws, shapes migrant workers' identity as 'worker-citizens'. However, while the identity of 'worker-citizen' borrows from the socialist 'working class' discourse, it also moves beyond it because it centres its claims on the request for migrants' belonging to the city as equal and rightful citizens. The construction of this identity reshapes migrant workers' role in structural citizenship, because it redrafts the hierarchical spatio-temporal imaginary between rural and urban. The NGOs' stories presented in this chapter also reveal that the migrant workers' culture, which is often perceived as apolitical, and therefore non-transformative, should indeed be seen as enabling the formation of political subjectivity among migrant workers. More than just a form of entertainment or leisure, cultural activities can become a tool of political dialogue and can have empowering qualities. Through the recasting of the history of China's reform period by emphasising the centrality of the migrant worker group, which is silenced, marginalised or manipulated by the mainstream narrative, NGOs help to develop a common identity of a marginalised group seeking to redress the injustice they suffer. In this way, the migrant workers' culture exerts a transformative impact on citizenship formulation in China. Yet, the struggle against the spatial hierarchy embedded in Chinese citizenship must transgress the discursive methods and discursive focus as presented in this chapter in order to fully address migrants' exclusion from the city. The next chapter explores how NGOs address the problem of migrants' spatial exclusion from material belonging to the city and the forms of activism which run within the material fabric of the city itself.

Notes

1 The water buffalo is a symbolic animal of the Chinese countryside.

2 In another poem by the same author, she reflects on the dissociation not just from the city, but also from her native village.

3 This data was supplied by NBW.

4 Mao Zedong's embalmed body lies in state in the mausoleum in the centre of Tiananmen Square.
5 See the final section of the next chapter for more details.
6 For instance, Julia Kwong states that the regular price is about 1,000–2,000 yuan a term (USD 154–309), which is a very high sum for most migrant workers (Kwong, 2011: 874).
7 Interview no. 5.
8 Interview no. 19.
9 NHC, like many others in this study, uses slogans which, while criticising the mistreatment of workers in China (in the form of 'overtime culture'), at the same time seek to incorporate Party language by the use of words such as 'promoting harmonious treatment of labour' to emphasise its support for the state – the strategy I label 'resistance through accommodation' in this book.
10 Taiwanese-owned factories have a rather grim reputation in China (as compared to 'Western'-owned factories) (Interview no. 17; Chan and Wang, 2004), with some of the most famous cases of resistance and strikes in recent history, such as the Foxconn suicides and the Yu Yuan strike, all taking place in Taiwanese-owned factories.
11 The characters of the word '清理*qingli*' clearly depict the word's embeddedness in the modernity discourse: 清*qing* means 'clean', while 理*li* means 'to order, to control'. As Arendt (1951) and Bauman (1989) argue, these values are integral to the modernity discourse, and bear dehumanising potential. The *suzhi* discourse, which points to the inferior position of migrant workers vis-à-vis the 'proper' urban citizens discourse, is one manifestation of the implementation of this modernisation project in China (as discussed in the introduction).
12 The translation is that of the museum.
13 I use the notion of 'worker identity' instead of 'class consciousness' because the notion of class is quite conflicted in the case of China (see Lee (2007) and Chan (2012b) for comparison on this). Migrant workers and NGO staff I interviewed do not use the word 'class' (*jieji*) to describe themselves. In fact, when talking to the NBW representative, who not only holds avowedly socialist (if not Maoist) sentiments, but also uses words like 'capitalist' and 'working people', he described his personal self-transformation from 'rural' to 'migrant worker group' identity (*dagong qunti*), rather than 'working class' (Interview no. 5). The notion of 'class' appears to be conflicted and confusing in the context of post-Communist China due to the idea having been previously used to depict city workers. Consequently, I prefer to employ the notion of 'identity', which is a wider concept that might also include the elements

of workers' solidarity to which the notion of 'class consciousness' appeals.

14 Interview no. 5.

15 Interview no. 5.

16 Interview no. 5.

17 Interview no. 9.

18 In a song version, the band sings '*Dagong dagong* is the most glorious'.

19 Interview no. 5.

20 See Sun (2014) for further discussion on the training and cultural activities of the NGO.

7

From urban exclusion to urban transformation

In November 2017, a fire claimed nineteen lives in an overcrowded building in Daxing, one of the most densely migrant-inhabited districts of Beijing. Shortly afterwards, an estimated 100,000 migrant workers labelled as 'low-end population' were thrown out into the bitter Beijing winter as urban villages in Daxing and other parts of the city were razed in the forty-day crackdown on 'illegal housing' (Phillips, 2017). The city authorities justified the destruction of urban villages, as in previous cases of similar removal, on the grounds of 'safety'. Yet, this 'clean-up' of migrant workers continued a process of gentrification and expulsion initiated much earlier by the municipal governments: it was simply the most recent event in the chain of the Beijing authorities' decisions to further the long-standing plan of turning the capital into a global city with no place for low-income population.

The demolition of urban villages in Daxing is just one example of how citizenship exclusion manifests not only discursively, but also materially, in migrant workers' experience of urban China. This chapter focuses on the NGOs' response to the material forms of that exclusion, and it therefore builds on Chapter 1's discussion of municipal policies towards migrant workers in relation to urban redevelopment. By investigating acts of citizenship around the material remaking of the city, it reveals how the city can be transformed from 'spaces of (citizenship) exclusion' to 'spaces of (citizenship) transformation'. A great part of this process is triggered by the desire to belong to the city, which stems from the migrants' long-term residence in the urban environment, but also from self-perception of their cultural and material contribution to the city.

In this chapter I discuss two acts which are particularly relevant to the remaking of citizenship around material inclusion in the city: the act of 'integrating' into the city and the act of 'claiming' the right to the city. An act of 'integrating' does not always challenge citizenship, and many NGOs are caught in the struggle between implementing the state vision of integration, and promoting integration which is more supportive of migrants' true needs. As this chapter shows, the state-prescribed form of integration promotes superficial markers of inclusion, such as 'cultural uniformity' between the rural and urban populations, which actually helps to sustain the current, hierarchical and exclusive citizenship formulation. Some NGOs succumb to this aspect of integration in their attempts to gain the state's acceptance and funders' support. However, I also reveal other forms of how NGOs struggle for more equitable integration projects which are responsive to the workers' material claims to the city space. When discussing the act of 'claiming' I adopt Henri Lefebvre's idea of 'the right to the city', by which he meant access to various rights of urban citizenship, such as access to political participation in decision-making forums, access to housing and clean water, social inclusion, recognition, but also the right to shape cities' policies, and even architecture (Lefebvre, 1996; Harvey, 2012, 2008). As I discuss in this chapter, the concept of the 'right to the city' can be employed to account for the claims of migrant workers – which include claims concerning rights to housing, spatial and social inclusion, work, recognition, representation and respect – to be accepted and included in the city as equal citizens. Both acts adopt forms of interaction with material spaces of the city which turn them into 'spaces of transformation'. This concept of spaces of transformation borrows much from Lefebvre's idea of 'representational spaces' (Lefebvre, 1991), that is spaces which are imagined or reappropriated with the aim of changing the dominant modes of spatial production defining the forms of urban belonging and citizenship.

Integrating into the city

The official approach to 'integration into the city' (*rongru chengshi*) is part of the wider policies of turning Chinese cities into 'global cities' discussed in Chapter 1. While the concept is only vaguely

Figure 7.1 'Behaving in the civilised manner starts from myself'. As seen on the streets of Beijing (note migrant women sitting in front of the sign) in 2015.

defined by the government, the campaigns and slogans visible in public spaces in Chinese cities shed a light on what is understood by the concept. From these campaigns, it is clear that the idea of 'integration into the city', with the repeated phrases encouraging city residents to 'adopt civilised [*wenming*] behaviour' and become 'polite citizens' (see Figures 7.1 and 7.2), follows the wider policy of *shiminhua* discussed in Chapter 1, which aims at 'civilising' migrant workers into urban citizenship.

While these slogans are visible to all residents in the city, it became clear to me during my internship in BWH that they are particularly targeted at migrant workers, as local governments enlist migrant NGOs to help spread the message. For instance, from as early as 2012, BWH has been receiving various educational materials from the Beijing Propaganda Bureau (the playing cards in Chapter 3 are one example), including a range of leaflets which adopt the exact same messages as the propaganda banners in Figures 7.1 and 7.2, with the clear purpose of expecting the NGO to forward these to

Figure 7.2 'Build a civilised city'. As seen in Hangzhou bus station in 2012.

migrant workers. In 2013 the NGO was tasked with distributing leaflets entitled 'Promote the Beijing Spirit: Making a Civilised, Polite Beijinger' (see Figure 7.3) promoting the use of 'three civilised phrases' ('thank you', 'I am sorry' and 'hello') and 'four civilised acts' ('politeness', 'helping the elderly', 'queuing' and 'recycling') as emblematic of Beijing's spirit. The implicit message was that for migrant workers to fit in the city, they should adopt such 'civilised' behaviours, even though the 'three civilised phrases' are quite alien to traditional Chinese culture so ardently promoted by Xi's campaign of 'moral education' (Erbaugh, 2008: 631).

Therefore, the idea of 'integration in the city' clearly carries undertones of a 'civilising mission', cognate with the *shiminhua* strategy. As such, the slogan reinforces the dominant citizenship discourse, which ultimately seeks to transform migrant workers into 'proper' citizens: urban, modern and 'civilised'. However, as in the case of the production of more inclusive discourses on migrant workers in official museum exhibitions, the official approach does not address the roots of material and social marginalisation of migrant

Figure 7.3 'Promote Beijing spirit; Becoming a civilised, polite Beijinger'.

workers in the cities, but rather intends to change migrants culturally to fit within the agenda of producing hypermodern, visually uniform and pristine cities, geared towards global competition.

The way NGOs interact with this officially promoted idea of 'integration into the city' takes both discursive and material forms: sometimes accommodating to and sometimes resisting the official understanding of 'integration into the city'. One such way in which NGOs undertake acts of integration starts from quite a different place than the official discourse would like to see it: from producing material spaces of belonging to the city.

NGOs as spaces of belonging and self-transformation

Unlike the official approach to integration understood primarily as a cultural process, NGOs often recognise the importance of the material forms of belonging, as more relevant to migrant workers. One such form of materially helping the process of integration is the production of spaces of belonging in the city. In order to redirect migrant workers' orientation towards life in the city and to help them belong to it in a more tangible sense than through just the verbal attempts at recasting the discursive element of citizenship, many NGOs seek to create their own 'spaces of belonging' to the city through community-building practices. These NGOs' community centres provide migrant workers with established meeting places in the city (usually in urban villages), and form a base where migrants can feel like they are included in the city. While these places are often of limited outreach, usually only catering for migrants in the given urban village, and they might be treated pragmatically, they nevertheless create a sense of belonging and community, which in some cases changes migrants' relationship to the city.

Informality is the hallmark of NGOs' spaces of belonging. In contrast to the government-run labour aid centres and quasi-GONGOs' official approach, the NGOs seek to make their meeting places friendly and intimate. The informality seems to provide a platform for a greater sense of belonging, because it allows migrants to feel equal and engaged in building the organisation. A comparison between LHC and the migrant worker-established NGOs is a case in point. LHC, though officially an NPO, is a legal advice organisation with close personal links to the party-state (it was set up by the head of one of the departments in ACLA under the Beijing Municipal Judicial Bureau, and uses government-provided lawyers to represent migrants in court). However, the organisation's environment differs greatly from the spirited and welcoming atmosphere of NHC, NBW, IMH and other NGOs' premises. The stark interior of its building contrasts with the colourful and picture-filled, family-like atmosphere of the grassroots organisations. Similarly, its bare walls, office desks and the backdoor office with very limited access (I was requested not to follow my interviewee into the office) form an atmosphere like a public office. The way the organisation's staff interact with migrants also differs from what I observed in other organisations: the desk separating migrants and lawyers, and the lawyers typing in the details of migrants' cases in an office-like manner, seem to especially strongly mimic the hierarchical and bureaucratic relationship between office clerks and applicants. It is reminiscent of the government-run public labour aid centres (*laodong zhan*) which are now proliferating, particularly in Shenzhen, as part of the state-introduced 'legal aid' system to resolve labour conflicts (Halegua, 2016: 27–28). These agencies were described by MWU and UA interviewees as 'unfriendly' and 'intimidating' to migrant workers:

> Migrants don't really feel supported by these agencies. The feeling you get there is very formal … these posh tables and chairs make you feel like you can't even sit down, you feel like 'oh, I am dirty'. So, no one feels comfortable there.[1]

Indeed, other studies confirm that migrant workers distrust government-run legal aid centres, and their staff are often underperforming and can even be ignorant about migrant workers' eligibility for legal aid (Halegua, 2016: 28–29). NGOs fill the gap that the government did not manage to adequately cover with the official legal centres. Apart from greater commitment to resolving legal cases (Halegua, 2016: 28), grassroots NGOs are also much better at providing workers with a nourishing environment for their overall integration into the city.

This nourishing environment is experienced through NGOs' everyday interactions with migrants. During my three-month-long fieldwork in BWH, I witnessed many encounters between migrant workers and NGOs, which struck me as providing a sense of comfort and understanding:

> Two people came to the office. They were welcomed with a mug of lukewarm water. Two regular employees handle their case. This discussion over their case lasts a long time [over 2 hours]. There is a spirit of trust, and the workers are not shy in their claims – they present their cases with strength and stand up for themselves. They do not seem like victims – more so, like people talking to their equals.[2]

And another:

> GL [a pro bono lawyer working for the NGO] is asking how much they're earning. One says that it varies; he pulled 200 yuan yesterday, today just 10 … when GL talks about how they will deal with the boss he acts out the sound of a whip being unleashed … it makes the migrants laugh … GL pats one migrant on the back in a friendly gesture and the overall happiness ensues.[3]

Some migrants visiting BWH openly complained about their bosses, gruelling working conditions and illegal practices in their workplaces. The topics included personal issues, such as hardships of life in the city, the pain of being parted from children, a husband's alcoholism or parents' illness. After the formalities of a particular legal problem were discussed, some of the migrants, if they were willing, were then taken to a separate room where a female employee, Ms Qin, herself a Yao minority migrant from Yunnan, conducted in-depth interviews with the workers. By the time I spoke to Ms Qin about her working experience, she had already interviewed two hundred migrants. I also witnessed Ms Qin taking an interview on a few occasions:

> Her lead of the conversation is admirable and she has a great deal of empathy ... In order to relax and ease her interviewee into the conversation she first tells them her own story or other people's stories, to make them feel like they have a shared experience. She makes the interview process positive and makes her interviewees feel good.[4]

It is important to note that the informality, so important in the formation of spaces of belonging, relies on the particular, gendered division of roles within the organisations. In BWH the male workers dealt with legal action and mediation, while the female employees, such as Ms Qin, were in charge of a more holistic and empathetic approach to migrant workers coming to the office or, like Ms Xu, were the NGO's 'external face' in fund procurement activities, showing an approachable and friendly face of the organisation. I also found the effects of this gendered character of services provided by NGOs among the women-run organisations, such as MWU and ET. These NGOs paid a lot of attention to the well-being and psychological comfort of migrant workers visiting their organisations. The gendered division of tasks seemed to be important to cater for the complex needs of migrant workers, both material and non-material, but it also reinforced the traditional attitudes to the social role of women as caterers.

As to the material construction of the spaces of belonging, this is often achieved through the location of the premises of NGOs in parts of the city directly accessible to migrant workers and the decoration of their interiors in a 'welcoming' fashion. As one enters the premises of NHC, NBW, IMH or AC in particular, what is striking to a newcomer is their home-like character: the inviting interiors with sofas, chairs and pictures on the walls, with all areas open to migrant workers to visit whenever they feel like it. For instance, NHC has a cosy little library for relaxing and a computer

Figure 7.4 Injured Migrants' Home's legal advice centre.

room to allow migrants access to the internet, while at Foshan-based IMH, which has two sites (a cultural and a legal advice centre), like NHC the walls are adorned with pictures of the migrants who participate in the community life centred around the NGO (see Figure 7.4).

The creation of 'spaces of belonging' is not only limited to material places and interactions with migrant workers: it also relies on the particular language that the organisations use. One example of this is the way NGOs seek to redefine the notion of 'home' into a more deterritorialised feeling of belonging to a group, for which they employ the common identity of worker-citizen, as discussed in the previous chapter. NBW does this especially forcefully by constructing this new identity through identification with other migrant workers as 'one family'. They do it first through the introduction of the word *jia* (meaning both 'family' and 'home') in their names (this practice is used by other NGOs as well, for example NHC and JM).[5] NBW and NHC also use the word throughout their activities, artistic objects and texts. For instance, a painting welcoming visitors to the premises of NBW, which is also used as a cover for many of the NGO's publications, represents migrant workers sitting in a circle on the ground surrounded by construction cranes and watching a cultural performance by the musicians who formed the organisation. The inscription within the painting states 'All migrant workers under heaven are one family' (*Tianxia dagong shi yi jia*). Similarly, NHC treats everybody who visits their centre 'like family': 'We are all just like family, like brothers and sisters.'[6] This family-like identity is also traceable in the use of the notion of 'worker-friend' (*gongyou*), which is perhaps the most frequent name for migrant workers used by NGOs. This word not only relates to the common identity of a 'worker', but also emphasises belonging to a community of friends/kin. This equation between 'home' and the community of friends/family and workers makes the idea of home deterritorialised and detached from the material foundation, which responds to migrants' inability to attain a material home.

The centres are commonly run based on principles of volunteerism and 'mutual aid' which further contribute to the formation of spaces of belonging. The ideal of mutual aid is the driving force behind migrants' active participation in the organisation's activities. Mutual aid is linked to citizenship and space in that it is a form of activist citizenship which remakes relationships between migrants in the alienating urban space, recreating the safety of rural kinship-like relations by showing migrants that they belong to one family. As such, mutual aid is enacted through the everyday encounters between migrant workers within the NGO. For NHC, mutual aid is empowering because it helps to change one's self-perception and the feeling of alienation:

> A lot of migrants have a feeling of inferiority ... we are quite candid about it with each other ... We want to help each other understand what our aims and needs are ... then, if we notice that somebody does not cope well, we will all try to help him. If that person then comes across other people who need help (s)he will help them as well.[7]

From the above quotation, we can see that mutual aid appears as the driver behind activist citizenship. It is also a leading factor in bringing about self-empowerment. MWU also emphasises the importance of networks as spaces which allow for empowerment through mutual aid:

> We are building networks, helping migrants to meet with each other, share stories, feelings and experiences. They will then think 'oh, there is somebody supporting me!' and then they would have this 'collective feeling'. Also, when visiting injured migrants in the hospitals, we do

> not employ professional counsellors. We find it much more effective if the workers who experienced injury themselves go to the hospital and talk to the workers. It is authentic and brings a real relief to them … You just need to help them understand what their rights are and also that it [the injury] is not their fault and to inform them that every person should get compensation or treatment for free. This is the idea of mutual support![8]

Here, mutual help is effective in spreading legal rights consciousness, an important aspect of empowering migrants as citizens. In many cases, such self-empowerment then leads to the desire to spread the knowledge and skills, and results in further instances of mutual help. As such, both the physical premises and the deterritorialised networks which the NGOs enable are important foundations of creating a sense of belonging within the city, allowing for the formation of new civic practices and activist forms of citizenship. In this way, acts of 'integrating' differ quite dramatically from the state-promoted concept of 'integration into the city'.

Integration our way

However, some NGOs do not seek to reinvent the concept of 'integration' in this way. When analysing NGOs' efforts at integration beyond the safe spaces of community and familiar networks, one which is linked to migrants' wider relationship to the city, some NGOs appear to take on board the state-promoted understanding of 'integration into the city' by either adopting the state-prescribed discourse of integration, or regurgitating the *shiminhua* narrative embedded within it. Despite their vocal attempts to resist the marginalisation of migrant workers, they also end up internalising the *suzhi* discourse, by pointing to the need for migrant workers to acquire certain 'civilised' characteristics to cope in the city. They often, perhaps unwittingly, promote the idea of the 'neoliberal citizen-subject' too. However, some NGOs use the state concept of 'integration into the city' in a 'resistance through accommodation' manner. They gladly incorporate the 'integration into the city' rhetoric in their mission statements, but they do this to legitimise various training courses and publications, many of which actually go beyond the state-prescribed idea of 'integration into the city' (Jakimów, 2017). Sometimes NGOs do both and change their strategies, alternating between these two approaches, and therefore their activism's impact on citizenship is difficult to judge.

BWH, for instance, is a case in point. As discussed in the previous section, the NGO participates in the distribution of government-published information packages and leaflets, such as the one educating migrant workers on 'the civilised ways of behaving in the city' (see Figure 7.3 above). The adoption of such understanding of 'integration' is also visible in the NGO's 'Integration into the City Manual', which refers back to the Confucian-like importance of fulfilling one's social role and adopts the modernist approach to citizenship as a process of becoming 'urban and modern'.[9] In this sense, the NGO is highly complicit in maintaining the dominant citizenship discourse on migrant workers' place in urban China.

Yet, notwithstanding the narratives BWH employs, the aim of their 'Manual' is indeed mainly to give practical advice to migrant workers on what to expect in Beijing, how to look for jobs, and how to utilise the law to protect themselves (including information on relevant labour laws and the employer's obligations). While the NGO does not encourage migrant workers to undertake collective action in their workplaces, it does see the possibility for migrant workers to become more empowered in the cities by simply being able to access the relevant resources (ranging from government-sponsored institutions such as the Labour Bureau to how to use public toilets). Such promotion of the idea of the informed and self-empowered citizen, who does not need to rely on the social system to provide him/her with rights of citizenship, regurgitates the state intentions behind the 'integration into the city' slogan – of turning migrants not only into culturally 'modern, urban citizens', but also into 'neoliberal citizen-subjects'. However, in conversation with me, the NGO's founder expressed some frustration stemming from the lack of state support to NGOs undertaking such training on migrants' self-empowerment, and completely abandoning migrant workers to fend for themselves:[10]

> They [migrant workers] need NGOs like ours to help them, to provide training ... also, the government should provide training to them ... like our training on how to integrate into the city, to help them get to know this city, to help them to get to know their own selves [*renshi ziji*], so when they have a problem they know who to turn to, where to find the resources, where to find the strength [*liliang*] to help

> themselves ... So that they are able to rely on themselves [*kao ziji*]. It is very tough for them to constantly go through the ordeal by themselves; it takes a lot of time to become self-reliant. So, they really need some external help ... but the government evidently has not done anything like this.[11]

Therefore, while the NGO clearly supports the state's policies, it says that the policy itself is not implemented sufficiently by the state, but relies on actors like NGOs to put it into action. While the NGO sees the production of the 'neoliberal citizen-subject' as a necessary prerequisite for migrants' integration into the city, it still criticises the lack of state-provided training and assistance for migrant workers to become such citizens. This approach does not easily fit within either the 'resistance through accommodation' or the simple succumbing to the state narrative, as while it supports the state-defined ideal of citizenship that migrant workers should attain, it criticises the fact that migrants are left to their own devices in this process and do not receive enough support from the government.

While BWH mainly promotes the central government-prescribed 'civilisation mission' embedded in the *shiminhua* and the *suzhi* discourse, and only occasionally incorporates a more critical stance towards it, some other NGOs have a more fundamental (and more socially, materially and legally inclined) understanding of the idea of integration into the city. What is interesting and perhaps different in NHC's activities is its two-way form of promoting integration: integrating does not only mean that the migrants should adapt to the city, but also that the local city residents could participate in the process of mutual integration by joining the NGO's activities:

> Our activities are orientated towards the local community [*shequ*], the neighbourhood of Hangzhou where our organisation is located. We don't have any barriers related to status; migrant workers or local people are all welcomed into our centre to watch our spectacle and participate. When it comes to acting [on stage], there is no division between local residents and migrant workers [*waidiren*]. We spend festivals together. Even the local security guards [*minbing*, *bao'an*] join our festivals and we all celebrate together ... These kinds of cultural activities result in a greater social dialogue and enable the presentation of our worker-friends' [*gongyou*] culture [*fengmao*] to the city residents; it presents that we are an active and healthy group.[12]

Moreover, in NHC's publications we read that 'integration into the city' is not just a matter of 'acculturation' (which is the way the integration is promoted by the state), but also a question of relations between the city-*hukou* population and the 'newcomers':

> The 'New Hangzhouers' has become a popular name for us these past years ... But what price do we have to pay to be treated equally with the city residents? This decision is not ours to make, but we keep on fighting for it ... Our organisation is aiming to create this model of how new (urban) citizens [*xin shimin*] can integrate into the city ... From your words and letters, we feel that the dream to 'integrate into the city' is still far away from coming true, that you don't even dare to think it can be possible ... even though this is the case, worker-friends [*gongyou*] all work very hard fighting for it ... And the city, is the city ready for us? What attitude does the city have towards us? Does it understand us, care for us, help us, support us? Is it ready to provide us with justice?[13]

The NGO recognises the importance of the material aspects of integration. In its internal publications, it gives voice to migrant workers who criticise the government-promoted idea of 'integration into the city' as acculturation, and the absence of state policies to allow migrant workers to belong to the city in a spatial and material sense:

> 'Integrating into the city', for me, is a very distant [possibility]. Everybody wants to 'integrate into the city', but it is not so easy. Concretely speaking, one has to at least have a stable job; otherwise life in the city is too hard. When it comes to adaptation to life in the city, this is possible with one's own effort. But to think of putting down roots [*zhagen*] in Hangzhou, at present, I don't even dare think about it. Let alone to buy a flat ... It is hard enough to rent a flat: you always have to cohabit with other people. If one starts a family, then the pressure is even greater ... integrating into the city is indeed a very far-fetched dream.[14]

The migrant understands 'integration into the city' clearly as a material ability to belong, which questions the government-promoted understanding of 'integration into the city' as primarily a cultural construct demanding that migrant workers be culturally 'turned into citizens'. As the letter above reveals, this focus obscures the material foundations of one's ability to belong to the city, and the importance of access to material space.

NHC, and as discussed earlier in the chapter, NBW, clearly understand 'integration into the city' as 'attaining the right to be treated equally' and 'attaining the right to the city space'. These interpretations of the slogan have not been propagated by the government at any stage of its use of the concept 'integration into the city'. NBW seems not to include the concept in their activities, as they view it as derogatively close to treating migrant workers as the 'uncivilised outsiders'. However, even NBW promotes the general idea of integration as inclusion, and it does so within the government-prescribed means and language. Yet the difference between the NGOs' deployments of the term is revealing of their struggle between 'managing' their relations with the government and empowering migrant workers.

The way that the NGOs' act of 'integrating' impacts migrant workers' citizenship varies between organisations, and even within one organisation. While some NGOs clearly regurgitate the state-promoted idea of what kind of citizen migrant workers should become, they strive to enable migrant workers to become active citizens. However, some NGOs question the state-promulgated idea of 'integration' as 'acculturation', and instead promote the two-way process of integration of migrant workers: one which also accepts the newcomers with their different identities, walks of life and culture, and especially highlights the need for their material participation in the fruits of urbanisation. Indeed, the promotion of migrants' integration and the discussion of the concept is not enough for some other NGOs, and these organisations tend to go further, and to actually claim the migrants' right to the city.

Claiming the right to the city: from resisting demolitions to circumventing the *hukou* system

'Claiming the right to the city' is another act which stems from the experience of cities as 'spaces of exclusion' and directly engages with both the material and legal aspects of that exclusion. At the material level, the idea of 'claiming the right to the city' is signified through the activism of MVD. MVD is a small, informal, Beijing-based, family-run grassroots organisation. The married couple who set it up are themselves migrants from Shaanxi and Hebei provinces,

Figure 7.5 The nursery inside the Migrant Village Defenders premises (later moved to a new urban village).

and they run the organisation with help from other migrants and volunteer university students. All the NGO's activities were initially located in their single-storey house in the middle of a migrant-inhabited urban village in Haidian district, north-west Beijing. The building originally contained a nursery for migrant children (see Figure 7.5) and an information hotline for migrant workers. Later, after the demolition of the urban village, the nursery was moved to the new migrant village further out in the outskirts of Beijing, and the hotline was closed due to the loss of migrant networks.[15]

The very location of the NGO's premises seemed symbolic of the spirit of perseverance. The view of this lone house surrounded by the guarded neighbourhood, where the modern blocks of flats are fenced off and securitised, typical of Beijing middle-class areas, is reminiscent of the inequality and spatial divisions between Beijing residents and migrant workers (see Figure 7.6). However, what makes this particular house especially relevant for this story is the fact that it is the only house left standing in the village. When I enquired how this was possible, the migrant couple told me that when the developers came to demolish the house, they physically defended

Figure 7.6 The house rented by Migrant Village Defenders in the demolished urban village, 2012.

it, standing in the way of the bulldozers. They also recorded the fight, and then posted it on Youku (a Chinese version of YouTube) and in the organisation's profile on Sina Blog. All the inhabitants of the village except MVD were forced to move further to the fringes of the Haidian district after the village was demolished, but this vocal couple remained. Though they seemed to have come to terms with the fact that their move, too, is unavoidable, I could not help but perceive a feeling of indignation still pulsing underneath the surface of their hospitality. They walked me around the ruins of the urban village showing me, for example, the torn-down walls of what clearly used to be a teenager's bedroom, still adorned with posters of Chinese pop stars, now exposed to the elements, which left an eerie impression of lost community and shattered dreams.

Because of the demolition of the original site, MVD moved their kindergarten activities to the new migrant village, where most of the migrant workers relocated. On my visit to that 'new village' I noticed many buildings with a character *chai* (for demolish) already painted on them, and when I enquired, it emerged that indeed this 'new' migrant village was also scheduled for demolition. The NGO's defence of their rented house and NBW's criticism of the demolitions discussed in the previous chapter are rare examples of attempting to interrupt the cycle of constant moving. They also illustrate these organisations' demands to be granted a right to a more permanent belonging to the city. Since the right to housing for migrant workers is not guaranteed, and access to housing depends largely on the individual's financial ability (or the possession of an urban *hukou*), by voicing these demands, the NGOs put forward a claim to a new kind of right to city space: the right to housing.

The restrictions on public health and education imposed by the *hukou* system are another major element in the NGOs' strategy of claiming the right to the city. To respond to the unequal access to education, NGOs design ways to claim the right to social rights, such as education and hospitalisation, not simply by breaching the *hukou* system, but more often by transgressing the material and psychological constraints that result from the combined impact of the *hukou* administration, the modernisation project and the influence of the capitalist market. They do so by, for instance, setting up alternative private schools, which cater for the migrant population in the absence of public schooling, or by collecting money for the hospitalisation of migrant workers in need.

Several NGOs I interviewed had set up their own community centres for migrant children or even their own schools. As previously mentioned, MVD has been running a nursery for migrant children, first in the house they rented in the village which was demolished, and then in the migrant village further towards the outskirts of Haidian district where the migrants had moved. The organisation had very limited funds to maintain the nursery, and sought support from the local government, without much success.[16]

Similarly, AC also created community-based after-school care for migrant children. The organisation was set up in 2006 by graduates of the Beijing Normal University (themselves originating from the countryside) with help from the university's teachers. At the time of the fieldwork, the NGO was located in a migrant village on the outskirts of the Changping district, beyond the fifth ring road. In 2013, the population of the village was 40,000 migrant workers, mostly employed in some type of service job (such as running small shops, street stalls or cleaning the local residents' flats). AC acted as a children's centre, enabling migrants to leave their children under the NGO's care when going to work. Apart from providing daily care and education, the NGO also conducted an activity called 'Reuniting with the countryside', where migrant children and local-*hukou* children were invited to go together to the nearby countryside for weekend activities – another example of the 'two-way integration' process. The NGO operated with quiet consent from the local government, but had no contacts with the state as such, and its funding came from both foreign and domestic foundations. The NGO cooperated closely with a private school for migrant children in the same urban village. In 2013, the school was run by migrant worker teachers (including these from the NGO) and student volunteers from Beijing University. That year alone, around 1,000 migrant children attended the classes there, paying RMB 1,000 (USD 154) a semester, which is much less pricey than the 'regular' private schools in Beijing. As of 2018, the village was targeted for removal, but the NGO still operated there.

NBW also runs a school for migrant children, founded with the income from the organisation's first album. In September 2012, the local government ordered the school to close. At the time the closure notice was issued, a total of 6,300 children had been educated in the school since its opening, and the number of current students was 660; the entire migrant village's youngest generation was supported by the school. As discussed in the previous chapter, for many of these children, themselves born and raised in Beijing, a return to the countryside – the only place where they could access schools for free – seemed a painful and scary prospect. In 2012, NBW defied the government's decision and took an extremely brave stance to continue schooling. In the process of defending their right to run the school, NBW mobilised its national and international networks of support. For instance, as the school continued operation, the local government cut off its water supply, to which the NGO responded by publicly asking inhabitants in the village and more widely in Beijing for water. Some other NGOs I interviewed, for instance MWU from Shenzhen, were familiar with and sympathetic towards NBW's situation.[17] Six months after the order to close the school was issued, classes were still being held, although, as the representative told me during the interview, 'we are always scared the school might be just arbitrarily closed any day'.[18] Indeed, as of 2019, the village is under constant threat of forced demolition, with neighbouring villages already razed. NBW has been under threat of closure for years, with most notably the forced closure notice issued by the local government in 2016. Yet, as of 2019, it was still operating in the village.

Setting up schools is a fragile act of citizenship, constantly subjected to the state's violence. The local government can easily close down migrant schools and interpret the collection of funds as embezzlement if they wish to undertake a crackdown on civil society groups, or simply if they seek to demolish the village for redevelopment. The September 2011 and August 2017 closures of migrant schools in Beijing provide one example of such arbitrary crackdowns (Jiang, 2011; *The Economist*, 2011; China Network Television, 2011; Huang and Han, 2017). The reason for the authorities' decision on those closures was not transparent; the usual argument given by local officials is that the schools' premises violated safety standards. However, a common observation is that the destruction of the schools is usually a prelude to the demolition of an entire urban village for new property development,[19] or, as a recent trend has it, to clear space for grassland and forests. The plans are for only sixty private schools for migrant children to remain in Beijing by 2020, out of 500 in the early 2010s (Huang and Han, 2017).

Several migrant worker NGOs have also undertaken attempts to mitigate the lack of access to healthcare. When a 23 year-old migrant worker from Anhui province fell ill with kidney disease, NHC helped to collect 100,000 yuan for his kidney transplant. They collected the funds among the population living in Hangzhou by performing in front of shops and setting up a bazaar with books and magazines. In this process of fundraising, the regulated and controlled city space became suddenly spaces of transformation, where the urban citizens could join migrant workers in their fight for another worker's access to healthcare. Yet, fundraising can fall on particularly sensitive ground in China. Public attitudes towards charity organisations are marked by distrust, which makes the state's ability to crack down on civic activism even more easily justified. An example of how fundraising activities can be easily used against organisations was the December 2015 arrest of the founder of IMH on charges of embezzlement. Some Chinese citizens I spoke to about the incident sided with the state, distrusting the 'benevolence' of the NGO. The fundraising attempts, similarly to setting up schools in the city, point to a dramatic problem with citizenship rights in China, and are examples of collective expressions of the spirit of mutual help which drives migrants' determination to find ways to circumvent the limitations of the *hukou* system.

As such, 'claiming the right to the city' should be regarded as one of the most daring acts of citizenship. It engages with the material and legal aspects of migrants' marginalisation in the city, both linked to their citizenship. Through resisting demolitions NGOs demand the right to a home in the city, and by circumventing the *hukou* system via setting up their own schools and collecting healthcare funds they claim rights to education and healthcare in the city. It is through this act that we find the inextricable connection between the citizenship discourse and regime and its embeddedness in the material fabric of the city. This act is performed through the use of city spaces in productive ways (the NGOs' premises, artistic activities, the communities, the networks, the buildings and the streets), and as such can be understood to turn city spaces into 'spaces of transformation'.

Conclusion

The city has always occupied a special place in the theorisation of citizenship. As discussed in Chapter 1, Max Weber's theory solidified the now contested belief in the urban as the only space where citizenship could be formed (Weber, 1930, 1963). Engin Isin (2002, 2009) showed that even when citizenship became equated with nationality and belonging to the state rather than the city, the characteristics of urban citizenship were retained in the characteristics of state citizenship (Isin, 2009: 374–375). Contemporarily, urban spaces are still linked to the formation of citizenship in the world, as the shrinking of space and time in modern cities leads to qualitatively different negotiations of citizenship than the processes which take place in rural areas or at the level of the nation state. Cities, rather than the nation state, are viewed as key nodes in the 'post-national' world, as they are the setting where citizenship is being remade through increase in networking speed and the variety of cultures, languages, allegiances and identities of groups within the city raising new claims for rights (Castells, 2000 [1996]; Harvey, 2012).

Chinese cities also provide new and unprecedented opportunities for the remaking of citizenship. Acts of citizenship are especially prominent in urban spaces, as these provide the environment in which the existing institutional forms of citizenship are questioned through 'experimentation with identities and cosmopolitan belonging' (Isin and Nielsen, 2008: 8). Migrants play a pivotal role in this dynamic, because as newcomers they bring the variety of identities, material positions and allegiances into the city and are both a subject and a distinct motor of transformative processes occurring in urban spaces. Migrants' self-organisation and group self-assertion can be viewed as a decisive step in designing ways to benefit from the city's possibilities for the restructuring of their position in society, often by issuing a call for the 'right to the city' (Qian and He, 2012; Ren, 2012). But, apart from this type of activism which directly puts forward claims to the 'right to the city', there are also forms of migrants' interaction with urban spaces, which lead to new forms of inclusion into the urban, going beyond the established forms of citizenship as legally recognised acquisition of urban *hukou* or the state-promoted notion of *shiminhua*. These can include quotidian practices of migrants' sojourning in the city spaces from which they are normally excluded and then identifying with them (Kochan, 2019: 11); interactions with 'microscopic places' within the city, such as cultural centres; as well as the projection of ideological commonality between migrants' own values and those projected through the city image, which they come across in such microscopic places (Qian and Zhu, 2014: 97).

Similarly to the existing studies mentioned above, this chapter has also traced interactions with spaces in the city, but I focused on the cases where NGOs turn these spaces into 'spaces of citizenship transformation'. These spaces are both material places directly present in the city and reappropriated (urban villages, streets and factories) or created anew by NGOs (such as physical NGO premises, cultural places of performance or NGO-created and supported schools for migrant children), and also deterritorialised spaces of networks and virtual (online) spaces of communication. It is through these spaces that NGOs question, challenge and eventually transform migrants' citizenship exclusion from the city. In this way, the performance of acts of 'integrating' and 'claiming' can transform the former exclusive character of urban spaces into spaces which are the containers of new, 'mobile' (Kochan, 2019) and deterritorialised forms of belonging and acting in urban China, making a new form of migrants' citizenship. These forms of citizenship are certainly different from the legally defined *hukou* status or acculturation to 'urban citizenship' promoted in the state vision of 'integration into the city'. They instead promote migrants' active engagement with city resources despite their exclusion from various rights of citizenship, telluric-like networks of mutual help which preserve rural forms of acting within the city, and self-formation of alternative resources and spaces, not normally provided to migrants by the state due to their rural *hukou*. In the process of performing of such acts of citizenship, the former, fixed urban 'spaces of exclusion' become 'spaces of citizenship transformation': the streets where workers felt oppressed can become spaces of protest and cultural performance for the cause of migrant workers; the urban village from which the migrants are to be evicted becomes a space of formation of telluric networks through the meeting spaces created by NGOs; and the exclusion from city education results in the production of migrants' own schools and places of integration.

While citizenship transformation in relation to space appears as a process taking place on the local scale of the city, it calls for change on the national (reform of citizenship legislation) and global levels (the reform of the global relations of production and capital accumulation through property development, which alienate people from access to the city itself). Yet, while Harvey sees such resistance as necessarily linked to the anti-capitalist struggle (Harvey, 2012: xvi), in the case of China's migrant workers, the struggle for the right to the city is wider than just that of an anti-capitalist movement: it is a struggle for recognition, identity and citizenship. And it is the transformation of the cities' relationship with migrant workers and their own relationship with the city which will ultimately shape the process of the remaking of citizenship in China.

Notes

1 Interview no. 17.
2 Fieldnote, 20 February 2012, BWH premises, Beijing.
3 Fieldnote, 8 March 2012, BWH premises, Beijing.

4 Fieldnote, 9 April 2012, BWH premises, Beijing.
5 I am referring to the real names of these organisations here.
6 Interview no. 9.
7 Interview no. 9.
8 Interview no. 17.
9 The manual is on file with the author.
10 Interview no. 4.
11 Interview no. 4.
12 Interview no. 9.
13 Excerpt from NHC's magazine published in September 2011.
14 A letter written by a rural migrant in Hangzhou, published in NHC's magazine in September 2011. On file with the author.
15 Interview no. 7.
16 Interview no. 7.
17 Interview no. 17.
18 Interview no. 5.
19 Interview no. 21.

Conclusion

Citizenship challenge, social inequality and the insecure state

The Chinese state has long insisted that the 'Chinese human rights' ethos prioritises social rights above political and civil rights. Yet, the modernisation project in China has been geared towards high economic growth to ensure the regime's survival, rather than protection of any rights, social or otherwise. Indeed, the economic growth was achieved precisely at the cost of limited citizenship rights, which created unprecedented levels of social inequality. The population that emerged on the losing side of this social divide, the rural migrants and peasants, are not only barred from attaining the material fruits of their contribution to this modernisation project, they also remain under-represented in the political decision-making process. Without political voice, migrant workers must rely on the whims of the policy-makers, who may occasionally improve their situation by introducing new possibilities of acquiring urban *hukou*, but who at the same time may take arbitrary decisions to displace hundreds of thousands of people overnight, as it happened in December 2017 in Beijing.

Contrary to the conventional wisdom that migrant workers' struggle is driven by economic factors alone, this book has illustrated that for the struggle to be effective, it has to engage with other aspects: political, social, spatial, legal and economic all at once. The three sites around which labour NGOs' activism concentrates – civic organising, labour and space – reflect these wider ramifications of migrant workers' struggle for rights. What unites these seemingly disparate foci is their underlying connection to the question of citizenship: what citizenship rights one has access to, how citizenship is practised, and who a citizen is. This book illustrates the ways in which migrant worker NGOs challenge the pre-given answer to that question. The acts of citizenship they conduct testify to the possibility of subaltern actors to co-shape the citizenship-making process, traditionally monopolised by the state.

Understanding when migrant NGOs' activism becomes acts of citizenship allows us to uncover the degree to which NGOs challenge and reshape the citizenship-related causes of social inequality suffered by migrant workers. This, in turn, allows us to uncover why and how acts of citizenship should not be viewed as a political challenge to the party-state. While NGOs' acts are a form of participation in politics, they are primarily intended to lead to migrant workers' greater access to the material fruits of reforms, rather than effecting regime change. In other words, by pushing for social equality, migrant worker NGOs are not destabilising the country, as Zeng Feiyang's accusers forced him to claim in court,[1] and if anything, they contribute to maintaining that social stability. This is because they channel the workers' grievances into legal mechanisms and encourage negotiation rather than outright defiance. By becoming self-appointed migrants' representatives, they help to strengthen the migrant workers' voices: they find and create channels to communicate these voices and they develop strategies to make them persuasive to both the wider public and the state. This process facilitates the inclusion of migrant workers in the wider political discussion and helps satisfy their demands for fuller recognition as an important social group in China without resorting to violence or illegal means. In this sense, the NGOs' activism is not against the state: it actually facilitates the state's aim of social control and 'stability maintenance'. Therefore, the party-state's inimical treatment of these organisations appears at odds with the actual intentions of labour activists, and the reason for it must be further explored.

One explanation for this apparent mismatch is the fact that the activist citizenship model that these organisations promote has become increasingly problematic in the context of the restructuring of the Chinese economy and rising social unrest. The social dissatisfaction of migrant workers has become one of the greatest challenges to the Party's capacity to maintain its rule. In response, since 2012,[2] after a more tolerant period during the Hu-Wen administration, the new Chinese leaders have initiated a clear shift in the state's approach to labour discontent. Instead of entering into a dialogue with migrant workers through migrant-run organisations, workers' representatives and ACFTU, as was sometimes the case under the previous leadership, the Party has taken tougher measures against striking workers and initiated an unprecedented crackdown on labour NGOs across China.

The acts of citizenship undertaken by NGOs also cut across some key political battles between the party-state's many agencies and different levels of government. As the central state is reconsolidating its power under Xi Jinping, local governments have ever more reasons to feel unsettled. During the anti-corruption campaign of 'hunting down both tigers and flies' (*fanfu yao 'laohu' 'cangying' yiqi da*) they witnessed a growing number of arrests and sentencing of even the most prominent central and local Party leaders. This has resulted in fearful reshuffling at local levels of government (Teets *et al.*, 2017); insecurity, which translated into a more prescriptive adoption of the central mandate to repress labour organisations, resulting in a more repressive environment towards NGOs. This interpretation makes sense if one contrasts the local state's approach to labour organisations under the two administrations (Hu-Wen's and Xi's). Prior to 2012 the state only occasionally and covertly repressed activists, mostly turning a blind eye as long as NGOs didn't cross outright taboos, such as the formation of organisations with a high membership rate or the encouragement of strikes and protests. Indeed, most of the labour activists from NGOs have regularly met with State Security agents,[3] were being monitored by them (Fu, 2017: 57) and sometimes even developed long-lasting relationships with them (Franceschini and Nesossi, 2018). However, since 2012, this attitude has changed, and my interlocutors often pointed to the central state as the driving actor putting pressure on the local state to crack down on NGOs.

Following the bureaucratic reshuffling between different agencies of the local and central state during the leadership transition period, ACFTU is sometimes singled out as the main driving force behind the severity of the post-2012 crackdowns and their concentration on labour NGOs in particular.[4] The central state has long recognised the institutional weakness of ACFTU, resulting in the widespread loss of legitimacy among its constituency (Friedman, 2014; Lee, 2007). The current economic transition from low-skill export manufacturing to the high-tech domestic consumption model, which is expected to bring high levels of civic unrest, has resulted in an ever-greater central push for the long overdue ACFTU reforms. In the process of this reshuffling, labour NGOs have emerged as problematic agents potentially undermining the reforms. By showcasing their efficiency in resolving labour disputes, their commitment to migrant workers' cause and particularly their potential to promote new citizenship practices as discussed in this book, migrant NGOs both highlighted ACFTU's own inadequacy as an institution proclaiming to serve the working class and their own suitability as a political representative of migrant workers.[5] As such, these NGOs have become increasingly perceived as competition to ACFTU rather than partners, as the discussion in Chapter 2 highlighted. And this shift in the unions' attitude towards migrant NGOs is particularly visible in Guangdong province, which is at the forefront of union reforms in China. As UA's example, discussed in Chapter 2, shows, in 2006 the local branch of ACFTU was learning from the NGO, while in the 2010s it labelled the same organisation an 'illegal institution' and dissuaded workers from receiving its assistance.

In the context of the economic restructuring and the unions' unwillingness to address labour conflict, the state views activist citizenship as a problematic conundrum. Structural characteristics of citizenship in China, such as the *hukou* system, the limited civic and political rights of citizenship, the discouragement of activist citizenship practices and the hierarchical citizenship discourse, have long helped to keep the docile force of migrant workers in check. The activism performed by these organisations, even when performed via the 'resistance through accommodation' strategy, which clearly helps to dissipate 'social conflict', clashes with the CCP's insecurity over its own ability to successfully control social unrest. This is apparent in the scope of the crackdown conducted against migrant NGOs in China: it was not only the labour movement-orientated NGOs in the PRD who suffered, but also less 'sensitive' migrant NGOs, such as Zhejiang-based SFI and BWH, who had largely engaged in a state-conciliatory type of activism, avoiding contentious areas such as collective bargaining.

Effectively, the prospects of NGOs continuing their transformational work appear uncertain at best, if not outright hopeless. The Xi period has seen a drift away from more contentious forms of activism, many of which comprise truly transformational work in terms of citizenship rights and practices (such as collective bargaining couching and standing in elections), towards activism which should be seen as maintaining, rather than challenging the status quo (such as the 'integration into the city' manuals which actually coach migrants in obedience to Confucian ideas of state–citizen relations). The narrow space afforded to activist citizenship in Xi's China points to acts employing a 'resistance through accommodation' strategy, which engages with state domination rather than fighting it, as perhaps the only viable way in which migrant NGOs are still able to effect change in citizenship structure.

However, the rising unrest among migrant workers is only bound to heighten in the years to come. With China becoming a world leader in the so-called 'Fourth Industrial Revolution', relying on the robotisation of workplaces, many of the low-skilled, blue-collar, rural migrants will soon be made redundant due to the increasing mechanisation of workplace (Huang and Sharif, 2017). This is likely to create a wave of job losses, which will result in heightened social unrest in China. The state has been preparing for this event for a while, with spending on public security exceeding that on national defence for the first time in 2013 (Kuo, 2013). Judging from the state's treatment of the growing social unrest and migrant worker NGOs, it will continue to deploy force against striking migrant workers. Yet, in the absence of NGOs who divert workers' grievances to legal channels, and who train them how to bargain effectively rather than resort to violence, workers will be increasingly inclined to take desperate actions, which will only heighten social instability in China.

Limitations to the NGO-led citizenship transformation

The migrant NGOs' acts of citizenship have great potential to bring about a more equitable and sustainable form of development. However, these acts ultimately defy the state-prescribed models of non-state actors' participation in China's modernisation, resulting in a sustained crackdown on these organisations. Yet, apart from the 'chilling effect' (Franceschini and Nesossi, 2018) brought about by the crackdown, there are also some other factors which put limitations on the NGOs' ability to transform citizenship. In order to understand the potential of NGOs to continue to transform citizenship despite the state crackdown it is important to further reflect on other trends and limitations to these NGOs' activism – those stemming from the problems related to NGOs' inner struggles as well as from structural concerns related to funding and the state approach.

The NGOs discussed throughout this book are all small, grassroots organisations, with the exception of LHC, which is a quasi-governmental NGO. As a result of their small size and reliance on volunteers, migrant NGOs suffer from high staff turnover and a lack of proper human resources to carry out a more profound role in society and politics. Some NGO staff's commitment to stay in the labour NGO sector can also be short-term. While migrant workers-turned-activists I interviewed have been mostly committed to continue their work, and often saw no other prospects for themselves beyond continuing in their jobs as labour activists, many other staff members, particularly university graduates and social work professionals, have hopped between organisations. In the years 2011–2016 I witnessed four of them leaving the sector – to undertake further studies or to work in jobs with better prospects, usually in another non-profit sector. The only organisation which was comparatively well-off and boasted a stable source of income and staff, LHC, the largest of them all, was closely associated with the state, and despite its advocacy and legal help work, it was not interested in pushing for change in citizenship practices and discourse.

Another problematic constraint for NGOs is the relationship with their proclaimed constituency. While there are many instances of empowering acts conducted by NGOs, such as education on rights of citizenship and extra-legal aspects of citizenship, it is clear that this relationship has its limits and problems (for instance, the training in law they provide often lacks empowering qualities). The number of migrant workers that migrant NGOs can reach is limited due to state policies, NGOs' own limited capacities and the distrust of migrant workers (see Franceschini, 2014 for further discussion). Some scholars criticise migrant labour NGOs for being more concerned with their own organisational survival than with addressing workers' needs. They may, for example, prioritise relations with the state over promoting genuine worker solidarity (e.g. Lee and Shen, 2011; Franceschini, 2014). The relationship between NGO staff (often professionalised migrant workers themselves) and migrant workers may at times incorporate unequal power relations, despite many NGOs' attempts to interact with migrants on an equal basis. Some scholars even point out that these NGOs may impose middle-class values and aspirations, seeking to co-opt migrants into neoliberal norms and practices rather than upholding the cultural importance of rural or workers' lifestyles (e.g. Zhan, 2019).

However, the majority of these internal limits to NGOs' successful relationship with migrant workers stem from the structural limitations to activist citizenship: the formal legal constraints to operating NGOs in China, the informal limitations to citizenship practices imposed by the state, and the limited access to funding, both domestic and foreign. The current legal developments concerning NGOs and other civic actors, as discussed in Chapter 2, limit organisations' ability to operate and therefore conduct activism which can transform citizenship. The 2016 Charity Law and the amendments to the 1998 Regulation on Management of Social Organisations being debated currently are introducing more relaxed opportunities for the functioning of organisations in sectors deemed non-threatening to the state. However, for migrant worker NGOs, which are perceived as 'politically sensitive' often regardless of how contentious they really are, access to government funding is being largely cut off. The rise of public procurement projects in the NGO sector is resulting in some NGOs already changing their activities and strategies to comply with the government's objectives, as indicated in Chapter 2. This trend of relabelling NGOs' work away from labour is further encouraged by the withdrawal of foreign funding from the labour sector, as part of the wider global decrease in funding for labour issues (discussed in Chapter 3). This is paired with the effects of the 2017 Overseas Management Law, which prevents entry of labour INGOs to China and limits labour NGOs' ability to access foreign funding and network with FAs.

Therefore, it is understandable that with the tightening of state regulations, the government's preference for a state-led civil society model and the withdrawal of foreign funds, labour NGOs fear tough days ahead and some of them are now facing difficulties in continuing their work or even surviving (Jakimów, 2017; Franceschini and Nesossi, 2018; Froissart, 2018). Without retaining both foreign and domestic funding explicitly for 'labour issues', it is hard to imagine a better future for these organisations. However, while the above-mentioned limitations impacting labour NGOs' ability to survive might draw a gloomy picture of their ability to continue to challenge structural citizenship, the NGOs' activism should be contextualised within a wider drive towards 'activist citizenship' in China in recent years, which leaves some hope that the citizen-driven transformation will continue.

Activist citizenship in China and beyond

The findings offered in this book allow for a new contribution to the study of citizenship in China and to the wider field of critical citizenship studies by taking it beyond the empirical and theoretical focus on Western democratic states. Acts of citizenship theory was originally developed in the Western, democratic context, and has been sparsely applied to the authoritarian context. However, people's engagement in politics through activist citizenship is a universal phenomenon, observed everywhere in the modern world, in both democratic and authoritarian states. As society is inherently political, and imbued with unequal power relations, it is characterised by a continuous contestation of citizenship. The study of acts of citizenship in the case of China sheds new light on the particularities of this process in an authoritarian context, which in turn highlights the limitations of the Western-centric critical theories of citizenship, including acts of citizenship, and points to the ways in which the theory can be reshaped and built upon by taking this context into account.

The 'resistance through accommodation' strategy, which is employed throughout all three sites of activist citizenship, is a particularly useful contribution to the acts of citizenship framework in the authoritarian context, as it helps in understanding acts of citizenship as having the ability to transform citizenship, even if they are performed within state-prescribed channels, such as the law. The findings highlight that in an authoritarian context the law can be a site of contention, as the actors utilise it to push for observance of citizenship rights where they are not respected and to further stretch the citizenship regime from within. The original declaration of the acts of citizenship framework conceives of citizenship transformation as possible only if an act goes beyond the established laws and conventions. However, the findings presented throughout this book clearly show that acting within the law and using the official narratives in the authoritarian context, which lacks a strong 'rule of law', often allows for the negotiation of wider changes and new practices of citizenship more effectively than open resistance would. The law can serve as an arbitrary mechanism of repression by the state, but it can also provide space for citizens' own negotiation of their interests. By abiding by the law and working within it, NGOs do not necessarily enforce the state's regime of rule by law. More often than not the NGOs use the space between legal and 'beyond legal' for negotiation of their activism with the state. The framework of acts of citizenship should see engagement with the law, especially in a state where law is a malleable and arbitrary institution, as a site of struggle for and production of activist citizenship.

Because it reinvents existing tools offered by the structure to subvert the dominant order, the 'resistance through accommodation' strategy is best understood as a 'tactic' in de Certeau's sense (de Certeau, 1984: xix, 37). But as with de Certeau's 'tactics', over time they can lead to new 'practices'. Rather than being just understood as singular acts, acts of citizenship can have long-term impact when they are embedded enough to form new civic practices. This book illustrates how some of these acts are turned into practices: organising, educating, claiming, etc. are much more effective in transforming citizenship when they become entrenched over time and space. But this process necessitates normalisation of these once new actions into acceptable practices in the eyes of the state and society alike. Being acts, they are performed differently each time, therefore they end up forming a patchwork of new behaviours and attitudes, which over time evolve into new practices, having more impact than singular acts of citizenship.

In terms of the relationship between activist citizenship and civic organising, this book has illustrated that for civil society organisations in authoritarian states, citizenship can be a negotiated process between the civic actors and the state. I have shown how instead of understanding civil society as functioning necessarily in conflict with and separation from the state (republican theories), or as necessarily co-opted by the state in the Chinese context (state corporatism), it is more accurate to look at state–society relations as fragmented, atomised, localised and uneven, shaped by particular actors within both society and the state. It is often through 'relational citizenship negotiation' that acts of citizenship can be effective in pushing for transformation of citizenship, not outside of that relationship.

Despite the particularity of migrant workers' struggle and its focus on the question of citizenship, the adapted acts of citizenship framework that I present in this book also offers useful theoretical tools to analyse the ways in which citizenship is being challenged by actors other than migrant NGOs in China. Since 2012, there has been an increasing number of instances of citizen action taking place, as the growing number of strikes and protests across various sectors indicates (White *et al.*, 2017: 4). Much of this was explicitly linked to the multilayered understanding of citizenship, as presented in this book.

The acts of citizenship such as organising and networking, and the accompanying 'resistance through accommodation'-like strategies which facilitate them, are a common strategy among the wider NGO sector in China (Ho, 2008a; Hildebrandt, 2013). These NGOs undertake some other acts as well, such as 'empowering', 'challenging' and 'constructing', though these do not centre on any of the three sites that NGOs target. 'Empowering' can be found in the environmental sector for instance, where NGOs empower citizens to stand up for their rights with regard to environmental degradation or to take collective action (Mertha, 2010). LGBT NGOs perform acts of 'challenging' and 'constructing'. They do so by challenging public attitudes to homosexuality and aiding the development of LGBT group's self-identity as that of equal citizens regardless of their sexual orientation. (Ho, 2010). They also perform acts of 'empowering' by building communities of marginalised groups which endow them with a feeling of belonging to a particular deterritorialised space of network, transforming their self-perception in a polity. Many NGOs undertake 'petitioning and advocacy' acts, which can transform the wider legal framework and change the position of citizens in the policy-making process (Lu, 2007; Mertha, 2010). These NGOs might also undertake other acts of citizenship which migrant NGOs do not undertake and utilise different sites to do so.

Acts of citizenship are also encouraged and conducted by intellectuals, and it is this group that arguably has the longest history of struggling for political rights of citizenship (Goldman, 2005; Goldman and Perry, 2002). Intellectuals may often more consciously and overtly engage in the cause of challenging citizenship than migrant NGOs. An academic from one of the universities in Beijing sympathetic to the migrant NGOs' mission, himself took part in local elections in order to promote the political participation of citizens, and he regularly coached his students about various aspects of activist citizenship.[6] His commitment to spreading civic consciousness echoed the call of the intellectuals who formed the New Citizen Movement (*Xin Gongmin Yundong*), perhaps the most prominent example of the rise of activism aimed explicitly at citizenship transformation in China in recent years. The New Citizen Movement emerged in May 2012 but was suppressed through waves of lawyers' arrests from 2013 through to 2015. It was organised predominantly by lawyers, such as Xu Zhiyong and Teng Biao, and its roots lay in the wider civil rights movement which originated with the 2003 case of Sun Zhigang's death. Moreover, the New Citizen Movement was supposed to be 'organised without organisations': the civic rights lawyers associated with the movement used channels such as organising 'citizen meals' and information-spreading through social media in order to enable interactions and momentum-building for the movement (see Xu, 2017). Both the origin of the movement and the way it was organised differ from the origins of migrant NGOs, yet certain goals and methods used by both converge. These intellectual circles often interact with migrant NGOs, as the example of the above-mentioned professor indicates. Also, some of the labour NGO activists also sympathised with the New Citizen Movement:

> We don't have direct connection to the New Citizen Movement, but I do keep in touch with some of the people in the movement. Of course, I support their cause. But we have slightly different methods: they want to build a citizen movement, while we focus on the 'rights defence'. From the social function point of view, there isn't much of a difference because labour rights are just part of wider citizenship rights: if you don't have the civil rights, your labour rights are also limited.[7]

As a result of his belief in the connection between citizenship and labour rights, Mr Zhao stood in local elections as an independent candidate in 2011, as discussed in Chapter 4. Therefore, activist citizenship performed around the site of civic organising is not particular to migrant NGOs: it is a unifying call for many types of social movements and NGOs in China.

The site of labour is widely used as a site of activist citizenship by other striking professionals around China, not only migrant workers. The wider unionisation of various workers, both rural migrants and the urban population, that is taking place in China is not only driven by NGOs or intellectuals, but also results from the emerging activist citizenship consciousness among the urban middle classes. For instance, in the years 2014–2016 there was a countrywide strike by teachers in both rural and urban China over wage arrears, low pay and the lack of social insurance. When protesting in the 2016 strike in Hengyang, Hunan over wage arrears, a couple of teachers' representatives were arrested for singing the national anthem and speaking to the media about their dissatisfaction with working conditions in schools. When the detainees were finally released, some of them refused to leave the prison, demanding the governments explain the reasons for their detention (China Labour Bulletin, 2016). These strikes and the civic stand that the teachers took in response to the government actions are just one of many examples of actors other than migrant workers performing activist citizenship around labour rights.

Space also serves as a rallying call for activist citizenship, particularly among the dispossessed rural population in China. Among the protests against land grabs, a particularly prominent case which offers a clear example of actions which had a transformative impact on citizenship is that of Wukan village. Wukan village, located in Guangdong province, was the site of unprecedented events in 2011, when the village residents protested against the local government's land grabs,[8] forcing the government out of power and successfully electing a new village chief. The villagers' claims concerned the matter of the dispossession of land, yet the methods they employed and the resulting impact on citizens' participation in politics was revolutionary. Curiously, it was the returned migrant workers who instigated the villagers' action and had brought with them the political consciousness and activist attitudes acquired from their experiences in urban China (Lu *et al.*, 2017). This binds well with the argument raised in the introduction about the importance of urban spaces in refashioning citizenship and the impact of migrants on the changing dynamics of activism.

Yet, despite the wider rise of activist citizenship in China in the last decade or so, the combination of claims around the sites of civic organising, labour and space visible in the acts of migrant

NGOs is quite particular to the social group of migrant workers. They employ tools (for example, cultural activism combined with labour rights training and collective bargaining cases) and a range of issues which are not normally present in this combination in other actors' activism. Unlike many other striking and protesting citizens, their claims bind more closely to demands for changes in structural citizenship. At least in part, this is a result of the rural–urban divide which underpins the *hukou* system and *suzhi* discourse and determines migrants' status as second-class citizens, which drives much of their activism. However, other motivations, such as social equality demands and pressure for extension of civil and political rights, are shared with the demands of some other social groups mentioned above. The combination of civic organising, labour and space as sites of performance of the acts of citizenship is particular to migrant worker NGOs and makes them crucial actors in the process of citizenship transformation in China. It also allows for new theoretical insights, which can inform cases of activist citizenship beyond China.

When applying the findings to the context beyond China, it appears that China is not unique in terms of the close relationship between labour and citizenship claims. In Chinese studies so far, the majority of research has treated migrant workers' activism as a form of labour activism, which focuses on labour disputes (Friedman, 2014; Chan, 2012b; Pringle, 2011).[9] However, as was the case with the struggle of the working class in many modernising and authoritarian states, labour struggle was usually accompanied by a wider struggle for citizenship rights (Steadman-Jones, 1983; Somers, 2008, 1996). In early nineteenth-century England, voting rights were bestowed on the aristocracy only, leaving the working class under-represented and marginalised in politics and the economy, which led to the Chartist movement. Through various examples, this book has shown that the case of Chinese workers' activism bears many similarities to that of the nineteenth-century English working class: the struggle for labour rights is a struggle for wider access to citizenship, as without it, labour rights, even if achieved, cannot be guarded as the interest of workers remains under-represented in politics. Therefore, the struggle for labour rights and labour identity of migrant workers is paralleled with their struggle for citizenship rights. This is ever more prominent in authoritarian states, as another example, that of the Polish Solidarność, shows. The Solidarność movement in Poland was organised by workers with the help of intellectuals, who jointly recognised that the struggle for economic rights was only possible if wider political and civil rights, such as access to political representation through trade unions (in the case of Solidarność, the independent trade unions), was acknowledged. These demands differ in democratic states, where the political, civil and sometimes cultural rights of citizenship are guaranteed, so the working-class struggle usually focuses on social, industrial or economic rights. As workers already possess access to political and civil rights, they are endowed with tools (at least in theory) to undertake struggle for social and economic rights. However, in this authoritarian state, the migrant workers must struggle for social as well as political, civil and cultural rights simultaneously, as the access to and effective implementation of their social rights often depends on the possession of the other rights of citizenship. This makes the relationship between activist citizenship and labour special in the case of authoritarian states, and this is why the case study of migrant NGOs is enlightening in this regard.

Similarly, this book provides some useful examples of how subaltern actors can address the vulnerability of internal migrants resulting from the differentiated citizenship status and discriminatory character of citizenship discourse that accompanies that status. I argued that migrant workers are discursively treated as inferior citizens because of the spatial, hierarchal imaginary between rural and urban scales in the modern understanding of citizenship in China. This imaginary can be found in other modernising contexts too, both historically and contemporarily. For instance, in nineteenth-century France, Germany or England (see Weber, 1976) and twentieth-century modernising countries all around the world, peasants have often been treated as inferior, and rural migrants to the cities were forced to adapt to this new modern, urban world which required them to leave their rural identities behind. Similarly, in present-day modernising states, regardless of the political regime type, the rural–urban divide determines the treatment of migrant workers as second-class citizens. The Indian government's recent treatment of rural migrants during the COVID-19 pandemic, including police brutality and the state's abandonment of rural migrants as they tried to reach their home destinations or faced job losses, illustrates the long-standing disregard for rural populations and migrant workers. The case of India, just like China, also highlights the hidden vulnerability of internal migrants, who cannot claim refugee status when displaced, and have no recourse if their own governments do not take responsibility for protecting their citizens and addressing long-standing citizenship discrimination (Nair, 2020).

This book shows how subaltern actors can challenge this hierarchical characteristic of the citizenship discourse, and address the vulnerability of internal migrants and the limits on their accessing rights to the city, which are both linked to it. I have provided examples of how migrant NGOs in China promote an alternative role of migrant workers and peasants in the citizenship discourse through activism involving cultural practices and mobilisation of resources available in the city. I also showed how migrant NGOs put forward claims to material and non-material aspects of space in the form of claims to belonging to the city, building a community within that city, defending their house from demolition and providing migrants with alternative communal services. However, while such struggle parallels the plight of other migrants globally, both domestic and transnational, this study has highlighted the distinct role of the law in the context of internal migrants' contestation of citizenship. The way in which NGOs use the existing law, including migrant workers' Chinese nationality status, in a process of claiming their right to the city and arguing for an end to discrimination against rural migrants, highlights the different tools that domestic and transnational migrants have at their disposal. China's case demonstrates that the language of citizenship is perhaps more often employed in the struggles of domestic migrant workers than in the context of transnational migrations. These insights contribute to studies of the space–migration nexus in the field of critical citizenship theories by pointing to the ways in which internal migrants defend the right to the city and reshape citizenship inequality in the process.

Looking back at the opening vignette of the book, the acts which NGOs undertake, whether the organisation of a festival of migrants' poetry and music or legal support provided to striking migrant workers, might appear as rather insignificant instances of rupture within the everyday status quo of the powerful state governing over the docile workforce of disenfranchised citizens. However, while these organisations are weak and represent only a small part of the migrant workers group, they are part of the wider process of the citizen-initiated contestation of citizenship in China and beyond. As they reshape our understanding of who should be defined as a citizen, how and why, their contribution is one of the most necessary, positioning these actors at the forefront of social and political change.

Notes

1 On 26 September 2016, a court in Guangzhou Panyu district sentenced Zeng Feiyang, a leader of Guangzhou-based labour NGO, Panyu Migrant Workers Centre, to a suspended prison sentence of three years for 'gathering a crowd to disrupt public order'. In the publicised statement from the trial he admitted that he received funding and training from 'foreign organisations hostile to China' and that he committed crimes against Chinese society.

2 Some of my interlocutors from NGOs place the beginning of this period in 2010, after the economic crisis (Interview no. 38).

3 Interview no. 39.

4 Interview no. 39. There is a similar argument in Froissart (2018: 14).

5 Interview no. 39.

6 Interview no. 6.

7 Interview no. 42.

8 The Wukan government officials sold RMB 700 million worth of the collective land to developers in the years 1993–2011. They pocketed the profits without compensating the villagers (Lu, Zheng and Wang 2017: 5).

9 With the exception of studies by Lee (2007) and Fu (2017).

Appendices

Appendix 1

Methodology: researching labour NGOs in China

The study of acts of citizenship in an authoritarian context is a challenging enterprise, requiring uneasy choices over the most effective versus most ethical ways of conducting the research. The methodology of the study in this book is a compromise between these two major challenges. From the sampling method to the very choices of actors who would become the main focus of the study, each decision was dictated by the negotiation between the limits of access, safety of the research subjects and the necessity to answer the research question in the most accurate way possible.

One such choice pertaining to methodology in particular was the decision, taken early on, to focus the enquiry on NGOs only, rather than a wider group of migrant workers. While a wider study of migrant workers' activism, beyond NGOs, could equally allow us to answer the research question, the focus on a particular group of migrant workers – those who set up NGOs, and therefore are easily identifiable activists – allowed for a greater focus and rigour of the enquiry. By focusing on NGOs only, I could undertake methodologically sound, manageable, coherent and in-depth fieldwork in China. Unlike strikes and protests, the formation of grassroots organisations brings with it a more institutionalised form of activism, which can better and more coherently help with the analysis of long-term ideas about citizenship and their implementation in practice, which is the focus of the book.

However, despite these advantages, the focus on NGOs rather than a wider group of migrant activists, has its limitations in answering the research question. One such limitation relates to the academic criticism of the validity of NGOs as a level of analysis of migrant activism. NGOs are traditionally understood to be agents representing certain groups or causes, rather than constituting these groups' forms of activism or places of belonging (see Reimann, 2005: 43). The NGOs discussed in this book undoubtedly take the position of migrants' representatives, despite not being democratically elected to do so, and therefore despite lacking the representativeness of a wider migrant workers group. Moreover, even if initially established by migrant workers, the particularities of agency, motivations, recognisability and self-identity of NGOs soon set them apart from the wider migrant workers group they profess to serve. Some even argue that these very NGO activists end up reproducing the class boundaries between the middle classes who they effectively become part of, and the workers themselves (Zhan, 2019). In the case of migrant organisations, it is the NGOs, rather than migrants, who ultimately decide which issues receive attention and who is to speak; therefore they entrench new power dynamics between NGO activists and migrant workers. However, while it is important to critically reflect on these issues, it is also essential to remember that even in the non-NGO context of migrant workers' activism, for example in the form of strikes, there are still power relations between leaders and followers, which inevitably obscure the intentions of many of the group members. Power relations inevitably pervade any form of social relationship. What is therefore essential for research like this, and I sought for it in this book, is to uncover and reflect on these power relations.

Another choice which dictated the way the research question was answered was the scope and variety of the sample. It was my explicit intention to conduct a study with as many NGOs in as many places across China as possible, to give the study a breadth of scale. Yet, I wanted to achieve this breadth without losing the depth of study afforded by a close observation of these organisations' activities. Due to the study's focus on the degree to which subaltern actors can transform citizenship, the findings presented in this book come mostly from the fourteen organisations that were set up by migrant workers. However, the remaining five non-migrant-founded organisations serve as control group, providing a comparative perspective. I would like to think that this study design provided balance between the breadth and depth that I hoped for.

The main research methods, semi-structured interviews and participant observation, were mutually reinforcing in the case of several NGOs, where the use of participant observation allowed me a more complete insight into the workings of these organisations. Indeed, it is the participant observation method that makes this research especially insightful, contributing to an emerging type of political ethnography as a new research method in Political Science.[1] The experience of fieldwork in BWH, in particular, confirmed many of the literature's findings on the high effectiveness of participant observation as a research method. This method allowed me to study first-hand interactions both within the organisations and with other bodies, and to investigate whether the claims put forward by the NGO concerning their achievement could be confirmed in everyday working life. The extended socialisation that I underwent through participant observation enabled greater openness of research subjects, and it allowed continuous questioning and readjustment of preconceived theories.

Last but not least, I was faced with some profound ethical concerns. What makes migrant/labour NGOs special, and what made the fieldwork challenging both in terms of access and ethical considerations, is the degree to which these organisations are perceived as 'politically sensitive' in China. The political sensitivity of these organisations meant that I was often faced with challenges of access to the field. The fact that I am ethnically non-Chinese made these issues even more pronounced and limited the kinds of activities I could participate in and observe. While working in an NGO office allowed me some important access to the day-to-day work of the organisation, such as meeting donors, taking part in the NGO's networking activities and conferences, and helping with translations, I was not able to participate in wage negotiations, as this could put my interlocutors unduly under the attention of the authorities and interfere in the processes observed. Due to my 'foreigner' status, I undertook special measures and adopted a high degree of cautiousness in order to avoid jeopardising the organisations I interacted with. In order to do so, I made sure not to participate in any events which would draw the attention of State Security to the organisations, always strived to meet the NGOs in secure locations for interviews, away from potentially prying eyes, and only used the Chinese language in my electronic correspondence. I also refrained from using an interpreter, and always visited the organisations by myself in order to ensure that none of the information they gave me in conversations was known to anybody else, and that I did not compromise the safety of an interpreter at any point. These challenges of access to the field, however, were overshadowed by the knowledge and experience gained in the process, and the ensuing satisfaction of connecting to the people who have devoted their lives to some of the most difficult struggles in contemporary China. The ability to observe their work and the daily challenges they faced, and being able to gain insight into their experiences, was the ultimate privilege and a precious gift, one that I can only hope to reciprocate with this study.

Notes

1 See Fu (2017) for another study of labour NGOs using this method.

Appendix 2

List of interviews

1. **Interview no. 1**, 24 September 2011, in Chinese, not recorded – **Students in Action** (head of organisation)
2. **Interview no. 2**, 18 November 2011, in Chinese, recorded – **AC 1** (a Chinese professor from Zhejiang University specialising in migrant issues)
3. **Interview no. 3**, 21 March 2012, in Chinese, recorded – **Beijing Workers' Hotline and its branch representatives from Shanghai, Shenzhen and Shenyang, Saving from Injury and Justice for the Miners** (group interview with heads and staff from these NGOs – ten people in total)
4. **Interview no. 4**, 29 March 2012, in Chinese, recorded – **Beijing Workers' Hotline** (head of organisation)
5. **Interview no. 5**, 13 April 2012, in Chinese, partially recorded – **New Beijing Workers** (one of the founders of the organisation)
6. **Interview no. 6**, 16 April 2012, in English, not recorded – **AC 2** (a Chinese professor from the Communication University of China in Beijing specialising in media studies)
7. **Interview no. 7**, 18 April 2012, in Chinese, partially recorded – **Migrant Village Defenders** (two of the heads of the organisation)
8. **Interview no. 8**, 19 April 2012, in Chinese, recorded — **Beijing Workers' Hotline** (organisation employee)
9. **Interview no. 9**, 20 April 2012, in Chinese, recorded – **New Hangzhou Citizens** (organisation employee)
10. **Interview no. 10**, 25 April 2012, in Chinese, recorded – **Solidarity with the Sick** (organisation employee)
11. **Interview no. 11**, 27 April 2012, in English, recorded – **FA 5** (head of the China Office)

12. **Interview no. 12**, 29 April 2012, in English, recorded – **FA 4** (head of the China Office)
13. **Interview no. 13**, 30 April 2012, in English, not recorded – **FA 1** (embassy employee)
14. **Interview no. 14**, 2 May 2012, in Chinese, recorded – **FA 6** (head of the China Office's division concerning NGOs)
15. **Interview no. 15**, 4 May 2012, in Chinese, not recorded – **Legal Help Centre** (organisation employee)
16. **Interview no. 16**, 4 May 2012, in English, not recorded – **FA 7 (EC)** (project managers on related projects)
17. **Interview no. 17**, 7 January 2013, in English, recorded – **Migrant Women United** (organisation employee)
18. **Interview no. 18**, 16 January 2013, in Chinese, recorded – **United in Action** (head of organisation)
19. **Interview no. 19**, 17 January 2013, in Chinese, recorded – **Empowered Together** (organisation employee)
20. **Interview no. 20**, 18 January 2013, in Chinese, recorded – **Injured Migrants' Home** (organisation employee)
21. **Interview no. 21**, 21 January 2013, in Chinese, not recorded – **Action for the Children** (head of organisation)
22. **Interview no. 22**, 22 January 2013, in English, not recorded – **FA 9 (UNDP)** (organisation employee)
23. **Interview no. 23**, 22 January 2013, in English, not recorded – **FA 9 (UNDP)** (organisation employee)
24. **Interview no. 24**, 23 January 2013, in English, recorded – **FA10 (ILO)** (two organisation employees)
25. **Interview no. 25**, 28 January 2013, in English, recorded – **FA 11** (organisation employee)
26. **Interview no. 26**, 29 April 2016, in English and Chinese, not recorded – **Beijing Workers' Hotline** (organisation employee)
27. **Interview no. 27**, 6 May 2015, in English, not recorded – **FA 7 (EC)** (a project manager in charge of one of the projects related to governance in China, and an intern)
28. **Interview no. 28**, 6 May 2015, in English, not recorded – **FA 7 (EC)** (a project manager in charge of one of the projects related to civil society in China)
29. **Interview no. 29**, 19 May 2015, in English, not recorded – **FA 7 (EC)** (a project manager in charge of one of the projects related to civil society in China)

30. **Interview no.** 30, 21 May 2015, in English, not recorded – **NGO 20** (organisation employee)
31. **Interview no.** 31, 25 May 2015, in English, not recorded – **FA 14** (China coordinator and implementer of projects)
32. **Interview no.** 32, 27 May 2015, in English, not recorded – **FA 5** (head of the China Office), follow-up
33. **Interview no.** 33, 27 May 2015, in English, not recorded – **FA 7 (EC)** (a project manager in charge of one of the projects related to civil society in China)
34. **Interview no.** 34, 10 June 2015, in English, not recorded – **FA 7 (EC)** (a project manager on a project related to trade)
35. **Interview no.** 35, 12 June 2015, in English, not recorded, Skype – **FA 7 (EC)** (former project manager in charge of one of the projects related to governance in China)
36. **Interview no.** 36, 16 June 2015, in English, not recorded – **FA 7 (EC)** (European External Action Services delegate working on human rights issues)
37. **Interview no.** 37, 16 June 2015, in English, not recorded – **FA 7 (EC)** (project manager in charge of one of the projects related to governance in China)
38. **Interview no.** 38, 20 June 2015, in English, not recorded – **Beijing Workers' Hotline** (organisation employee), follow-up
39. **Interview no.** 39, 4 July 2016, in English, recorded, Hong Kong – **FA 15** (organisation employee)
40. **Interview no.** 40, 6 July 2016, in English, recorded, Shenzhen – **FA 16** (intern)
41. **Interview no.** 41, 7 July 2016, in Chinese, recorded, Shenzhen – **AC 3** (an academic from Shenzhen University specialising in law)
42. **Interview no.** 42, 8 July 2016, in Chinese, recorded, Shenzhen – **United in Action** (head of organisation), follow-up
43. **Interview no.** 43, 9 July 2016, in Chinese, recorded, Shenzhen – **Safer Construction** (head of organisation)
44. **Interview no.** 44, 11 July 2016, in Chinese, recorded, Guangzhou – **AC 4** (an academic from one of the Guangzhou-based universities specialising in labour and NGOs)
45. **Interview no.** 45, 12 July 2016, in Chinese, recorded, Guangzhou – **AC 4** (an academic from one of the Guangzhou-based universities specialising in labour and NGOs), follow-up and fieldwork in migrant village

46. **Interview no. 46**, 15 July 2016, in Chinese, recorded, Shenzhen – **Empowered Together** (head of organisation, leaving the organisation at the time of the interview)

Interviews conducted via social media:

47. **Interview no. 47**, 15 October 2012, with **Justice for the Miners** (head of organisation), follow-up
48. **Interview no. 48**, 24 April 2012, with **Justice for the Miners** (head of organisation), follow-up
49. **Interview no. 49**, 15 January 2013, with **Saving from Injury** (head of organisation), follow-up
50. **Interview no. 50**, 23 January 2013, with **Justice for the Miners** (head of organisation), follow-up

Appendix 3

List of participant observation sites

1. Participant observation of cultural activities conducted with **Students in Action, Hangzhou:** several occasions in October and December 2011.
2. Participant observation of cultural activities conducted with **New Hangzhou Citizens, Hangzhou:** several times in October and December 2011.
3. Participant observation of cultural activities conducted with **New Beijing Workers, Beijing:** several times in October 2011, April and May 2012.
4. Participant observation of **Beijing Workers' Hotline, Beijing** through part-time internship (3–4 days a week) in the organisation in the period between February and May 2012.
5. Fieldwork trip to a **migrant village** located in the Changping district of Beijing, 21 January 2013.
6. Fieldwork trip to a **migrant village** located in the Shipaicun district of Guangzhou, 12 July 2016.

Appendix 4

Tables

Table A4.1: Breakdown of Chinese NGOs who participated in the study

Guangdong-based organisations						
Pseudonym of organisation	Province, city, district	Date started	Started by	Sources of funding	Relationship with the government	Activities
Fighting for Justice (FJ)[1]	Guangdong, Guangzhou	1998	• a migrant worker • later included other professionals (e.g. lawyers)	• foreign (Hong Kong, other)	• suffered crackdown in 2015	• legal training and advice • mediating labour conflicts and coaching strike leaders • court representation

1 While I did not formally interview this NGO, I spoke to some of its representatives at the joint events organised by Beijing Workers' Hotline in March 2012 in Beijing. I also collected information on the organisation from its website and from interviews with other NGOs.

Table A4.1: Breakdown of Chinese NGOs who participated in the study (Continued)

Guangdong-based organisations						
Pseudonym of organisation	Province, city, district	Date started	Started by	Sources of funding	Relationship with the government	Activities
Migrant Women United (MWU)	Hong Kong, Guangdong, Shenzhen	1997	• academics and activists from Hong Kong	• foreign (Hong Kong, UK)	• registered in Hong Kong	• visiting injured workers in hospital • supporting migrant women in particular • labour law education, feminist rights, occupational health and safety training • cultural activities

United in Action (UA)	Guangdong, Shenzhen (also a branch in Dongguan, Guangdong province)	2005/2006 (a continuation of organisation set up in 2004)	• migrant worker from Hunan province (rural *hukou*)	• foreign (Hong Kong and USA) • in the past some domestic (ACFTU)	• registered as business under SAIC • suffered government crackdown since 2012	• mediating labour disputes in factories • directing court cases to lawyers • representing labour dispute cases in courts and arbitration courts • leading collective bargaining with employers and in courts

Table A4.1: Breakdown of Chinese NGOs who participated in the study (Continued)

Pseudonym of organisation	Province, city, district	Date started	Started by	Sources of funding	Relationship with the government	Activities
Guangdong-based organisations						
Empowered Together (ET)	Guangdong, Shenzhen	2003	• migrant worker (male) from Hubei (left organisation in 2008) • now run by 3 migrant women and 1 man, from various provinces, plus social workers, university graduates and others	• foreign (Hong Kong)	• registered as business under SAIC • suffered government's crackdown since 2012 and split in 2015 into 4 specialised NGOs, each dealing with specific area of work in relation to migrant workers	• cultural activities • community centre • health and safety education • entertainment (films, library etc.) • legal education and arbitration/litigation procedure training • representation in court; arbitration and litigation • legal advice • visiting injured workers in hospital • phone inquiries

						• managed to register as NPO under MOCA in 2014	• group counselling, group discussions and civic and class identity-building
Beijing Workers' Hotline (Shenzhen branch) (BWH)	Guangdong, Shenzhen	2006		• a migrant worker from Henan province	• foreign (19 foreign donors)	• registered as a non-profit organisation with MOCA	• legal training and advice, hotline • educational campaigns, health and safety training, accident and pneumoconiosis prevention

Table A4.1: Breakdown of Chinese NGOs who participated in the study (Continued)

Pseudonym of organisation	Province, city, district	Date started	Started by	Sources of funding	Relationship with the government	Activities
Guangdong-based organisations						
Injured Migrants' Home (IMH)	Guangdong, Foshan	2012 (earlier the founder was involved with FJ since the early 2000s)	• migrant workers who experienced injury themselves	• foreign (Germany)	• registered as non-profit under MOCA	• visits to injured workers in hospital and legal advice on compensation • large-scale training on legal advice, particularly in relation to industrial injury and compensation • training in work skills for workers with disabilities and injuries • training on self-empowerment and ability to cope in the city

Pseudonym of organisation	Province, city, district	Date started	Started by	Sources of funding	Relationship with the government	Activities
						• outdoor activities • court hearing simulations • hotline advice
Beijing-based organisations and their branches						
New Beijing Workers (NBW)	Beijing, outskirts of Chaoyang district (urban village)	2002	• a group of migrants from different parts of China	• domestic (local branch of ACFTU) • foreign (ILO, Hong Kong)	• no formal links with the government • organises events in cooperation with the local government and the local branch of ACFTU	• music band and theatre productions • training centre for migrant workers • school for migrant children • second-hand shop • weekly magazine for migrant children • museum of migrant workers

Table A4.1: Breakdown of Chinese NGOs who participated in the study (Continued)

Pseudonym of organisation	Province, city, district	Date started	Started by	Sources of funding	Relationship with the government	Activities
Beijing-based organisations and their branches						
Beijing Workers' Hotline (BWH)	Beijing, central	1999	• a migrant worker from Henan province	• foreign (19 foreign donors)	• received authorisation from the local government to set up Mediation Committee • registered under SAIC as a business in 2007	• mediating timely and fair pay on behalf of migrants at construction sites and in factories • legal training, educational campaigns • legal advice, hotline • capacity building for NGOs across China

Legal Help Centre (LHC)	Beijing, central Fengtai, 27 other offices	2005	• a lawyer (head of All China Lawyers' Federation and a CCP member)	• domestic (ACFTU, Public Interest Lottery Fund for legal aid programmes, China Legal Aid Foundation) • foreign (UNDP, Belgian Embassy)	• set up by the Beijing Municipal Judicial Bureau: very close links to the government • seen as a form of GONGO by some other NGOs • registered officially as a non-profit organisation under MOCA	• advocacy with the government • reports and research • legal representation for migrants in court (government-dispatched lawyers)

Table A4.1: Breakdown of Chinese NGOs who participated in the study (Continued)

Beijing-based organisations and their branches						
Pseudonym of organisation	Province, city, district	Date started	Started by	Sources of funding	Relationship with the government	Activities
Migrant Village Defenders (MVD)	Beijing, outskirts of Haidian district (former and new urban villages)	2003	• a migrant worker from Hebei province • his wife, a migrant from Shaanxi province, joined in 2010	• domestic	• no formal links to the government, but hoping for government support • registered as a business under SAIC	• advice hotline, focused mainly on emotional support and employment advice to other workers • free nursery for migrant workers' children

Solidarity with the Sick (SWS)	Beijing, central Haidian district	2011	• a professor associated with a number of universities across China	• domestic	• registered as a non-profit organisaton under MOCA	• provide education on prevention of, compensation for and access to medical help for workers with pneumoconiosis • train volunteers carry out this work in locations with a concentration of mines • advocate with intellectuals and ruling elites to increase the social outreach of awareness on pneumoconiosis

Table A4.1: Breakdown of Chinese NGOs who participated in the study (Continued)

Beijing-based organisations and their branches						
Pseudonym of organisation	Province, city, district	Date started	Started by	Sources of funding	Relationship with the government	Activities
Action for the Children (AC)	Beijing, Changping district (urban village)	2006	• 5 migrant workers from various provinces[2]	• domestic (ACFTU and 2 foundations) • foreign (Hong Kong and USA)	• registered as a business under SAIC	• local community centre for education and culture, mainly providing education to migrant children • organisation of 'day in the countryside' events for migrant children and Beijing-*hukou* children

2 As of 2013.

							• providing volunteer teachers for a local private school (run by a businessman and charging migrant children a fee) • local community entertainment centre
Safer Construction (SC)	Beijing, Daxing	2010		• specialised social worker and migrant worker	• domestic (Beijing trade unions, Gingko Foundation, Nerada Foundation, online fundraising among citizens) • Foreign (Germany)	• registered as a business under SAIC (Beijing) • registered as a non-profit organisation under MOCA (Shenzhen), but registered as a community work NGO, not labour NGO	• preventative health and safety and occupational health training to workers in construction industry • policy advocacy and advice (government level) • improving enterprise-level health and safety training, CSR measures and introducing industry standards

Table A4.1: Breakdown of Chinese NGOs who participated in the study (Continued)

Zhejiang-based organisations						
Pseudonym of organisation	Province, city, district	Date started	Started by	Sources of funding	Relationship with the government	Activities
Students in Action (SA)	Zhejiang, Hangzhou, Xihu district	2006	• students from Zhejiang University	• domestic (university fund)	• attached to Zhejiang University as an association, not registered	• organising cultural events for migrants • teaching migrant children in schools
New Hangzhou Citizens (NHC)	Zhejiang, Hangzhou, Jianggan district	2006	• a migrant worker from Jiangxi province	• domestic (local branch of ACFTU)	• up until 2010 independent, unregistered NPO • from 2010 was subordinated to the local branch of ACFTU	• music band and cultural/leisure activities • collecting funds for workers in need of hospitalisation • legal advice and training; forwarding to trade union lawyers

Saving From Injury (SFI)	Zhejiang, Yongkang	2009	• a migrant worker who experienced injury in the workplace himself	• foreign	• registered as a business under SAIC	• legal advice • education on labour rights and health and safety • helping injured migrants to seek compensation from employers

Organisations based in other parts of China

Pseudonym of organisation	Province, city, district	Date started	Started by	Sources of funding	Relationship with the government	Activities
Justice for the Miners (JM)	Hubei, Shiyan	2008	• a migrant worker from Hubei	• domestic (local branch of ACFTU)	• registered as a business under SAIC • maintains contacts with ACFTU	• civil representation of migrant workers in court (arbitration) • legal training and education • legal advice, hotline • advocacy with the government • contact with media to propagate migrant workers' cause

Table A4.1: Breakdown of Chinese NGOs who participated in the study (Continued)

Organisations based in other parts of China						
Pseudonym of organisation	Province, city, district	Date started	Started by	Sources of funding	Relationship with the government	Activities
Beijing Workers' Hotline (Shenyang branch) (BWH)	Liaoning, Shenyang	2006	• a migrant worker from Henan province	• foreign (19 foreign donors)	• registered as a business under SAIC	• legal training and advice, hotline • educational campaign, health and safety, accident and pneumoconiosis prevention • day centre for migrant children
Beijing Workers' Hotline (Shanghai branch) (BWH)	Shanghai	2011	• a migrant worker from Henan province	• foreign (19 foreign donors)	• registered as a business under SAIC	• educational campaigns • legal advice, hotline

Other NGOs (non-labour)						
Pseudonym of organisation	Province, city, district	Date started	Started by	Sources of funding	Relationship with the government	Activities
NGO 20 This is not a labour NGO, therefore it is not included in the sample	Beijing	1996	• 13 members in two language sections[3]	• 4 permanent foreign founders (USA, Germany) • project-based funding mostly from the EC	• registered as a business under MOCA	• provides information on voluntary sector and NGOs across China • information platform

3 As of 2015.

Table A4.2: Breakdown of FAs included in the study

	Type of FA	Location (HQ)	Cooperation with labour NGOs	Types of projects supported	Mission/aims/ motivation (in relation to migrant workers)
FA 1[4]	Embassy of a foreign country	Beijing	Beijing Workers' Hotline; other NGOs dealing with migrant worker issues in Beijing who were not included in this book	• provide funding for law training and law manuals for migrant workers to be distributed through NGOs	• aiding Chinese development
FA 2[5]	Embassy of a foreign country	Beijing	Beijing Workers' Hotline	• cooperation with the Chinese government through intergovernmental project 'Social Security for Migrant Workers' • funding research on social security in China in cooperation with Chinese universities	• aiding Chinese Social Security system reform • aiding Chinese development

4 Information about FA 1 was collected through Interview no. 13.

5 Information about FA 2 was collected through personal face-to-face informal communication on several occasions between February and May 2012 and email exchange on 28 February 2012.

FA 3[6]	Embassy of a foreign country	Beijing	Beijing Workers' Hotline	• supporting education on rights among migrant workers, also through text messages and media channels • support for migrant women • supporting capacity of labour NGOs	• support for human rights, civil society and democratisation
FA 4[7]	INGO (Germany)	Beijing	Beijing Workers' Hotline; Saving From Injury; several other NGOs dealing with migrant worker issues who were not included in this study	• project-based support for labour NGOs (among other types of NGOs) • support for children of migrant workers • occupational illness support for migrant workers • legal training • CSR and ethics in business	• poverty alleviation through harnessing the potential of the so-called 'poor' • alleviation of suffering • support for solidarity • support for transparency

6 Information about FA 3 was collected through an email exchange on 23 May 2012 and the relevant websites.
7 Information about FA 4 was collected through Interview no. 12 and the organisation's publications.

Table A4.2: Breakdown of FAs included in the study (Continued)

	Type of FA	Location (HQ)	Cooperation with labour NGOs	Types of projects supported	Mission/aims/ motivation (in relation to migrant workers)
FA 5[8]	INGO (Germany)	Beijing	Beijing Workers' Hotline; Safer Construction	• inter-university projects, contributing to academic discussion • project-based support for labour NGOs (among other types of NGOs) • empowerment through legal training • community centres for migrant workers	• social justice • alternatives to capitalist development model • sustainable development

8 Information about FA 5 was collected through Interview no. 11 and the organisation's publications.

FA 6[9]	INGO (UK/ Hong Kong)	Hong Kong/ Beijing	New Beijing Workers; Beijing Workers' Hotline; Migrant Women United; United in Action; Empowered Together; Action for the Children; altogether in its history has supported 30 labour NGOs across China	• inter-university research projects and training • long-term orientated support for labour NGOs (among other types of NGOs) • also supports local community centres • labour rights-related training, advice, protection, court representation • change in societal approaches to migrant workers, support for cultural and community-building activities • empowerment of migrant workers	• poverty alleviation and support for development

9 Information about FA 6 was collected through Interview no. 14 and the organisation's publications.

Table A4.2: Breakdown of FAs included in the study (Continued)

	Type of FA	Location (HQ)	Cooperation with labour NGOs	Types of projects supported	Mission/aims/ motivation (in relation to migrant workers)
FA 7[10]	IO (European Commission (EC))	Beijing	FA 11, FA 14, NGO 20	• in the past cooperated with the Chinese government through intergovernmental projects regarding migrant workers and NGOs: 'EU–China Civil Society Dialogue Project', 'No Child Left-Behind' and 'Governance for Equitable Development', among others	• aiding sustainable development in China • defending human rights, supporting welfare and governance reforms (information from the website)

10 Information about FA 7 was collected from the organisation's website and several interviews.

FA 8[11]	Austrian Federation of Trade Unions	Austria	-not materially supporting any NGOs	• training and supporting Austrian companies working in China • dialogue platform on issues of globalisation, working in China • CSR measures	• transnational and inter-institutional dialogue and cooperation on globalisation and labour issues, particularly in the context of China–Austria business cooperation • CSR measures in China

11 Information about FA 8 was collected through the organisation's leaflets and a face-to-face exchange on 30 March 2012 with representatives visiting Beijing.

Table A4.2: Breakdown of FAs included in the study (Continued)

	Type of FA	Location (HQ)	Cooperation with labour NGOs	Types of projects supported	Mission/aims/ motivation (in relation to migrant workers)
FA 9[12]	IO (UNDP)	Beijing	Legal Help Centre	• cooperation with the Chinese government, EC and research institutions (universities and think tanks) through intergovernmental projects regarding migrant workers and NGOs: 'Legal Aid for Migrant Workers' and 'Governance for Equitable Development', among others.	• supporting China's development • poverty alleviation • democratic governance • legal system reforms

12 Information on FA 9 was collected through Interviews no. 22 and no. 23.

FA 10[13]	IO (ILO)	Beijing	New Beijing Workers; Beijing Workers' Hotline; other NGOs who were not included in this study	• assessing capacity of labour NGOs in China • cooperating with NGOs to assess the situation of migrant workers • cooperating with trade unions (on a local level) to improve the situation in factories • cooperating with ministries and policy-makers	• promoting social dialogue

13 Information on FA 10 was collected through Interview no. 23.

Table A4.2: Breakdown of FAs included in the study (Continued)

	Type of FA	Location (HQ)	Cooperation with labour NGOs	Types of projects supported	Mission/aims/ motivation (in relation to migrant workers)
FA 11[14]	INGO (UK)	Beijing (HQ), Shanghai, Yunnan (Kunming), Xinjiang (Hetian)	not materially supporting any NGOs	• implementing EC-sponsored project 'No Child Left Behind'; supporting maternity health and childcare for children below the age of 5 • cooperating with local community centres, community-based NGOs and GONGOs • cooperating with local government	• supporting children's welfare

14 Information on FA 11 was collected through Interview no. 24.

FA 12[15]	TNC (Ireland)	Guangdong, Shenzhen	Beijing Workers' Hotline	• enables Beijing Workers' Hotline to disseminate information on hotline assistance it provides in the factories subcontracting for FA 12, and to communicate workers' issues back to the company's management	• enhancing own CSR standards
FA 13[16]	Embassy of a foreign country	Beijing	unknown	unknown	unknown

15 Information on FA 12 is based on the meeting organised by Beijing Workers' Hotline between FA 12 management and factory workers' management in Shenzhen, 18 January 2013.
16 I did not interview this actor, only attending several of their events.

Table A4.2: Breakdown of FAs included in the study (Continued)

	Type of FA	Location (HQ)	Cooperation with labour NGOs	Types of projects supported	Mission/aims/ motivation (in relation to migrant workers)
FA 14[17]	INGO (Italy)	Existed as an institute attached to one of the Italian trade unions since 1983	Saving From Injury	• work on workers' rights in partnership with local NGOs and trade unions (in China only with NGOs as ACFTU is not recognised by the trade union that this INGO is affiliated with)	• promoting trade union association • promoting development of civil society • protection of vulnerable groups, especially women and migrants • combating trafficking • sustainable socio-economic development • education on trade unions and labour rights

17 Information on FA 14 was collected through Interview no. 31 and the organisation's publications.

FA 15[18]	INGO	Hong Kong, set up in 1994 by a labour activist from the mainland	United in Action; Fighting for Justice; other NGOs who were not included in this study	• international advocacy • reports and research on labour conditions in China • supporting grassroots labour organisations • strengthening collective bargaining mechanisms	• China-focused establishment of democratic trade union elections • supporting activist workers in China • development of unionist consciousness • establishment of sustainable collective bargaining mechanism in China

18 Information on FA 15 was collected through Interview no. 39 and the organisation's publications.

Table A4.2: Breakdown of FAs included in the study (Continued)

	Type of FA	Location (HQ)	Cooperation with labour NGOs	Types of projects supported	Mission/aims/ motivation (in relation to migrant workers)
FA 16[19]	INGO	New York, USA, set up in 2000 by a labour activist from the mainland	unknown	• research on workplace abuse in China • international advocacy • offices in China also provide advice and counselling to workers • work with TNCs to pressure local suppliers to conform to labour regulations and standards	• defending workers' rights in China • increasing transparency of supply chains • supporting the Chinese labour movement

19 Information on FA 16 was collected through Interview no. 40 and the organisation's publications.

Table A4.3: Table created by the author based on statistics collected in Beijing Workers' Hotline (Beijing branch) premises (1999–2011)

	Number of hotline enquiries	Number of visits[20] to NGO premises	Number of cases[21] resolved	Number of migrant workers benefited	Sum of remittances mediated (approx.)
Average per day	12	5	N/A	N/A	N/A
2011	3,284	N/A	361	2,293	RMB 4.7 million (USD 727,385)[22]
2004–2011	unknown	unknown	2,814	27,588	RMB 91.884 million (USD 14.22 million)
2006–2011	unknown	16,420	unknown	unknown	unknown
1999–2011	130,000	unknown	unknown	unknown	unknown

20 The number of visits is not equal to the number of workers: most of these are group visits of two or more migrant workers.

21 Some cases tackled by the NGO concern several migrant workers, so the number of cases is not equivalent to the number of migrant workers.

22 This calculation is based on the average exchange rate for 2011 according to the World Bank (6.4615/1 USD/RMB).

Appendix 5

Glossary

bao'an 保安 – security guards
bendiren 本地人 – local residents
bianyuan 边缘 – to marginalise
bu wenming de 不文明的 – uncivilised
butie 补贴– regular allowances, subsidy
chai 拆 – to demolish
chengbiancun 城边村 – urban village by the city
chengguan 城管 – city guards
chengxiang de niudai he qiaoliang 城乡的纽带和桥梁 – links and bridges between city and countryside
chengxiang jiehebu 城乡结合部 – rural–urban fringe zones
chengzhongcun 城中村 – urban village within the city
dage 大哥– brother
dagong 打工 – working for a boss, doing work for others
dagong qunti 打工群体 – migrant worker group
dagongzhe 打工者 – (lit. contingent workers) migrant worker
daili 代理 – to represent (in the context of this book: to represent cases in court)
dailiquan 代理权 – in this book: used to describe the right to civil representation in courts by NGOs
danwei 单位 – work unit
dazhangqigu 大张旗鼓 – clearly and in a loud voice
diaomin 刁民 – unruly people
diceng 底层 – low level
diduan renkou 低端人口 – low-end population
duli gonghui 独立工会 – independent trade unions
*fanfu yao 'laohu' 'cangying' yiqi da*反腐要"老虎""苍蝇"一起打 – 'to hunt down both tigers and flies' (anti-corruption campaign)

fanggong jijin 放公积金 – housing provident fund
fansi jiaban wenhua, changdao hexie yonggong 反思加班文化，倡导和谐用工 – rethinking the culture of overtime, promoting harmonious treatment of workers
fanwei 范围 – space
fengbi guanli 封闭管理 – (lit. sealed management) the practice of walling off migrant villages in the city
fengmao 风貌 – culture
fuwuxing 服务型 – service type [NGO]
gongkai 公开 – open and widely publicised, public openness
gongmin 公民 – (lit. public people) citizen
gongmin shehui 公民社会 – civil society
gongmin zige 公民资格 – citizenship status
gongminquan 公民权 – citizenship (possessing rights of citizenship)
gongren 工人 – workers
gongren jieji 工人阶级 – working class
gongren shehui 工人社会 – workers' society
*gongyi*公益 – public interest
gongyi cishan 公益慈善 – public interest philanthropy
gongyi jigou 公益机构 – public interest organisations
gongyi weiquan 公益维权 – defending rights for public interest
gongyou 工友 – worker-friends
gongyou shehui 工友社会 – workers' society
*gongyunxing*工运型 – labour movement type [NGO]
goufang ruhu 购房入户 – acquisition of an urban *hukou* through purchase of a property
goumai fuwu 购买服务 – purchase of social services (public procurement of services from NGOs)
guakao danwei 挂靠单位 – sponsoring unit, 'mother-in-law institution'
guanxi 关系 – connections, relationships
guanxixue 关系学 – the science of guanxi
guobao 国保 – state security
guomin 国民 – (lit. people of the state) citizens
hefa quanyi 合法权益 – legal rights
hengfu 横幅 – banner (in context in the book, the interviewee meant a banner containing a petition)
hexie 和谐 – harmony
hukou 户口 – household registration number
jia 家 – family, home

jiantao 检讨 – 'self-criticism statement'
jieji 阶级 – (social) class
jiji fengzi 积极分子 – active agent, activist
jijinhui 基金会 – foundation
jiliang 脊梁 – backbone
*jiti tanpan*集体谈判 – collective bargaining
junzi 君子 – morally superior person
juzhuzheng 居住证 – residence permit
kaifang 开放 – openness
kaifang gaige 开放改革 – 'opening to the world reforms'
kangyi 抗议 – to protest
kao ziji 靠自己 – relying on one's self
laodong paiqian 劳动派遣 – dispatch agencies
laodong zui guangrong 劳动最光荣 – 'labour is the most glorious'
laodongju 劳动局 – Labour Bureau
laodong zhan 劳动站 – government-run public labour agencies (types of GONGOs)
laojiao 劳教 – 're-education through labour'
laoxiang 老乡 – friend from one's home town
lianghui 两会 – the most important yearly session of the NPC and the CPPCC
liliang 力量 – strength
lingdao 领导 – leader
liudong renkou 流动人口 – transient population
liyi 利益 – benefits
meiyou wenhua de 没有文化的 – uneducated, uncultured
minbing 民兵 – People's militia
minjian liliang 民间力量 – grassroots force
minjian zuzhi 民间组织 – civic organisation
minyue 民约 – harmonious pact
niangjia 娘家 – institution like a married woman's family
nongmin 农民 – peasant
nongmingong 农民工 – (lit. peasant workers) rural migrant workers
qi bu jiang 七不讲 – 'seven speak-nots' (a campaign under Xi Jinping aimed at eradicating 'Western concepts' from higher education in China)
qidi 启迪 – (lit. inspire enlightenment) inspire change
qing hecha 请喝茶 – 'to invite for tea' (a euphemism for state security interrogation)

qingli 清理 – clear up
qingshi 请示 – instructions (from the Party)
quanmin gongyi 全民公益 – everyone's public interest
qunti 群体 – group
renda daibiao 人大代表 – representatives of the NPC
renkou suzhi 人口素质 – population quality
renshi ziji 认识自己 – to know one's own self
rongru chengshi 融入城市 – integration into the city
ruoshi qunti 弱势群体 – weak and vulnerable group
shangfang de ren 上访的人 – petitioners
shehui fuwu jigou 社会服务机构 – social service organisation
shehui tuanti 社会团体 – social association
shehui xinyong tixi 社会信用体系 – Social Credit System
shehui zhidu 社会制度 – social system
shengmin pinzhi zhi cheng 生活品质之城 – 'the city with quality of life'
shequ 社区 – local community
shimin 市民 – (lit. city people) urban citizen, citizen
shiminhua 市民化 – being turned into an urban citizen
shixin 失信 – untrustworthy
shunmin 顺民 – obedient citizen
suzhi 素质 – quality
suzhi di 素质低 – low quality
teji 特级 – (lit. special) in context in this book: classified
tianxia 天下 – all under heaven
Tianxia dagong shi yi jia 天下打工是一家 – 'All migrant workers under heaven are one family'
*tongzhi*通知 – (lit. message), in the context of this book: internal memo
touming 透明 – transparency
toutoumomo 偷偷摸摸 – in a stealthy, secretive way
waidiren 外地人 – (lit. external people) in the context of this book: migrant workers
waigongrenyuan 外公人员 – (lit. external workers) in the context of this book: migrant workers
weiquan 维权 – defending rights
weiquanxing 维权型 – rights protection type [NGO]
weiwen 维稳 – maintaining stability
wenming 文明 – civilised

women gongyou 我们工友 – our worker-friend
wujing 武警 – armed police, a Chinese equivalent of SWAT (Special Weapons and Tactics)
wuzhengfu zhuyi 无政府主义 – anarchism
xin gongmin 新公民 – new citizen
xin gongren 新工人 – new workers
xin Hangzhouren 新杭州人 – new Hangzhouers, new inhabitants of Hangzhou
xin laodong 新劳动 – new labour
xin shimin 新市民 – new urban citizens
xueyuan guanxi 血缘关系 – (lit. blood relationship) kinship, relationship by blood
*yifa zhiguo*依法治国 – to rule the country in accordance with the law
yundong zhongxin 运动中心 – exercise ground
zhagen 扎根 – to put down roots in a place
Zhifubao 支付报 – an online payment system, a Chinese equivalent of PayPal
zhonghua minzu de jiliang 中华民族的脊梁 – (lit. the backbone of the Chinese nation) holding up the whole nation
zifang 资方 – capitalists
ziji de gonghui 自己的工会 – [migrants'] own trade unions
ziwojuexing 自我觉醒 – self-awareness
ziwotuanjie 自我团结 – solidarity
ziwozuzhi 自我组织 – self-organisation
zixiaershang 自下而上 – bottom-up
zizhu chuangye 自主创业 – self-employed
zougou 走狗 – lapdog

References

Amnesty International. 2019. *Laws Designed to Silence: The Global Crackdown on Civil Society Organizations*. London: Amnesty International. Available at: www.amnesty.org/download/Documents/ACT3096472019ENGLISH.PDF [Accessed 6 May 2020].

Arendt, Hannah. 1951. *The Origin of Totalitarianism*. New York: Harcourt Brace Jovanovich.

Bakken, Børge. 2018. '"Chinese Dream" and Chinese reality; voices from the margins' in Børge Bakken (ed.) *Crime and Chinese Dream*. Hong Kong: Hong Kong University Press, pp. 1–19.

Batra, Nidhi. 2012. 'Village in the city – new slums? – China's and India's approach', *Terra Urban* website. Urban Forum by Society for Participatory Research in Asia (SPRA) and Society for the Promotion of Area Resource Centres (SPARC). Available at: http://terraurban.wordpress.com/tag/urban-village/ [Accessed 1 November 2013].

Bauman, Zygmunt. 1989. *Modernity and the Holocaust*. Cambridge: Polity Press.

Benney, Jonathan. 2016. '*Weiwen* at the grassroots: China's stability maintenance apparatus as a means of conflict resolution', *Journal of Contemporary China* 25(99), pp. 389–405.

Benney, Jonathan. 2013. *Defending Rights in Contemporary China*. London and New York: Routledge.

Bottomore, Tom. 1992. 'Citizenship and social class, forty years on' in T. H. Marshall and Tom Bottomore, *Citizenship and Social Class*. London, Pluto Press, pp. 53–93.

Brandtstadter, Susanne. 2011. 'The law cuts both ways: rural legal activism and citizenship struggles in neosocialist China', *Economy and Society* 40(2), pp. 266–288.

Branigan, Tania. 2014. 'China reforms *hukou* system to improve migrant workers' rights', *The Guardian*, 31 July. Available at: www.theguardian.com/world/2014/jul/31/china-reform-hukou-migrant-workers [Accessed 4 August 2014].

Butollo, Florian and ten Brink, Tobias. 2012. 'Challenging the atomization of discontent: patterns of migrant-worker protest in China during the Series of Strikes in 2010', *Critical Asian Studies* 44(3), pp. 419–440.

Cai, Jingcheng. 2008. 'Nongmingong shiminhua cujin chengshi hexie' [Turning peasant workers [migrants] into (urban) citizens promotes harmony in the city], *Hubei di'er shifan xueyuan xuebao* [*Journal of Hubei University of Education*] 25(4), pp. 68–70.

Callahan, William A. 2012. 'Shanghai's alternative futures: the World Expo, citizen intellectuals, and China's new civil society', *China Information* 26(2), pp. 251–273.

Castells, Manuel. 2000 [1996]. *The Rise of the Network Society*. Oxford: Blackwell Publishers.

CECOC (Congressional-Executive Commission on China). 2006. 'ACFTU measures promote migrant benefits, also aim to curb independent groups', 8 December. Available at: www.cecc.gov/publications/commission-analysis/acftu-measures-promote-migrant-benefits-also-aim-to-curb [Accessed 20 June 2020].

Chan, Anita and Wang, Hong-zen. 2004. 'The impact of the state on workers' conditions: comparing Taiwanese factories in China and Vietnam', *Pacific Affairs* 77(4), pp. 629–646.

Chan, Kam Wing. 2019. 'China's hukou system at 60: continuity and reforms' in Ray Yep, June Wang and Thomas Johnson (eds) *Handbook on Urban Development in China*. Cheltenham: Edward Elgar Publishing, pp. 59–79.

Chan, Kam Wing. 2014. 'China's Urbanization 2020: a new blueprint and direction', *Eurasian Geography and Economics* 55(1), pp. 1–9.

Chan, Kris King-Chi. 2012a. 'Community-based organizations for migrant workers' rights: the emergence of labour NGOs in China', *Community Development Journal* 48(1), pp. 6–22.

Chan, Kris King-Chi. 2012b. 'Class or citizenship? Debating workplace conflict in China', *Journal of Comparative Asia* 42(2), pp. 308–327.

Chen, An. 2010. 'Rising class politics and its impact on China's path to democracy', *Democratization* 10(2), 141–162.

Chen, Feng and Yang, Xuehui. 2017. 'Movement-oriented labour NGOs in South China: exit with voice and displaced unionism', *China Information* 31(2), pp. 155–175.

Chen, Mingxing, Gong, Yinghua, Lu, Dadao, and Ye, Chao. 2019. 'Build a people-oriented urbanization: China's new-type urbanization and Anhui model', *Land Use Policy* 80, pp. 1–9.

Chen, Mingxing, Liu, Weidong, Lu, Dadao, Chen, Hao and Ye, Chao. 2018. 'Progress of China's new-type urbanization construction since 2014: a preliminary assessment', *Cities* 78, pp. 180–193.

Chen, Yingfang. 2005. 'Nongmingong: zhidu anpai yu shenfen rentong' [Peasant labourers: the system's arrangement and identity], *Shehuixue yanjiu* [*Sociological Studies*] 3, pp. 119–132.

Cheng, Hao. 2010. '"Caogen Zhijia": nongmingong jingshende jia' ['Grass-roots Home': the peasant-workers' spiritual home], *Zhejiang Renda* 8, pp. 52–54.

China Daily. 2017. 'Final closure of Beijing Zoo market set at year-end', *China Daily*, 28 June. Available at: www.chinadaily.com.cn/china/2017-06/28/content_29921648.htm [Accessed 5 January 2018].

China Development Brief. 2018. 'The new draft on the registration of social organisations: 15 points to note', 15 August. Available at: http://chinadevelopmentbrief.cn/news/the-new-draft-on-the-registration-of-social-organisations-15-points-of-note/ [Accessed 10 September 2019].

China Development Brief. 2014. 'People-oriented urbanization? Three events in May', 8 July. Available at: http://chinadevelopmentbrief.cn/articles/people-oriented-urbanization-three-events-in-may/ [Accessed 8 December 2018].

China Development Brief. 2013. 'How far has philanthropy sector reform come since 2011? The experts debate', 6 September. Available at: http://chinadevelopmentbrief.cn/articles/how-far-has-philanthropy-sector-reform-come-since-2011-the-experts-debate/ [Accessed 11 December 2017].

China Labour Bulletin. 2017. *China's Social Security System*. Available at: www.clb.org.hk/content/china%E2%80%99s-social-security-system [Accessed 15 November 2017].

China Labour Bulletin. 2016. *China's Teachers Continue to Fight for Decent Work*. Available at: www.clb.org.hk/content/china%E2%80%99s-teachers-continue-fight-decent-work [Accessed 29 January 2018].

China Labour Bulletin. 2013. *Migrant Workers and Their Children*. Available at: www.clb.org.hk/en/content/migrant-workers-and-their-children [Accessed 16 September 2014].

China Network Television. 2011. 'Gongban xuexiao: menlin taigao, shoufei taigui. Minban xuexiao: shenfen gangga, chang beiqudi' [Public schools: threshold too high, fees too high. Private schools: embarrassing position, often banned], *China Network Television (CNTV)*. Available at: http://news.cntv.cn/special/uncommon/11/0817/index.shtml [Accessed 18 November 2012].

Cohen, Myron L. 1993. 'Cultural and political inventions in modern China: The case of the Chinese "peasant"', *Daedalus* 122(2), pp. 151–170.

CPPCC (Chinese People's Political Consultative Conference). 2013. 'Communiqué on the Current State of the Ideological Sphere', *China File*, 8 November. Available at: www.chinafile.com/document-9-chinafile-translation [Accessed 13 May 2020].

Creemers, Rogier. 2018. 'China's social credit system: an evolving practice of control'. Published online: https://ssrn.com/abstract=3175792.

Davis, Meg. 2010. 'China's new non-profit regulations: season of instability', *Asia Catalyst*, 14 June. Available at: https://asiacatalyst.org/blog/2010/06/14/chinas_new_nonprofit_regulations_season_of_instability/ [Accessed 6 October 2020].

De Certeau, Michel. 1984. *The Practice of Everyday Life*. Berkeley: University of California Press.

Doyon, Jérôme. 2012. 'The "Guangdong model": towards the real NGOs?', *China Perspectives 2012/2*. Published online: http://journals.openedition.org/chinaperspectives/5898.

Duan, Yi. 2015. 'Gongyunxing laogong NGO de qianjing yu tiaozhan' [Prospects and challenges for labour-movement-type labour NGOs], *Gongmin*, 20 May. Available at: https://xgmyd.com/archives/17927 [Accessed 28 October 2019].

Duara, Prasenjit. 2000. 'Local worlds: the poetics and politics of the native place in modern China', *South Atlantic Quarterly* 99(1), pp. 13–45.

Dutton, Michael. 1992. *Policing and Punishment in China: From Patriarchy to the People*. New York: Cambridge University Press.

Enjuto Martinez, Regina. 2016. 'Within and against the law. The politics of labour law in China's adaptive authoritarianism'. PhD thesis, Department of International Development, London School of Economics and Political Science.

Erbaugh, Mary S. 2008. 'China expands its courtesy: saying "hello" to strangers', *Journal of Asian Studies* 67(2), pp. 621–652.

Fan, Wei and Mao, Dan. 2008. 'Tili laodong: gonggong fuwu shijiao toushi' [Physical labour: perspective from public services], *Jingying Guanlizhe* [*Manager's Journal*] 11, p. 50.

Fan, Yongling, Allen, Ryan and Sun, Tieshan. 2014. 'Spatial mismatch in Beijing, China: Implications of job accessibility for Chinese low-wage workers', *Habitat International* 44, pp. 202–210.

Fang, I-Chieh. 2011. 'Growing up and becoming independent: an ethnographic study of new generation migrant workers in China'. PhD thesis, London School of Economics and Political Science.

Fong, Vanessa and Murphy, Rachel. 2006. 'Introduction: Chinese experiences of citizenship at the margins' in Vanessa Fong and Rachel Murphy (eds) *Chinese Citizenship: Views from the Margins*. New York: Routledge, pp. 1–8.

Ford, Peter. 2010. 'Law chokes Chinese NGOs' foreign funding', *The Christian Science Monitor*, 20 May. Available at: www.csmonitor.com/World/Asia-Pacific/2010/0520/Law-chokes-Chinese-NGOs-foreign-funding [Accessed 19 April 2013].

Foucault, Michel. 1991. 'Governmentality' in G. Burchell, C. Gordon and P. Miller (eds) *The Foucault Effect: Studies in Governmentality*. London: Harvester Wheatsheaf, pp. 87–104.

Foucault, Michel. 1972. *The Archaeology of Knowledge*. London: Tavistock.

Franceschini, Ivan. 2014. 'Labour NGOs in China: a real force for political change?', *The China Quarterly* 218, pp. 474–492.

Franceschini, Ivan and Nesossi, Elisa. 2018. 'State repression of Chinese labor NGOs: a chilling effect?', *The China Journal* 80, pp. 111–129.

Fraser, Nancy. 1995. 'From redistribution to recognition? Dilemmas of justice in a "post-socialist" age', *New Left Review* 212, pp. 68–93.

Friedman, Eli. 2014. *Insurgency Trap: Labour Politics in Postsocialist China*. Ithaca, NY: Cornell University Press.

Friedman, Eli and Lee, Ching Kwan. 2010. 'Remaking the world of Chinese labour: a 30-year retrospective', *British Journal of Industrial Relations* 48(3), pp. 507–533.

Froissart, Chloé. 2018. 'Negotiating authoritarianism and its limits: worker-led collective bargaining in Guangdong Province', *China Information*, November, 32(1), pp. 23–45.

Froissart, Chloé. 2014. 'Using the law as "harmonious weapon": the ambiguities of legal activism in favour of migrant workers in China', *Journal of Civil Society* 10(3), pp. 255–272.

Frolic, Michael B. 1997. 'State-led civil society' in Timothy Brook and Michael B. Frolic (eds) *Civil Society in China*. Armonk, NY: East Gate Books.

Fu, Diana. 2017. *Mobilizing Without the Masses: Control and Contention in China*. Cambridge: Cambridge University Press.

Fu, Diana and Distelhorst, Greg. 2017. 'Grassroots participation and repression under Hu Jintao and Xi Jinping', *The China Journal* 79, pp. 100–122.

Fulda, Andreas. 2013. 'Government procurement of CSO services in the PR China: doing the Party's work?' China Institute Policy Paper 2013: No. 4. Nottingham: University of Nottingham.

Gallagher, Mary. 2017. *Authoritarian Legality in China: Law, Workers, and the State*. Cambridge: Cambridge University Press.

Gallagher, Mary. 2006. 'Mobilizing the law in China: "informed disenchantment" and the development of legal consciousness', *Law & Society Review* 40(4), pp. 783–816.

Gleiss, Marielle Stigum. 2015. 'Speaking up for the suffering (br)other: Weibo activism, discursive struggles and minimal politics in China', *Media, Culture and Society* 37(4), pp. 513–529.

Gleiss, Marielle Stigum. 2014. 'How Chinese labour NGOs legitimize their identity and voice', *China Information* 28(3), pp. 362–381.

Goldman, Merle. 2005. *From Comrade to Citizen: The Struggle for Political Rights in China*. Cambridge, MA: Harvard University Press.

Goldman, Merle and Perry, Elizabeth J. 2002. 'Introduction: political citizenship in modern China' in Merle Goldman and Elizabeth J. Perry (eds) *Changing Meaning of Citizenship in Modern China*. Cambridge, MA: Harvard University Press, pp. 1–22.

Gore, Lance L. P. 2012. 'China in search of a new development model: Guangdong or Chongqing?' EAI Background Brief No. 701. Singapore: East Asian Institute.

Gow, Michael. 2017. 'The core socialist values of the Chinese Dream: towards a Chinese integral state', *Critical Asian Studies* 49(1), pp. 92–116.

Guang, Lei. 1996. 'Elusive democracy: conceptual change and the Chinese democracy movement, 1978–79 to 1989', *Modern China* 22(4), pp. 417–447.

Guo, Zhonghua. 2015. 'The emergence of the citizen concept in Modern China. 1899–1919' in Zhonghua Guo and Sujian Guo (eds) *Theorizing Chinese Citizenship*. Lanham, MD: Lexington Books, pp. 3–22.

Guo, Zhonghua and Liang, Tuo. 2017. 'Differentiating citizenship in urban China: a case study of Dongguan city', *Citizenship Studies* 21(7), pp. 773–791.
Habermas, Jürgen. 1989. *The Structural Transformation of the Public Sphere: An Inquiry into a Category of Bourgeois Society*. Cambridge, MA: MIT Press.
Halegua, Aaron. 2016. *Who Will Represent China's Workers? Lawyers, Legal Aid, and the Enforcement of Labour Rights*. New York: US–Asia Law Institute, New York University School of Law.
Hand, Keith. 2006. 'Using law for a righteous purpose: the Sun Zhigang incident and evolving forms of citizen action in the People's Republic of China', *Columbia Journal of Transnational Law* 45(1), pp. 115–147.
Hann, Chris and Dunn, Elizabeth (eds). 1996. *Civil Society: Challenging Western Models*. London: Routledge.
Hardt, Michael and Negri, Antonio. 2000. *Empire*. Cambridge, MA: Harvard University Press.
Harvey, David. 2012. *Rebel Cities: From the Right to the City to the Urban Revolution*. London: Verso.
Harvey, David. 2008. 'The right to the city', *New Left Review* 53, pp. 23–40.
Hayward, Jane. Forthcoming. 'Building city walls: reordering the population through Beijing's upside-down villages', *Modern China*.
Hayward, Jane and Jakimów, Małgorzata. Forthcoming 2021. 'Who makes the city? Beijing's urban villages as sites of ideological contestation', *positions: asia critique*.
He, Baogang. 2003. 'The making of a nascent civil society in China' in David C. Schak and Wayne Hudson (eds) *Civil Society in Asia*. Hampshire: Ashgate, pp. 114–139.
He, Na. 2010. 'Migrants put behind fences', *China Daily*, 6 May. Available at: www.chinadaily.com.cn/china/2010-05/06/content_9814616.htm [Accessed 18 December 2011].
He, Zengke. 2012. 'Institutional barriers to the development of civil society in current China' in Jianxing Yu and Sujian Guo (eds) *Civil Society and Governance in China*. New York: Palgrave Macmillan, pp. 157–173.
Hildebrandt, Timothy. 2013. *Social Organizations and the Authoritarian State in China*. Cambridge: Cambridge University Press.
Ho, Loretta Wing Wah. 2010. *Gay and Lesbian Subculture in Urban China*. London and New York: Routledge.
Ho, Peter. 2008a. 'Introduction: embedded activism and political change in a semi-authoritarian context' in Peter Ho and Richard Louis Edmonds (eds) *China's Embedded Activism: Opportunities and Constraints of a Social Movement*. London and New York: Routledge, pp. 1–19.
Ho, Peter. 2008b. 'Self-imposed censorship and de-politicized politics in China: green activism or a color revolution?' in Peter Ho and Richard Louis Edmonds (eds) *China's Embedded Activism: Opportunities and Constraints of a Social Movement*. London and New York: Routledge, pp. 20–43.

Ho, Peter. 2001. 'Greening without conflict? Environmentalism, NGOs and civil society in China', *Development and Change* 32(5), pp. 893–921.

Ho, Virginia Harper. 2003. *Labor Dispute Resolution in China: Implications for Labor Rights and Legal Reforms*. Berkeley, CA: Institute of East Asian Studies, University of California.

Howell, Jude. 2015. 'Shall we dance? Welfarist incorporation and the politics of state–labour NGO relations in China', *The China Quarterly* 223, pp. 702–723.

Howell, Jude. 2012. '*Civil society, corporatism and capitalism in China*', *Journal of Comparative Asian Development* 11(2), pp. 271–297.

Howell, Jude. 2009. 'Civil society and migrants in China' in Rachel Murphy (ed.) *Labour Migration and Social Development in Contemporary China*. London and New York: Routledge, pp. 171–194.

Howell, Jude. 2004. *Governance in China*. Maryland: Rowman & Littlefield.

Hsu, Carolyn L. 2017. *Social Entrepreneurship and Citizenship in China: The Rise of NGOs in the PRC*. London and New York: Routledge.

Hsu, Jennifer. 2017. *State of Exchange: Migrant NGOs and the Chinese Government*. Vancouver: UBC Press.

Hsu, Jennifer. 2009. 'Quietly, quietly, quietly: Beijing's migrant civil society organisations' in Melissa Butcher and Selvaraj Velayutham (eds) *Dissent and Cultural Resistance in Asia's Cities*. London and New York: Routledge, pp. 53–71.

Hsu, Jennifer, Hsu, Carolyn and Hasmath, Reza. 2016. 'NGO strategy in an authoritarian context, and their implications for citizenship: the case of People's Republic of China'. Paper presented at the American Sociological Association Annual Meeting, Seattle, USA, 20–23 August.

Hu, Yinbing. 2010. 'Closed-off villages bad idea', *China Daily*, 29 April. Available at: www.chinadaily.com.cn/cndy/2010-04/29/content_9789183.htm [Accessed 17 July 2011].

Huang, Wenhai. 2017. *Xiongnian zhipan* [*We, the Workers*], Zeng Jinyan and Huang Wenhai Production [film].

Huang, Yan. 2012. 'Chuangxin gongminquan: laogong NGO de nihe celüe' [Innovating citizenship: labour NGOs' mixed strategy], *Guojia xingzheng xueyuan xuebao* [*Journal of Chinese Academy of Governance*] 14, pp. 100–106.

Huang, Yu and Sharif, Naubahar. 2017. 'From 'labour dividend' to 'robot dividend': technological change and workers' power in south China', *Agrarian South: Journal of Political Economy* 6(1), pp. 1–26.

Huang, Ziyi and Han, Wei. 2017. 'Schools for migrant children vanishing as Beijing combats population growth', *Caixin*, 21 August. Available at: www.caixinglobal.com/2017-08-21/schools-for-migrant-children-vanishing-as-beijing-combats-population-growth-101132981.html [Accessed 4 December 2019].

Hudson, Wayne. 2003. 'Problematizing European theories of civil society' in David C. Schak and Wayne Hudson (eds) *Civil Society in Asia*. Hampshire: Ashgate, pp. 9–19.

Hui, Elaine Sio-ieng. 2016. 'The labour law system, capitalist hegemony and class politics in China', *The China Quarterly* 226, pp. 431–455.

ICNL (The International Center for Not-for-Profit Law). 2017. *Civic Freedom Monitor: China*. Available at: www.icnl.org/research/monitor/china.html [Accessed 13 December 2017].

Isin, Engin F. 2009. 'Citizenship in flux: the figure of the activist citizen', *Subjectivity* 29, pp. 367–388.

Isin, Engin F. 2008. 'Theorizing acts of citizenship' in Engin F. Isin and Greg M. Nielsen (eds) *Acts of Citizenship*. London: Zed Books, pp. 15–43.

Isin, Engin F. 2002. *Being Political: Genealogies of Citizenship*. Minneapolis: University of Minnesota Press.

Isin, Engin F. and Nielsen, Greg M. 2008. 'Introduction: acts of citizenship' in Engin F. Isin and Greg M. Nielsen (eds) *Acts of Citizenship*. London: Zed Books, pp. 1–12.

Isin, Engin F. and Wood, Patricia K. 1999. *Citizenship and Identity*. London: Sage Publications.

Jacka, Tamara, Kipnis, Andrew and Sargeson, Sally. 2013. 'Citizenship, household registration and migration' in Tamara Jacka, Andrew Kipnis and Sally Sargeson (eds) *Contemporary China: Society and Social Change*. Cambridge: Cambridge University Press, pp. 65–82.

Jakimów, M. 2017. 'Resistance through accommodation: a citizenship approach to migrant worker NGOs in China', *Journal of Contemporary China* 26(108), pp. 915–930.

Jakimów, M. 2015. 'Understanding citizenship beyond the *Hukou* system: the role of migrant worker NGOs in transformation of citizenship in China' in Zhonghua Guo and Sujian Guo (eds) *Theorizing Chinese Citizenship: Challenges Facing Chinese Political Development*. Lanham, MD: Lexington Books, pp. 111–132.

Jakimów, M. 2012. 'Chinese citizenship "after" Orientalism. Academic narratives on internal migrants in China', *Citizenship Studies* 16(5&6), pp. 657–671.

Jakimów, M. and Barabantseva, E. 2016. '"Othering" in the construction of Chinese citizenship' in Lion König and Bidish Chaudhuri (eds) *The Politics of the 'Other': Western Concepts in Non-Western Contexts*. London: Routledge, pp. 167–178.

Janoski, Thomas. 1998. *Citizenship and Civil Society: A Framework of Rights and Obligations in Liberal, Traditional and Social Democratic Regimes*. Cambridge: University of Cambridge.

Jiang, Chengcheng. 2011. 'In Beijing, students in limbo after migrant schools closed', *Time*, 14 September. Available at: http://content.time.com/time/world/article/0,8599,2093175,00.html [Accessed 6 October 2020].

Jones, Gareth A. 2004. 'The geopolitics of democracy and citizenship in Latin America' in Clive Barnett and Murray Low (eds) *Spaces of Democracy*. London: Sage Publications, pp. 161–184.

Kang, Yihong. 2010. 'Kang, Yihong' in Qiang Xu, Deyuan Luo and Zhongcun Chen (eds) *2009–2010 Zhongguo dagong shige jingxuan* [2009–

2010 Selection of Chinese Dagong Poetry]. Shanghai: Shanghai Wenyi, pp. 7–9.

Keck, Margaret E. and Sikkink, Kathryn. 1998. *Activists beyond Borders: Advocacy Networks in International Politics*. London: Cornell University Press.

Kennedy, Kerry J. 2013. 'Introduction. Educating Chinese citizens for the 'Chinese century' – views from the inside' in Kerry J. Kennedy, Gregory Fairbrother and Zhengzhou Zhao (eds) *Citizenship Education in China: Preparing Citizens for the Chinese Century*. London and New York: Routledge, pp. 1–8.

Kerr, David. 2015. 'Civil society and China's governance dilemmas in the era of national rejuvenation' in David Kerr (ed.) *China's Many Dreams: Comparative Perspectives on China's Search for National Rejuvenation*. Basingstoke: Palgrave, pp. 35–64.

Kochan, Dror. 2019. 'Spatiality, belonging, and citizenship in the age of migration in contemporary China', *Asia Pacific Viewpoint*. Published online: https://doi.org/10.1111/apv.12233.

Kostka, Genie and Antoine, Lukas. 2020. 'Fostering model citizenship: behavioral responses to China's emerging social credit systems', *Policy & Internet* 12(3), 256–289.

Kovacheva, Vesela, Vogel, Dita, Zhang, Xiaonan and Jordan, Bill. 2012. 'Comparing the development of free movement and social citizenship for internal migrants in the European Union and China – converging trends?', *Citizenship Studies* 16 (3–4), pp. 545–561.

Kubat, Aleksandra. 2018. 'Morality as legitimacy under Xi Jinping: the political functionality of traditional culture for the Chinese Communist Party', *Journal of Current Chinese Affairs* 47(3), pp. 47–86.

Kuo, Lily. 2013. 'China is spending more on policing its own people than on its defense budget', *Quartz*, 5 May. Available at: https://qz.com/59367/china-is-spending-more-on-policing-its-own-people-than-on-its-defense-budget/ [Accessed 30 January 2018].

Kwong, Julia. 2011. 'Education and identity: the marginalisation of migrant youths in Beijing', *Journal of Youth Studies* 14(8), pp. 871–883.

Lau, Clement Chu S. 2009. 'The role of NGOs in China', *Journal of Ideology* 31 (3&4), pp. 1–18.

Lau, Stuart. 2017. 'Beijing unveils vision for "downsized", liveable city with cleaner air', *South China Morning Post*, 29 September. Available at: www.scmp.com/news/china/policies-politics/article/2113458/beijing-unveils-vision-downsized-liveable-city-cleaner [Accessed 29 November 2019].

Lee, Ching Kwan. 2007. *Against the Law: Labor Protests in China's Rustbelt and Sunbelt*. Berkeley: University of California Press.

Lee, Ching Kwan and Shen, Yuan. 2011. 'The anti-solidarity machine?: Labour nongovernmental organisations in China' in Sarosh Kuruvilla, Ching Kwan Lee and Mary E. Gallagher (eds) *From Iron Rice Bowl to Informalization: Markets, Workers and the State in a Changing China*. Ithaka and London: Cornell University Press, pp. 173–187.

Lefebvre, Henri. 1996. *Writings on Cities*. Oxford: Blackwell Publishers.
Lefebvre, Henri. 1991. *The Production of Space*. Oxford: Blackwell.
Li, Bingqin, Chen, Chunlai and Hu, Biliang. 2016. 'Governing urbanization and the New Urbanization Plan in China', *Environment and Urbanization* 28(2), pp. 515–534.
Liang, Lavinia. 2019. 'The uncertain future of a migrant school in Beijing', *CityLab*, 24 June. Available at: www.citylab.com/equity/2019/06/china-migrant-school-beijing-subway-expansion-hukou-children/592312/ [Accessed 20 November 2019].
Lin, Delia. 2017. *Civilising Citizens in Post-Mao China: Understanding the Rhetoric of Suzhi*. Oxon: Routledge.
Lin, Sainan. 2016. 'Socio-spatial segregation in China and migrants' everyday life experiences: the case of Wenzhou', *Urban Geography* 38(7), pp. 1019–1038.
Liu, Yong, Yue, Wenze and Fan, Peilei. 2011. 'Spatial determinants of urban land conversion in large Chinese cities: a case of Hangzhou', *Environment and Planning B: Planning and Design* 38(4), pp. 706–725.
Lu, Yao, Zheng, Wenjun and Wang, Wei. 2017. 'Migration and popular resistance in rural China: Wukan and beyond', *The China Quarterly* 229, pp. 1–22.
Lu, Yiyi. 2007. 'Environmental civil society and governance in China', *International Journal of Environmental Studies* 64(1), pp. 59–69.
Mao, Dan. 2010. 'Zhengfu chuangxin: dui guomin shenghuo fangshi de yingxiang' [The innovativeness of the government: the impact on citizens' lifestyles], *Hangzhou (Women)* [*We, Hangzhou*] 11, pp. 27–28.
Mao, Dan. 2008. 'Xijie gaijin yifen, pinzhi tishen yibu' [The details improve little by little, the quality advances step by step], *Hangzhou Tongxun (Shenghuo Pinzhi Ban)* [*Hangzhou Communicate (Life Quality Edition)*] 1, p. 52.
Mao, Zedong. 1940. 'On new democracy' in *Selected Works of Mao Tse-Tung*, Volume 2. Peking: Foreign Language Press. Available at: www.marxists.org/reference/archive/mao/selected-works/volume-2/mswv2_26.htm [Accessed 15 September 2014].
Marshall, Thomas H. 1992 [1950]. 'Citizenship and social class' in T. H. Marshall and Tom Bottomore (eds) *Citizenship and Social Class*. London: Pluto Press, pp. 1–52.
Mertha, Andrew C. 2010. *China Water Warriors: Citizen Action and Policy Change*. Ithaca, NY: Cornell University Press.
Mertha, Andrew C. 2008. '"Fragmented authoritarianism 2.0": political pluralisation in the Chinese policy process', *The China Quarterly* 200, pp. 995–1012.
Miller, Byron. 2004. 'Space of mobilization: transnational social movements' in Clive Barnett and Murray Low (eds) *Spaces of Democracy*. London: Sage Publications, pp. 223–246.
Mouffe, Chantal. 1993. *The Return of the Political*. London: Verso.

Murphy, Rachel. 2004. 'Turning Chinese peasants into modern citizens: "population quality", demographic transition, and primary schools', *The China Quarterly* 177, pp. 1–20.

Nair, Parvati. 2020. 'India's internal migrants are citizens too – the government must protect them', *The Conversation*, 15 June. Available at: https://theconversation.com/indias-internal-migrants-are-citizens-too-the-government-must-protect-them-140295 [Accessed 20 June 2020].

National Bureau of Statistics of China. 2019. *2018 nian nongmingong lance diaocha baogao* [*The Report of 2018 Survey of Migrant Workers*]. Available at: www.stats.gov.cn/tjsj/zxfb/201904/t20190429_1662268.html [Accessed 4 December 2019].

Noakes, Stephen. 2018. *The Advocacy Trap: Transnational Activism and State Power in China*. Manchester: Manchester University Press.

Oakes, Tim and Schein, Louisa. 2006. 'Translocal China: an introduction' in Tim Oakes and Louisa Schein (eds) *Translocal China: Linkages, Identities, and the Reimagining of Space*. London and New York: Routledge, pp. 1–35.

O'Brien, Kevin and Li, Lianjiang. 2006. *Rightful Resistance in Rural China*. Cambridge: Cambridge University Press.

Ong, Aihwa. 2006. *Neoliberalism as Exception: Mutations in Citizenship and Sovereignty*. Durham, NC: Duke University Press.

Ong, Aihwa. 1999. *Flexible Citizenship: The Cultural Logics of Transnationality*. Durham and London: Duke University Press.

Page, Jeremy. 2011. 'Unease in "Happy Guangdong"', *The Wall Street Journal*, 18 June. Available at: http://online.wsj.com/articles/SB10001424052702303499204576389453425121490 [Accessed 18 November 2014].

Palmer, James. 2020. 'China's coronavirus success is made possible by Xi's brutality', *Foreign Policy*, 14 May. Available at: https://foreignpolicy.com/2020/05/14/china-coronavirus-pandemic-lockdown-xi-jinping/ [Accessed 20 June 2020].

Palmer, James. 2017. 'How to destroy the heart of a Chinese city', *Foreign Policy*, 31 May. Available at: https://foreignpolicy.com/2017/05/31/how-to-destroy-the-heart-of-a-chinese-city-beijing/ [Accessed 28 May 2018].

Peerenboom, Randall. 2002. *China's Long March Toward Rule of Law*. Cambridge: Cambridge University Press.

Phillips, Tom. 2017. 'The gentrification of Beijing: razing off migrant villages spells end of China dream', *The Guardian*, 8 December. Available at: www.theguardian.com/world/2017/dec/08/beijing-gentrification-china-migrant-villages-destroyed?CMP=share_btn_fb [Accessed 6 October 2020].

PRC Government. 2014. 'Guojia xinxing chengzhenhua guihua (2014–2020 nian)' [National New-type Urbanisation Plan (2014–2020)], 16 March. Available at: www.gov.cn/zhengce/2014–03/16/content_2640075.htm [Accessed 6 October 2020].

Pringle, Tim. 2011. *Trade Unions in China: The Challenge of Labour Unrest*. London and New York: Routledge.

Pun, Ngai. 2005. *Made in China: Women Factory Workers in a Global Workplace*. Durham, NC: Duke University Press.
Qian, Junxi and Guo, Junwan'guo. 2019. 'Migrants on exhibition: the emergence of migrant worker museums in China as a neoliberal experiment on governance', *Journal of Urban Affairs* 41(3), pp. 305–323.
Qian, Junxi and He, Shenjing. 2012. 'Rethinking social power and the right to the city amidst China's emerging urbanism', *Environment and Planning A* 44(12), pp. 2801–2816.
Qian, Junxi and Zhu, Hong. 2014. 'Chinese urban migrants' sense of place: emotional attachment, identity formation, and place dependence in the city and community of Guangzhou', *Asia Pacific Viewpoint* 55(1), pp. 81–101.
Qian, Yingyi and Weingast, Barry R. 1997. 'Federalism as a commitment to preserving market incentives', *Journal of Economic Perspectives* 11(4), pp. 83–92.
Reimann, Kim D. 2005. 'Up to no good? Recent critics and critiques of NGOs' in Oliver P. Richmond and Henry F. Carey (eds) *Subcontracting Peace: The Challenges of NGO Peacebuilding*. Aldershot: Ashgate, pp. 37–54.
Ren, Xuefei. 2012. 'Dancing with the state: migrant workers, NGOs, and the remaking of urban citizenship in China' in Michael Peter Smith and Michael Mcquarrie (eds) *Remaking Urban Citizenship: Organizations, Institutions, and the Right to the City*. New Brunswick: Transaction Publishers, pp. 99–108.
SACOM. 2012. 'Open letter to the Guangdong government'. Available at: http://sacom.hk/archives/953 on 20/06/2013 [Accessed 12 May 2013].
Saich, Tony. 2000. 'Negotiating the state: the development of social organizations in China', *The China Quarterly* 161, pp. 124–141.
Said, Edward. 1978. *Orientalism*. London: Penguin Books.
Salmenkari, Taru. 2013. 'Theoretical poverty in the research in Chinese civil society', *Modern Asian Studies* 47 (2), pp. 682–711.
Shenzhen Bureau of Statistics. 2019. *Shenzhenshi 2018nian guomin jingji he shehui fazhan tongji gongbao* [*2018 Shenzhen Statistical Communique on National Economic and Social Development*]. Available at: www.sz.gov.cn/tjj/tjsj/tjgb1/201904/t20190419_16908575.htm [Accessed 15 June 2020].
Shenzhen Evening News. 2013. '2012 Shenzhen changzhu renkou 1300.18 wan zengjia le 29.59 wan' [2012 Shenzhen residents number climbs to 13 m, increase of 295,900], *Shenzhen Wan Bao* [*Shenzhen Evening News*]. Available at: http://esf.sz.fang.com/newsecond/news/9410923.htm?utm_source=szblog&utm_medium=click&utm_term=%E6%96%B0%E9%97%BB&utm_content=xinwen&utm_campaign=P2013.1.22 [Accessed 25 August 2014].
Shi-Kupfer, Kristin and Lang, Bertram. 2017. 'Overseas NGOs in China: left in a legal limbo', *The Diplomat*, 4 March. Available at: https://thediplomat.com/2017/03/overseas-ngos-in-china-left-in-legal-limbo/ [Accessed 6 October 2020].

Shieh, Shawn. 2009. 'Beyond corporatism and civil society. Three modes of state–NGO interactions in China' in Jonathan Schwartz and Shawn Shieh (eds) *State and Society Responses to Social Welfare Needs in China: Serving the People*. London and New York: Routledge, pp. 22–42.

Shin, Hyun Bang. 2013. 'The right to the city and critical reflections on China's property rights activism', *Antipode* 45, 5: 1167–1189.

Shin, Hyun Bang and Li, Bingqing. 2012. 'Migrants, landlords and their uneven experience of the beijing olympic games', CASE paper (CASE/163), Centre for Analysis of Social Exclusion. London: London School of Economics.

Simon, Karla. 2013. *Civil Society in China: The Legal Framework from Ancient Times to the 'New Reform Era'*. Oxford: Oxford University Press.

Spires, Anthony. 2011. 'Contingent symbiosis and civil society in an authoritarian state: understanding the survival of China's grassroots NGOs', *American Journal of Sociology* 117 (1), pp. 1–45.

State Administration of Foreign Exchange. 2010. *Notice of the State Administration of Foreign Exchange on Issues concerning the Administration of Foreign Exchange Donated to or by Domestic Institutions*. Beijing: State Administration of Foreign Exchange. Available at: www.apccsl.org/pubs/Notice_of_the_State_Administration_of_Foreign_Exchange_20100226.pdf [Accessed 10 April 2011].

State Council. 2014. *Shehui xinyong tixi jianshe guihua gangyao (2014–2020 nian)* [*Planning Outline for the Construction of a Social Credit System (2014–2020)*]. Available in English at: https://chinacopyrightandmedia.wordpress.com/2014/06/14/planning-outline-for-the-construction-of-a-social-credit-system-2014-2020/ [Accessed 3 December 2019].

Steadman-Jones, Gareth. 1983. *Languages of Class: Studies in English Working Class History, 1832–1982*. Cambridge: Cambridge University Press.

Solinger, Dorothy. 1999. *Contesting Citizenship in Urban China: Peasant Migrants, the State, and the Logic of the Market*. Berkeley: University of California Press.

Somers, Margaret. 2008. *Genealogies of Citizenship: Markets, Statelessness, and the Right to Have Rights*. Cambridge: Cambridge University Press.

Somers, Margaret. 1996. 'Class formation and capitalism. A second look at a classic', *European Journal of Sociology* 37(1), pp. 180–202.

Song, Yan, Yves, Zenou and Chengri Ding. 2008. 'Let's not throw the baby out with the bath water: the role of urban villages in housing rural migrants in China', *Urban Studies* 45(2), pp. 313–330.

Sun, Wanning. 2014. *Subaltern China: Rural Migrants, Media, and Cultural Practices*. Lanham, Boulder, New York and London: Rowman & Littlefield.

Sun, Wanning. 2009. *Maid in China: Media, Morality, and the Cultural Politics of Boundaries*. New York: Routledge.

Swider, Sarah. 2015. 'Reshaping China's urban citizenship: street vendors, chengguan and struggles over the right to the city', *Critical Sociology* 41(4–5), pp. 701–716.

Tang, Didi. 2014. '30,000 workers are striking at China's biggest shoe factory in one of country's biggest strikes ever', *Business Insider*, 17 April. Available at: www.businessinsider.com/30000-workers-striking-at-chinas-biggest-shoe-factory-2014-4#ixzz3DY9ntQzl [Accessed 17 September 2014].

Teets, Jessica. 2014. *Civil Society under Authoritarianism: The China Model.* Cambridge: Cambridge University Press.

Teets, Jessica, Hasmath, Reza and Lewis, Orion. 2017. 'The incentive to innovate? The behaviour of local policymakers in China', *Chinese Journal of Political Science* 22, pp. 505–517.

The Economist. 2014. 'Danger zone', *The Economist*, 26 April. Available at: www.economist.com/news/china/21601291-huge-strike-southern-china-shows-migrant-workers-are-starting-demand-more-just?fsrc=scn%2Ftw_ec%2Fdanger_zone [Accessed 12 May 2014].

The Economist. 2011. 'School's out', *The Economist*, 3 September. Available at: www.economist.com/node/21528301 [Accessed 18 November 2012].

Unger, Jonathan and Chan, Anita. 1995. 'Corporatism in China: a developmental state in an East Asian context' in Barrett L. McCormick and Jonathan Unger (eds) *China After Socialism: In the Footsteps of Eastern Europe or East Asia?* Armonk and New York: East Gate Books, pp. 95–129.

Walters, William. 2008. 'Acts of demonstration: mapping the territory of (non-)citizenship' in Engin F. Isin and Greg M. Nielsen (eds) *Acts of Citizenship*. London: Zed Books, pp. 182–206.

Wang, Fei-ling. 2010. 'Conflict, resistance and the transformation of the *hukou* system' in Elizabeth Perry (ed.) *Chinese Society: Change, Conflict and Resistance*. London: Routledge, pp. 80–100.

Wang, Mingming. 2014. *The West as the Other: A Genealogy of Chinese Occidentalism*. Hong Kong: The Chinese University Press.

Wang, Xiaozhang. 2009. 'Cong "shengcun" dao "chengren": gongminquan shiyuxia de nongmingong wenti' [From 'existence' to 'recognition': issues of peasant workers in the view of citizenship], *Shehuixue Yanjiu* [*Sociological Studies*] 1, pp. 121–138.

Weber, Eugen. 1976. *Peasants into Frenchmen: The Modernization of Rural France, 1870–1914*. Stanford: Stanford University Press.

Weber, Max. 1963. *Economy and Society: An Outline of Interpretative Sociology*, Vol. 2. Berkeley: University of California Press.

Weber, Max. 1930. *Protestant Ethic and the Spirit of Capitalism*. London: George Allen and Unwin Ltd.

White, Stephen, McAllister, Ian and Munro, Neil. 2017. 'Economic inequality and political stability in Russia and China', *Europe Asia Studies* 69(1), pp. 1–7.

Whyte, Martin K. and Parish, William L. 1984. *Urban Life in Contemporary China*. Chicago: University of Chicago Press.

Wong, Tai-Chee and Liu, Ran. 2017. 'Development urbanism, city image branding, and the 'right to the city' in transitional China', *Urban Policy and Research* 35 (2), pp. 210–223.

Woodman, Sophia. 2017. 'Legitimating exclusion and inclusion: "culture", education and local urban citizenship in Tianjin and Lanzhou', *Citizenship Studies* 21(7), pp. 755–772.

Wu, Cherry. 2018. 'How to get a Shenzhen *hukou*', *China Briefing*, 21 November. Available at: www.china-briefing.com/news/chinas-hukou-system-benefits-and-application-process-in-shenzhen/ [Accessed 2 June 2020].

Wu, Fengshi. 2017. 'An emerging group name "Gongyi": ideational collectivity in China's civil society', *China Review* 17(2), pp. 123–150.

Xia, Ying and Guan, Bing. 2017. 'Practicing democratic citizenship in an authoritarian state: grassroots self-governance in urban China', *Citizenship Studies* 21(7), pp. 809–823.

Xiang, Biao. 2005. *Transcending Boundaries: Zhejiangcun: The Story of a Migrant Village in Beijing*. Leiden: Brill.

Xinhua. 2019. '2682wan renci yin shixin bei xianzhi chengji' [2.682 m people are denied plane tickets due to untrustworthiness], *Xinhuanet*, 17 July. Available at: www.xinhuanet.com/fortune/2019-07/17/c_1124761947.htm [Accessed 10 December 2019].

Xiong, Yihan and Li, Miao. 2017. 'Citizenship education as NGO intervention: turning migrant children in Shanghai into "new citizens"', *Citizenship Studies* 21(7), pp. 792–808.

Xu, Yi. 2013. 'Labour non-governmental organizations in China: mobilizing rural migrant workers', *Journal of Industrial Relations* 55 (2), pp. 243–259.

Xu, Zhiyong. 2017. *To Build a Free China: A Citizen Journey*. Boulder, CO: Lynne Reiner Publishers.

Xu, Zu'e. 2013. 'Rang "shenghuo pinzhi zhi cheng" de yangguangxi xiang meiyiwei xin Hangzhouren: "Hangzhoushi liudong renkou fuwu guanli tiaoli" shishi qingkuang diaocha' [Let the sunshine of 'the city of life quality' reach every new Hangzhouer: the investigation of the implementation of the 'Hangzhou Floating Population Service Management Regulation'], *Chenshixue yanjiu* [*Urban Studies*] 5, pp. 102–108.

Yan, Hairong. 2008. *New Masters, New Servants: Development, Migration, and Women Workers*. Durham, NC: Duke University Press.

Yang, Jianjun, He, Youjoun, Pauleit, Stephan, Spiekermann, Martin and Burkhardt, Irene. 2008. 'Analysis and assessment of regional and local government and planning strategies: Hangzhou Case Study', part of a report entitled *Governance and Strategic Planning Scenarios, Module 3*. Available at: http://spool.tudelft.nl/index.php/spool/article/downloadSuppFile/629/29 [Accessed 15 August 2014].

Yang, Mayfair. 2011. 'Postcoloniality and religiosity in modern China: the disenchantments of sovereignty', *Theory Culture Society* 28(2), pp. 3–45.

Yang, Mayfair. 1994. *Gifts, Favors and Banquets: The Art of Social Relationships in China*. Ithaca and London: Cornell University Press.

Yang, Miaoyan. 2017. 'Learning to be safe citizens: state-run boarding schools and the dynamics of Tibetan identity', *Citizenship Studies* 21(7), pp. 824–841.

Yeh, Wen-hsin. 1997. 'Shanghai modernity: commerce and culture in a republican city', *The China Quarterly* 150, pp. 375–394.

Yu, Tianlong. 2020. 'Does democracy still have a chance? Contextualizing citizenship education in China', *Chinese Education & Society* 53 (1–2), pp. 14–24.

Yu, Tianlong. 2008. 'The revival of Confucianism in Chinese schools: a historical-political review', *Asia Pacific Journal of Education* 28(2), pp. 113–129.

Yuan, Zhenlong. 2011. 'Beijing chengxiang jiehe shequ anquan guanli de tansuo yu chuanxin – yi Daxingqu nunzhuang shequhua quanli wei li' [Exploration and innovation in community security management: the case of village communitization management in Daxing District] in *Beijing gonggong fuwu fazhan baogao 2010–2011* [*Blue Book Annual Report on Public Service of Beijing 2010–2011*]. Beijing: Beijing Academy of Social Sciences, pp. 241–251.

Yuval-Davis, Nira. 2011. *The Politics of Belonging: Intersectional Contestations*. Los Angeles: Sage Publications.

Zai, Liang. 2013. 'Understanding the puzzle of shortage of migrant labor in the Pearl River Delta region'. Paper presented for the Pearl River Delta Social Research Centre, Department of Sociology, Chinese University of Hong Kong, 10 January 2013.

Zeng, Hui, Yu, Xiaofen and Zhang, Juanfeng. 2019. 'Urban village demolition, migrant workers' rental costs and housing choices: evidence from Hangzhou, China', *Cities* 94, pp. 70–79.

Zeng, Jinghan. 2014. 'The debate on regime legitimacy in China: bridging the wide gulf between Western and Chinese scholarship', *Journal of Contemporary China* 23(88), pp. 612–635.

Zhan, Yang. 2019. 'Gifting as governance: NGO service projects and disciplinary power in rural migrant settlements in China', *Anthropological Forum* 29 (2): pp. 153–171.

Zhang, Li. 2007. 'Living and working at the margin: rural migrant workers in China's transitional cities' in Heather Xiaoquan Zhang, Bin Wu and Richard Sanders (eds) *Marginalisation in China: Perspectives on Transition and Globalisation*. Aldershot: Ashgate, pp. 81–96.

Zhang, Li. 2002. 'Spatiality and urban citizenship in late socialist China', *Public Culture* 14(2), pp. 311–334.

Zhang, Li. 2001. *Strangers in the City: Reconfiguration of Space, Power and Social Networks within China's Floating Population*. Stanford: Stanford University Press.

Zhao, Suisheng. 1998. 'A state-led nationalism: the patriotic education campaign in post-Tiananmen China', *Communist and Post-Communist Studies* 31(3), pp. 287–302.

Zhejiang News. 2012. 'Hangzhoushi liudong renkou fuwu guanli tiaoli' [The Hangzhou Floating Population's Service Management Regulation], *Zhejiang Xinwen* [*Zhejiang News*], 29 May. Available at: http://zjnews.zjol.com.cn/05zjnews/system/2012/05/29/018528729.shtml [Accessed 6 August 2014].

Zhejiang Provincial Bureau of Statistics. 2014. *2010 Population Census Data*. Available at: www.geohive.com/cntry/cn-33.aspx [Accessed 6 August 2014].

Zhou, Benshun. 2011. 'Shehui guanli buneng luoru "gongmin shehui" xianjing' [The management of society should not fall into the pitfall of 'civil society']. 求是 [*Seeking Truth*], 17 May. Available at: http://wenku.baidu.com/view/fe3b070403d8ce2f006623bd.html [Accessed 17 May 2014].

Zhu, Qian. 2012. 'Post-reform urban restructuring in China: the case of Hangzhou 1990–2010', *Town Planning Review* 83(4), pp. 431–455.

Index

EU authorised representative for GPSR:
Easy Access System Europe, Mustamäe tee 50,
10621 Tallinn, Estonia
gpsr.requests@easproject.com

www.ingramcontent.com/pod-product-compliance
Ingram Content Group UK Ltd.
Pitfield, Milton Keynes, MK11 3LW, UK
UKHW011005120926
8556IPUK00027B/96
9781526153999